I0018491

CompTIA Security+ SY0-701 Practice Tests

Hundreds of challenging mock exam questions aligned with the latest SY0-701 exam objectives

Mark McGinley

CompTIA Security+ SY0-701 Practice Tests

Author: Mark McGinley

Reviewers: Julio Casablanca and Dr. Gaurang Panchal

Publishing Product Manager: Anindya Sil

Development Editor: Richa Chauhan

Presentation Designer: Shantanu Zagade

Editorial Board: Vijin Boricha, Megan Carlisle, Simon Cox, Ketan Giri, Saurabh Kadave, Alex Mazonowicz, Gandhali Raut, and Ankita Thakur

First Published: December 2024

Production Reference: 1231224

Published by Packt Publishing Ltd.
Grosvenor House
11 St Paul's Square
Birmingham
B3 1RB

ISBN: 978-1-83664-685-3

www.packtpub.com

Contributors

About the Author

Mark McGinley was born in Glasgow, Scotland. After gaining a BSc in Physics, he entered the Royal Navy's Dartmouth College as a Naval Officer. He specialized as an engineering instructor and, after periods of training technicians in electronics, became the Lead Trainer in the Microprocessor Section of the Navy's Marine Engineering School, where he taught assembly language and computer science.

After nine years in the Navy, Mark transitioned to the computer consultancy field. He holds several industry certifications, including CompTIA's Net+, Sec+, and Cyber Security Analyst+, Cisco's CCNA, and Microsoft's MCSE and MCT. He is currently part of Ian Neil's team, which trains US Forces Europe specifically in Security+ at a very high success rate and contracts for the British Army training server systems and CCNA networking.

Mark lives in southern England with his wife Alison and their son Callum. He enjoys long walks in the countryside and is learning golf.

About the Reviewers

Julio Casablanca is an accomplished cybersecurity professional with over 30 years of experience in the tech industry. As a Senior Cybersecurity Advisor at World Wide Technology (WWT), Julio leads initiatives to elevate cybersecurity maturity across WWT's customer base. His career includes key roles as a Senior Systems Engineer, adjunct professor, and technical instructor and he has contributed his expertise to renowned organizations such as Palo Alto Networks and Tarrant County College. Julio holds a Master of Science in Information Assurance and multiple industry certifications, including CISSP and C|CISO, which reflects his deep commitment to advancing cybersecurity standards and best practices.

Dr. Gaurang Panchal is a cybersecurity expert with over 15 years of experience specializing in product security, security control development, gap analysis, and threat modeling. His work focuses on secure coding (SAST), comprehensive architecture review, and security maturity assessments. Dr. Panchal earned his Ph.D. in Computer Science and Engineering from the Indian Institute of Technology Kharagpur (IIT Kharagpur), where he contributed to cryptographic protocols for key management in data storage security. His expertise combines technical rigor with strategic security solutions, driving robust security practices across complex systems and environments.

Table of Contents

Preface

Cybersecurity is an essential aspect of every organization's infrastructure. With the growing number and increasing sophistication of cyber threats, there is a high demand for cybersecurity engineers, as well as network and systems administrators with strong security skills.

Cybersecurity is not merely the domain of specialized IT staff; it is a shared responsibility that impacts every level of an organization. As ransomware attacks, phishing exploits, and data breaches regularly make headlines, identifying and mitigating threats has become a critical skill set for all IT professionals, regardless of their role.

From small businesses to global enterprises, organizations look to certifications like *CompTIA Security+ SY0-701* to validate the skills of trusted and up-to-date security personnel. Widely recognized as a foundational credential in cybersecurity, Security+ certifies core knowledge of security concepts, tools, and procedures, serving as a stepping stone to more advanced roles in IT security.

This book is designed with a single purpose: to help candidates with preparation for the Security+ exam by offering high-quality realistic practice exams.

Each question has been meticulously crafted to reflect the quality and scope of the actual CompTIA Security+ SY0-701 exam. This resource allows candidates to gauge their understanding, identify knowledge gaps, and strengthen their grasp of key concepts by simulating real exam scenarios. Consistent practice with these high-quality questions is an effective way to build confidence and excel on exam day.

The *CompTIA Security+ SY0-701 Practice Tests* aim to ensure that you earn a respected credential and gain a robust understanding of the security practices and principles that safeguard data, networks, and systems. By covering core areas like risk management, incident response, and secure network architecture, this book equips you with the tools needed to tackle the exam with confidence.

Preparing for an exam can be daunting, especially one as comprehensive as the Security+. This book is structured to provide you with a clear path to success. Each question in the six mock exams is accompanied by detailed explanations to solidify your understanding of complex topics, ensuring you learn from every attempt. Whether you are a beginner entering the IT field or a seasoned professional seeking to validate your expertise, this book is a valuable companion on your journey to certification and beyond.

This book will help you achieve certification through diligent study and practice. Welcome to the first step in advancing your cybersecurity career!

Who This Book Is For

This book is for all the IT and cybersecurity professionals preparing for the *CompTIA Security+ SY0-701* certification exam. It is specifically designed for network administrators, systems administrators, and cybersecurity analysts who need realistic practice questions to assess their understanding of security concepts. By focusing on high-quality practice questions with detailed explanations, this book helps build confidence and ensures that you are well prepared for the *CompTIA Security+ SY0-701* exam.

Get in Touch

Feedback from our readers is always welcome.

General feedback: If you have any questions about this book, please mention the book title in the subject of your message and email us at customercare@packt.com.

Errata: Although we have taken every care to ensure the accuracy of our content, mistakes do happen. If you have found a mistake in this book, we would be grateful if you could report this to us. Please visit www.packtpub.com/support/errata and complete the form. We ensure that all valid errata are promptly updated in the GitHub repository at https://packt.link/SY0-701PTGithub.

Piracy: If you come across any illegal copies of our works in any form on the internet, we would be grateful if you could provide us with the location address or website name. Please contact us at copyright@packt.com with a link to the material.

If you are interested in becoming an author: If there is a topic that you have expertise in and you are interested in either writing or contributing to a book, please visit authors.packtpub.com.

Share Your Thoughts

Once you've read *CompTIA Security+ SY0-701 Practice Tests*, we'd love to hear your thoughts!
Scan the QR code below to go straight to the Amazon review page for this book and share your
feedback:

https://packt.link/r/1836646852

Your review is important to us and the tech community and will help us make sure we're delivering
excellent-quality content.

CompTIA Security+ SY0-701 Mock Exam 1

1. A company wants to ensure that its internal database servers are inaccessible from the public internet. What type of firewall rule should be configured?

    A. Allow all incoming traffic.

    B. Deny all outbound traffic.

    C. Deny all incoming traffic to the database server.

    D. Allow all traffic on port 80.

2. What is the benefit of using a centralized proxy for web filtering?

    A. It requires no configuration on user devices.

    B. It encrypts all web traffic.

    C. It reduces the need for antivirus software.

    D. It increases bandwidth consumption.

3. What is an access control vestibule, commonly called a "mantrap", used for in physical security?

    A. To restrict vehicle access to a facility

    B. To trap unauthorized personnel between two doors until identification is verified

    C. To monitor and log all access attempts to a secure area

    D. To provide emergency exits during a security breach

4. A network administrator must install an intrusion detection system (IDS) to improve the company's security posture. Which control type is an IDS?

    A. Corrective

    B. Physical

    C. Detective

    D. Managerial

5. After a security incident, the CISO needs the security team to be more specific about each control. How do directive security controls differ from preventive security controls?

    A. Directive controls prevent security incidents, while preventive controls guide behavior to follow security policies.

    B. Directive controls guide user behavior, while preventive controls are designed to stop security incidents before they occur.

    C. Directive controls provide real-time alerts of security breaches, while preventive controls document security events.

    D. Directive controls focus on protecting data from loss, while preventive controls focus on compliance with regulations.

6. Which core principle best defines the zero-trust security model?

    A. Trust but verify

    B. Least privilege

    C. Implicit trust within the network

    D. Access based on location

7. An intrusion prevention system (IPS) differs from an intrusion detection system (IDS) primarily in which of the following ways?

    A. An IPS only monitors network traffic without taking any action.

    B. An IPS can actively block malicious traffic, whereas an IDS only detects it.

    C. An IPS requires manual intervention, while an IDS does not.

    D. An IPS is designed only for outbound traffic monitoring.

8. How does threat scope reduction help in improving network security?

    A. By expanding the network's attack surface to gather more intelligence

    B. By reducing the number of potential attack vectors through segmentation and isolation

    C. By increasing the number of open ports to enhance communication

    D. By using complex encryption algorithms for all network traffic

9. What is the main purpose of deploying a honeypot in a network security environment?

    A. To increase network bandwidth

    B. To attract and trap attackers for monitoring and analysis

    C. To provide a backup for critical data

    D. To enforce access control policies

10. Which detection method does an intrusion detection system (IDS)/intrusion prevention system (IPS) use to identify known attack patterns?

    A. Anomaly-based detection

    B. Signature-based detection

    C. Heuristic detection

    D. Behavioral analysis

11. The CISO wants the security team to analyze data gaps. What is the primary purpose of conducting a gap analysis in a security context?

    A. To identify and document the differences between current security practices and desired security goals.

    B. Comparing current security measures with vulnerability scans.

    C. Implementing encryption across all data systems.

    D. Conducting a vulnerability assessment of the network.

12. A disgruntled employee who intentionally leaks confidential information is best described as which type of threat actor?

    A. Shadow IT

    B. Nation-state

    C. Insider threat

    D. Organized crime

13. Which of the following best describes the primary purpose of using access control lists (ACLs) in a firewall?

    A. To increase network speed

    B. To define rules for allowing or denying traffic

    C. To monitor network performance

    D. To store encryption keys

14. A security consultant discovers that an organization's email system has been compromised by attackers using malicious attachments. What is this type of attack best described as?

   A. Image-based attack

   B. File-based attack

   C. Voice call attack

   D. Message-based attack

15. An attacker exploits a company's outdated software vulnerability to gain unauthorized access to its network. What is the most likely form of this attack vector?

   A. Unsupported systems and applications

   B. Vulnerable software

   C. Removable device

   D. Message-based attack

16. Employees receive phishing emails with malicious links to steal login credentials. What kind of attack is this?

   A. Image-based attack

   B. File-based attack

   C. Message-based attack

   D. Voice call attack

17. A security administrator notices that an application is vulnerable to an attack where arbitrary code is injected into memory, allowing the attacker to execute it. What type of vulnerability is this?

   A. Buffer overflow

   B. Cross-site scripting (XSS)

   C. XML injection

   D. Structured Query Language injection (SQLi)

18. During a security audit, the administrator finds that a web application fails to properly validate input, allowing attackers to execute malicious code in the browser of users who view the affected web page. What type of vulnerability is this?

   A. Buffer overflow

   B. Race conditions

   C. Memory injection

   D. Cross-site scripting (XSS)

19. An attacker exploits a vulnerability in a web application's database query handling by injecting malicious SQL statements into an input field. What type of attack does this describe?

    A. Memory injection

    B. Buffer overflow

    C. Structured Query Language injection (SQLi)

    D. Cross-site scripting (XSS)

20. A security administrator identifies that a program is susceptible to an attack where more data can be input to the buffer than it can hold, leading to potential system crashes or the execution of malicious code. What vulnerability is this?

    A. Race conditions

    B. Buffer overflow

    C. Cross-site scripting (XSS)

    D. Structured Query Language injection (SQLi)

21. A security team must restrict incoming traffic to a web server on the company's network to only allow HTTP and HTTPS traffic. Which firewall rule should they implement?

    A. Allow traffic on port 25 and port 110.

    B. Allow traffic on port 53 and port 123.

    C. Allow traffic on port 80 and port 443.

    D. Allow traffic on port 21 and port 22.

22. A security consultant at a large company notices that several computers on the network are performing file encryption while showing a text message demanding payment to restore access. What type of malicious activity does this indicate?

    A. Virus

    B. Trojan

    C. Ransomware

    D. Bloatware

23. A security consultant notices an unusual amount of failed login attempts on the company's authentication server within a short period. What type of attack does this indicate?

    A. Environmental attack

    B. RFID cloning

    C. Phishing

    D. Brute force

24. A security administrator detects an attacker successfully exploiting an application vulnerability to input arbitrary commands into a database query. What type of attack is this an example of?

    A. Buffer overflow

    B. Injection

    C. Privilege escalation

    D. Directory traversal

25. A security administrator notices that attackers have forced a communication session to use a less secure version of a cryptographic protocol than what the server typically supports. What type of attack is this?

    A. Birthday attack

    B. Downgrade attack

    C. Collision attack

    D. Replay attack

26. A security administrator notices many failed login attempts on a user account spread over a long period, using different passwords each time. What type of password attack does this scenario best describe?

    A. Brute-force attack

    B. Dictionary attack

    C. Password spraying

    D. Rainbow table attack

27. What is the primary purpose of a web filter in an enterprise environment?

    A. To speed up web page loading times

    B. To block access to unauthorized or malicious websites

    C. To encrypt all outbound traffic

    D. To manage user credentials for web access

28. A security administrator notices several user accounts being locked out repeatedly due to failed login attempts from different IP addresses. What does this likely indicate?

    A. Concurrent session usage

    B. Account lockout due to a brute-force attack

    C. Impossible travel

    D. Resource consumption

29. A security consultant sets up rules to specify which users can access a network resource based on IP addresses and protocols. Which access control method is the consultant implementing?

   A. Role-based access control (RBAC)

   B. Access control list (ACL)

   C. Mandatory access control (MAC)

   D. Discretionary access control (DAC)

30. A security consultant advises a company on preventing unauthorized applications from running on its network. Which mitigation technique should the consultant recommend to allow only approved software to execute?

   A. Application allow list

   B. Firewall rules

   C. Block list

   D. Antivirus scanning

31. A security consultant advises a company on handling outdated hardware that the vendor no longer supports. What is the best mitigation technique for reducing the risk associated with these legacy servers?

   A. Apply the latest security patches.

   B. Increase their physical security.

   C. Use the servers in a test environment.

   D. Decommission and replace with modern hardware.

32. A security consultant is implementing hardening measures on company servers. What is a key benefit of installing endpoint protection software?

   A. It increases network bandwidth.

   B. It provides encryption for data in transit.

   C. It helps detect and block malware and other malicious threats.

   D. It simplifies user access management.

33. A company is considering moving its infrastructure to a public cloud environment. What is one of the primary security implications of adopting a public cloud architecture?

    A. Increased control over the physical security of hardware

    B. Reduced responsibility for managing underlying infrastructure

    C. Complete control over all software and hardware configurations

    D. Increased complexity in managing internal network security

34. What is a typical security challenge in a decentralized architecture model where multiple independent systems operate without a central authority?

    A. Difficulty in managing individual system configurations

    B. Centralized control over data access and encryption

    C. Simplicity in scaling and expanding the infrastructure

    D. Unified logging and monitoring across all systems

35. When evaluating a cloud-based architecture, which of the following is a significant consideration regarding availability?

    A. The cloud provider guarantees 100% uptime.

    B. Availability depends on the provider's service-level agreement (SLA) and redundancy measures.

    C. Availability is managed entirely by the company's internal IT team.

    D. Availability is irrelevant for cloud services due to their inherent flexibility.

36. For a large-scale e-commerce application, which architecture consideration is most important for ensuring resilience?

    A. Implementing high-capacity storage solutions

    B. Using a single data center with extensive security controls

    C. Deploying a multi-region architecture with failover capabilities

    D. Minimizing the use of backup systems to reduce complexity

37. When designing a network security architecture, which consideration is most important for effectively managing the attack surface?

    A. Limiting the number of physical devices in the network

    B. Ensuring all devices are placed in a single security zone

    C. Minimizing the number of exposed services and interfaces that attackers could target

    D. Increasing the physical security of the data center facilities

38. In a secure enterprise network design, which factor is crucial when determining device placement?

    A. Placement should be based on the cost of the devices.

    B. Devices should be placed in locations that maximize their accessibility for administrators.

    C. Devices should be placed according to their function within different security zones to control access and limit exposure.

    D. Placement should prioritize reducing the amount of cabling required.

39. When planning for failure modes in a network infrastructure, which approach helps ensure continued operations?

    A. Deploying single points of failure to simplify troubleshooting

    B. Implementing redundant systems and failover mechanisms to maintain functionality during failures

    C. Avoiding the use of backup systems to reduce complexity

    D. Centralizing all critical systems in one location to streamline management

40. What is the primary function of remote access solutions in enterprise security?

    A. To provide users with secure access to applications and data outside the corporate network.

    B. To monitor and control network traffic based on predefined security rules

    C. To manage and enforce security policies on endpoint devices

    D. To encrypt data stored on disk drives within the data center

41. A security administrator needs to protect sensitive data that is subject to government regulations such as General Data Protection Regulation (GDPR) or Health Insurance Portability and Accountability Act (HIPAA). What type of data is this?

    A. Intellectual property

    B. Trade secret

    C. Regulated

    D. Human-readable

42. A security administrator is implementing controls to protect data that, if disclosed, could seriously damage the organization's reputation and operations. What classification best fits this type of data?

    A. Public

    B. Restricted

    C. Critical

    D. Confidential

43. A security administrator is implementing encryption for files stored on a company's servers to protect them against unauthorized access. Which term best describes this type of data?

    A. Data in use

    B. Data in transit

    C. Data at rest

    D. Data sovereignty

44. What is it known as when a company sets out to mask its data?

    A. Hashing

    B. Obfuscation

    C. Certification

    D. Encryption

45. A security administrator wants to ensure that sensitive data is rendered unreadable during transmission, even if intercepted. Which of the following methods should they implement?

    A. Masking

    B. Hashing

    C. Encryption

    D. Tokenization

46. A security administrator is conducting capacity planning for a new disaster recovery site. Which of the following should be considered to ensure enough human resources to operate the site during an emergency?

    A. Network bandwidth

    B. Staffing levels

    C. Data replication

    D. Power supply

47. What is the primary purpose of an intrusion detection system (IDS) in a corporate network?

    A. To block all incoming network traffic

    B. To detect and alert on potential security breaches

    C. To encrypt all network communications

    D. To manage user authentication

48. A security administrator wants to evaluate the company's incident response plan without disrupting operations. Which testing method should be used to achieve this?

    A. Failover

    B. Tabletop exercise

    C. Parallel processing

    D. Simulation

49. A security administrator decides where to store backups to ensure data is not lost in case of a physical disaster at the main office. What type of backup location should be prioritized?

    A. Onsite

    B. Offsite

    C. Local drive

    D. Cloud only

50. A security consultant ensures that new servers adhere to the company's security standards before they are put into production. What is the first step in this process?

    A. Deploy the servers with default settings.

    B. Conduct regular vulnerability scans.

    C. Maintain security updates for the servers.

    D. Establish security baselines for the servers.

51. After defining the security baselines for computing resources, which step involves applying these standards to systems as they are deployed?

    A. Establish

    B. Deploy

    C. Maintain

    D. Review

52. A company implements a policy allowing employees to use their personal devices for work while maintaining control over security policies and data access. Which mobile solution best supports this policy?

    A. Corporate-owned personally enabled (COPE)

    B. Bring your own device (BYOD)

    C. Choose your own device (CYOD)

    D. Mobile device management (MDM)

53. A security consultant wants to implement the latest and most secure encryption standard for a company's Wi-Fi network. Which protocol should be used?

    A. Wi-Fi Protected Access 2 (WPA2)

    B. Wired Equivalent Privacy (WEP)

    C. Wi-Fi Protected Access 3 (WPA3)

    D. Extensible Authentication Protocol (EAP)

54. What is a standard method for authenticating systems or devices in a network?

    A. VPN credentials

    B. Digital certificates

    C. Security questions

    D. Biometric data

55. A security consultant reviews a web application's code to ensure it does not contain vulnerabilities that attackers could exploit. Which technique involves analyzing the code without executing it?

    A. Static code analysis

    B. Dynamic code analysis

    C. Penetration testing

    D. Code signing

56. A security administrator is responsible for maintaining department hardware assets. What is this process known as?

    A. Configuration management

    B. Bring your own device (BYOD)

    C. Data encryption

    D. Incident response

57. An administrator is classifying a set of documents that contain sensitive company information. What classification label is most appropriate for these documents?

    A. Public

    B. Restricted

    C. Confidential

    D. Internal

58. A security administrator is responsible for keeping an updated list of all hardware devices connected to the company's network. What is this process known as?

    A. Inventory management

    B. Software licensing

    C. Data encryption

    D. Vulnerability scanning

59. A security administrator must ensure that sensitive data on retired hard drives cannot be recovered. What is the most secure method for achieving this?

    A. Formatting the hard drives

    B. Using a secure erase utility

    C. Encrypting the hard drives

    D. Physically destroying the hard drives

60. What is the primary goal of data sanitization in the context of decommissioning hardware?

    A. To improve the performance of the storage device

    B. To completely remove all data so it cannot be recovered

    C. To upgrade the hardware to the latest standards

    D. To maintain compliance with software licenses

61. Which of the following processes involves certifying that a piece of hardware has been sanitized according to industry standards?

    A. Data encryption

    B. Data destruction

    C. Data certification

    D. Data retention

62. A security administrator wants to detect known vulnerabilities in the company's network without exploiting them. Which method should be used?

    A. Penetration testing

    B. Vulnerability scan

    C. Bug bounty program

    D. Dynamic analysis

63. Which method involves analyzing code to find potential security vulnerabilities without executing it?

    A. Dynamic analysis

    B. Static analysis

    C. Vulnerability scan

    D. Bug bounty program

64. A vulnerability scan reports a security flaw in a system, but further investigation reveals that the vulnerability does not exist. What is this scenario an example of?

    A. False negative

    B. True positive

    C. False positive

    D. True negative

65. How do the control plane and data plane interact in a network?

    A. The control plane directly transmits user data while the data plane makes routing decisions.

    B. The data plane executes the routing decisions made by the control plane and handles user data traffic.

    C. The control plane encrypts user data while the data plane decrypts it.

    D. The control plane and data plane operate independently without interacting.

66. A company has an acceptable use policy (AUP) for employees using their mobile devices. Which of the following security control types does this best represent?

    A. Detective

    B. Compensating

    C. Corrective

    D. Preventive

67. Which term describes a vulnerability that exists in a system but was not detected by a security scan?

    A. True positive

    B. False positive

    C. False negative

    D. True negative

68. A security administrator has identified several company systems vulnerabilities. What is the first step the administrator should take to address these vulnerabilities?

    A. Perform rescanning to ensure the vulnerabilities are still present

    B. Apply patches to the affected systems

    C. Purchase cyber insurance to mitigate financial risk

    D. Report the vulnerabilities to senior management

69. After applying patches to systems, what should an administrator do to mitigate the vulnerabilities effectively?

    A. Apply additional compensating controls

    B. Segregate the network to isolate the patched systems

    C. Rescan the systems to verify that the vulnerabilities are no longer present

    D. Purchase insurance for any residual risk

70. After applying patches to critical systems, what should a security administrator do to validate the remediation's success?

    A. Conduct rescanning to check for any remaining vulnerabilities

    B. Segregate the patched systems into a different network

    C. Apply compensating controls as an extra measure

    D. Report the patch application to senior management

71. A security team is responsible for monitoring the company's infrastructure to detect anomalies. Which tool is best suited for monitoring server health and performance?

    A. Intrusion detection system (IDS)

    B. Network access control (NAC)

    C. Security information and event management (SIEM)

    D. Simple Network Management Protocol (SNMP)

72. Which monitoring tool is primarily used to gather all log files from various devices to identify potential security incidents?

    A. Virtual private network (VPN)

    B. Security information and event management (SIEM)

    C. Firewall

    D. Web application firewall (WAF)

73. A security team wants to centralize the collection and analysis of logs from multiple systems across the network. Which activity best describes this process?

    A. Scanning

    B. Log aggregation

    C. Alert tuning

    D. Archiving

74. Which activity is focused on identifying vulnerabilities in a company's network and systems by actively probing them?

    A. Alerting

    B. Quarantine

    C. Reporting

    D. Scanning

75. Which tool is used to automate security compliance assessment by evaluating systems against security benchmarks?

    A. Vulnerability scanner

    B. Security Content Automation Protocol (SCAP)

    C. Data loss prevention (DLP)

    D. NetFlow

76. Which of the following is most likely to conduct cyberattacks for political or social causes rather than financial gain?

    A. Organized crime

    B. Hacktivist

    C. Nation-state

    D. Shadow IT

77. A security team is considering using a tool that does not require installation on each monitored device but collects data from network traffic. Which tool best fits this requirement?

    A. NetFlow

    B. Security information and event management (SIEM)

    C. Data loss prevention (DLP)

    D. Vulnerability scanner

78. A security consultant recommends placing critical servers on separate network segments to prevent unauthorized access from the leading corporate network. Which technique is being used to enhance security?

    A. Air-gap

    B. Demilitarized zone (DMZ)

    C. Virtual local area network (VLAN)

    D. Proxy server

79. What is the primary purpose of file integrity monitoring (FIM)?

    A. To encrypt files for confidentiality

    B. To detect unauthorized changes to files

    C. To back up critical files to the cloud

    D. To optimize file storage and management

80. A security team is implementing a data loss prevention (DLP) solution to prevent sensitive information from being sent outside the company through email. What specific feature should the DLP solution include to achieve this?

    A. Monitoring of network bandwidth

    B. Scanning and inspecting email attachments for sensitive data

    C. Blocking all outgoing emails

    D. Encrypting all inbound emails

81. What is the primary purpose of a quarantine network in a network access control (NAC) environment?

    A. To provide a separate network for guest users

    B. To isolate non-compliant computers until they are remediated

    C. To enforce bandwidth limits on specific devices

    D. To create a secure communication channel for sensitive data

82. What is the primary function of an endpoint detection and response (EDR) solution in a corporate environment?

    A. To manage network traffic based on predefined rules

    B. To monitor and detect suspicious activity on endpoints such as workstations and servers

    C. To enforce access control policies across the network

    D. To provide centralized backup and recovery services

83. A security administrator is tasked with choosing a recovery site that is fully operational and can immediately take over operations in case of a primary site failure. Which type of site should be chosen?

    A. Cold site

    B. Warm site

    C. Hot site

    D. Geographic dispersion

84. A security consultant detects an unusually high volume of traffic directed toward the company's web server, originating from numerous IP addresses. What type of attack is this most likely indicative of?

    A. Reflected attack

    B. Distributed denial-of-service (DDoS)

    C. Wireless attack

    D. Credential replay attack

85. Which type of threat actor will likely have substantial resources and expertise to conduct sophisticated attacks on critical infrastructure?

    A. Hacktivist

    B. Insider threat

    C. Nation-state

    D. Unskilled attacker

The answers to this mock exam are provided in the Solutions chapter on page **109**.

2

CompTIA Security+ SY0-701 Mock Exam 2

1. What is a key characteristic of agent-based web filtering?

    A. It relies on a centralized server to manage all rules.

    B. It requires installation on each user's device.

    C. It is only effective for mobile users.

    D. It does not support URL scanning.

2. What would be the likely benefit for a security administrator if IPS systems were integrated with a Security Information and Event Management (SIEM) solution?

    A. Reduced need for manual configuration of firewall rules

    B. Enhanced capability for real-time threat detection and response

    C. Automatic encryption of all network traffic

    D. Improved physical security of network infrastructure

3. An intrusion prevention system (IPS) can be configured to block traffic based on specific criteria. What is a common use case for this functionality?

    A. Allowing all traffic during business hours.

    B. Blocking IP addresses associated with known malicious activity.

    C. Encrypting data in transit.

    D. Allowing unrestricted access to all external websites.

4. What is one of the primary benefits of automating security operations in terms of time management?

    A. Increased need for manual reviews

    B. Reduced efficiency and longer resolution times

    C. Time-saving through quicker response and task completion

    D. Higher risk of human error

5. What is the primary security function of fencing around a facility?

    A. To improve the aesthetic appearance of the facility

    B. To support video surveillance equipment

    C. To deter unauthorized entry and provide a physical barrier

    D. To guide visitors to the main entrance

6. Which remediation technique involves breaking a network into separate pieces to reduce the impact of a vulnerability?

    A. Patching

    B. Segmentation

    C. Rescanning

    D. Reporting

7. Which of the following methods is primarily used to ensure the confidentiality of data?

    A. Digital signatures

    B. Hashing

    C. Encryption

    D. Redundancy

8. What is a common security concern related to the control plane in network security?

    A. Unauthorized access to user data while in transit

    B. Compromising routing protocols leading to incorrect routing decisions

    C. Data leakage through unencrypted channels

    D. Inadequate physical security of network hardware

9. Which authorization model grants access based on predefined roles assigned to users?

    A. Discretionary access control (DAC)

    B. Role-based access control (RBAC)

    C. Mandatory access control (MAC)

    D. Attribute-based access control (ABAC)

10. How does a honeynet differ from a single honeypot in network security?

    A. A honeynet is a collection of multiple honeypots designed to simulate a larger network environment.

    B. A honeynet only monitors network traffic without any interaction with attackers.

    C. A honeynet is a type of firewall used to protect against attacks.

    D. A honeynet consists of only one honeypot that can simulate different vulnerabilities.

11. If a cybersecurity contractor has reviewed the various server logs within a company in detail, what type of security control has been used?

    A. Corrective

    B. Preventive

    C. Detective

    D. Deterrent

12. Which activity should a security team implement for their logs to maintain compliance and preserve historical data for future analysis?

    A. Alert tuning

    B. Scanning

    C. Archiving

    D. Quarantine

13. Which scripting technique is commonly used to ensure consistency and efficiency when automating and creating new user accounts in a large organization?

    A. Manual entry

    B. User provisioning scripts

    C. Security group updates

    D. Ticket creation

14. To minimize false positives, which aspect of IDS/IPS tuning should a security team focus on?

   A.   Increasing the number of signatures loaded

   B.   Fine-tuning the sensitivity of anomaly detection

   C.   Allowing all outbound traffic by default

   D.   Blocking all incoming traffic by default

15. A company using an IDS configured to generate alerts based on predefined signatures. What is the potential risk when using this solution?

   A.   Missing new and unknown threats

   B.   Generating alerts for every packet passing through the network

   C.   Overloading network bandwidth with excessive data

   D.   Automatically blocking legitimate traffic

16. Which protocol should be used to transfer files over the internet securely?

   A.   File Transfer Protocol (FTP)

   B.   Hypertext Transfer Protocol (HTTP)

   C.   Secure File Transfer Protocol (SFTP)

   D.   Telnet

17. What is the primary role of reputation-based filtering in web security?

   A.   To block websites that have been reported as malicious

   B.   To allow access to any website with a high visitor count

   C.   To provide a log of all accessed URLs

   D.   To encrypt all outbound web traffic

18. A company wants to inspect all web traffic for malicious content before reaching the user. Which web filtering method should be implemented?

   A.   Agent-based filtering

   B.   URL scanning

   C.   Block rules

   D.   Centralized proxy

19. What type of access control model does SELinux implement?

    A. Discretionary Access Control (DAC)

    B. Role-Based Access Control (RBAC)

    C. Mandatory Access Control (MAC)

    D. Attribute-Based Access Control (ABAC)

20. In which access control model are permissions assigned based on the user's organizational role?

    A. Mandatory access control (MAC)

    B. Role-based access control (RBAC)

    C. Attribute-based access control (ABAC)

    D. Discretionary access control (DAC)

21. A security team needs to dispose of sensitive documents. What method should be used to ensure that the information cannot be reconstructed?

    A. Shredding

    B. Recycling

    C. Filing

    D. Emailing copies to stakeholders

22. Which tool provides a centralized platform for collecting, analyzing, and correlating logs and events from various sources across an enterprise network?

    A. Security information and event management (SIEM)

    B. Simple Network Management Protocol (SNMP) traps

    C. Security Content Automation Protocol (SCAP)

    D. Data loss prevention (DLP)

23. Which transport method does the Secure Sockets Layer (SSL) primarily use to secure data?

    A. UDP

    B. TCP

    C. ICMP

    D. FTP

24. What should a security administrator do to ensure data retention policies are followed during decommissioning?

    A. Review the inventory list of all software

    B. Conduct regular audits to verify compliance

    C. Increase the physical security of the servers

    D. Change user permissions

25. When comparing on-premises infrastructure to a public cloud model, what is an on-premises architecture's key advantage regarding data security?

    A. Reduced responsibility for data privacy and compliance

    B. Simplified integration with third-party applications

    C. Complete control over physical and network security measures

    D. Greater flexibility in scaling resources up or down

26. A security administrator implements Infrastructure as Code (IaC) to automate network infrastructure deployment. What is a significant security consideration with IaC?

    A. It provides automatic updates to security patches.

    B. It centralizes control over network configurations.

    C. It introduces the risk of code injection if the IaC scripts are not properly validated.

    D. It ensures the physical security of network devices.

27. Which factor most directly impacts cost when selecting between on-premises and cloud solutions?

    A. The total cost of ownership, including Hardware, Software, and maintenance versus subscription costs.

    B. The geographic location of data centers

    C. The type of data encryption used

    D. The size of the network's bandwidth

28. For applications that require responsiveness, which architectural feature is most critical?

    A. Using a centralized database

    B. Implementing content delivery networks (CDNs) and edge computing solutions

    C. Relying solely on server-side processing

    D. Limiting the number of application servers

29. In the context of network security, what does a fail-open mechanism ensure?

    A. Systems and services usually operate even if a security device fails but may become vulnerable.

    B. Systems and services shut down completely to prevent unauthorized access when a security device fails.

    C. All user accounts are automatically disabled in the case of a failure to prevent unauthorized access.

    D. All network traffic is encrypted to prevent data breaches when a device fails.

30. Which password complexity requirement ensures that passwords include a mix of different character types?

    A. Length

    B. Reuse

    C. Expiration

    D. Complexity

31. What is a potential drawback when implementing a fail-open security design?

    A. Increased risk of unauthorized access due to the continuation of service despite a failure

    B. Increased complexity in managing and monitoring security policies

    C. Higher costs associated with redundant systems and failover mechanisms

    D. Higher likelihood of service interruptions and downtime during security device failures

32. Tunneling is a technique used in secure communication. What does tunneling primarily do?

    A. It secures communication between endpoints by encapsulating data within another protocol.

    B. It filters and blocks malicious traffic based on predefined security rules.

    C. It monitors network traffic for suspicious activities and alerts administrators.

    D. It manages and controls access to network resources based on user permissions.

33. Which type of data represents confidential business information that gives a company a competitive edge and is often protected by non-disclosure agreements?

    A. Financial information

    B. Trade secrets

    C. Legal information

    D. Non-human-readable

34. What is the primary purpose of just-in-time (JIT) permissions in privileged access management?

    A. To provide permanent access to critical systems

    B. To grant temporary access only when needed

    C. To store passwords securely

    D. To log all user activity continuously

35. What is a key factor in determining a company's risk tolerance?

    A. The accuracy of its vulnerability scanning tools.

    B. The severity of potential threats it is willing to accept.

    C. The number of employees dedicated to security.

    D. The size of its IT infrastructure.

36. A security administrator implements Transport Layer Security (TLS) encryption to cover data being sent over the network. What type of data is being protected in this scenario?

    A. Data sovereignty

    B. Data in use

    C. Data in transit

    D. Data at rest

37. Which method is most appropriate for replacing sensitive data with a unique identifier to reduce exposure but retain the ability to retrieve the original information?

    A. Obfuscation

    B. Tokenization

    C. Geographic restrictions

    D. Permission restrictions

38. What is considered a best practice for password length to enhance security?

    A. At least 6 characters

    B. At least 8 characters

    C. At least 12 characters

    D. At least 16 characters

39. Which type of recovery site typically requires the longest time to become operational after a disaster because it lacks the necessary hardware and software?

    A. Hot site

    B. Warm site

    C. Cold site

    D. Geographic dispersion

40. During a disaster recovery test, a security administrator switches from the primary data center to a backup site to ensure continuity of operations. What type of test is being conducted?

    A. Simulation

    B. Tabletop exercise

    C. Failover

    D. Parallel processing

41. Which backup method involves taking a point-in-time copy of a virtual system's data to allow fast restoration of files or systems?

    A. Replication

    B. Snapshot

    C. Incremental backup

    D. Differential backup

42. A security administrator must create a firewall rule to prevent all external hosts from accessing internal SSH services. What should this rule specify?

    A. Deny inbound traffic on port 22

    B. Allow outbound traffic on port 21

    C. Deny inbound traffic on port 80

    D. Allow inbound traffic on port 443

43. A security consultant should focus on which phase of managing secure baselines to ensure ongoing compliance with security standards after initial deployment?

    A. Establish

    B. Deploy

    C. Maintain

    D. Document

44. Which of the following is the correct sequence for managing secure baselines for computing resources?

   A. Deploy, Maintain, Establish

   B. Maintain, Establish, Deploy

   C. Establish, Deploy, Maintain

   D. Deploy, Establish, Maintain

45. Which deployment model should be used to ensure secure access and management of mobile devices owned by the company but used for personal activities as well?

   A. Bring your own device (BYOD)

   B. Corporate-owned, personally enabled (COPE)

   C. Choose your own device (CYOD)

   D. Mobile device management (MDM)

46. To manage wireless network access and ensure secure user authentication, which protocol should a company implement to centralize authentication, authorization, and accounting?

   A. Remote Authentication Dial-In User Service (RADIUS)

   B. Wi-Fi Protected Access 3 (WPA3)

   C. Simple Network Management Protocol (SNMP)

   D. Transport Layer Security (TLS)

47. Which technique should be employed to protect the integrity of an application's code and ensure that it has not been altered?

   A. Input validation

   B. Code signing

   C. Secure cookies

   D. Static code analysis

48. What is the primary benefit of assigning clear ownership of data assets within an organization?

   A. It ensures regular software updates.

   B. It reduces network traffic.

   C. It provides accountability for asset management.

   D. It improves user authentication.

49. Which of the following classifications would be used for data that is meant to be accessible to the general public without restrictions?

    A. Private

    B. Public

    C. Confidential

    D. Sensitive

50. Which of the following is the primary goal of asset enumeration in a corporate environment?

    A. To identify all available software updates

    B. To monitor user activity on the network

    C. To catalog all devices and software in use

    D. To enforce security policies on mobile devices

51. A company must dispose of old servers containing sensitive customer data. Which method ensures the data is unrecoverable?

    A. Overwriting the data multiple times

    B. Deleting all files from the hard drives

    C. Reformatting the hard drives

    D. Disconnecting the servers from the network

52. What is the purpose of a data retention policy in a corporate environment?

    A. To ensure all data is immediately deleted

    B. To define how long data should be kept based on legal and business requirements

    C. To ensure data is encrypted

    D. To improve data accessibility

53. When a security administrator needs to dispose of old mobile devices, what method should be used to ensure the data is unrecoverable?

    A. Perform a factory reset

    B. Encrypt the device

    C. Physically destroy the device

    D. Disable the device remotely

54. What is the primary purpose of dynamic analysis in vulnerability management?

    A. To detect vulnerabilities in live environments by monitoring behavior during execution

    B. To analyze software code without running the program

    C. To automatically update vulnerable packages

    D. To collect data from third-party sources

55. An organization subscribes to a service that provides regular updates on emerging threats and vulnerabilities. What type of identification method is this?

    A. Package monitoring

    B. Open source intelligence (OSINT)

    C. Threat feed

    D. Static analysis

56. What does the Common Vulnerability Scoring System (CVSS) primarily help an organization determine?

    A. The financial cost of a security breach

    B. The effectiveness of antivirus software

    C. The severity of a vulnerability

    D. The number of false positives

57. When classifying vulnerabilities, which of the following factors is not typically considered?

    A. Potential impact

    B. Exploitability

    C. Risk tolerance

    D. Network traffic

58. What is the purpose of using compensating controls in vulnerability management?

    A. To provide an additional layer of security when direct remediation isn't possible

    B. To replace the need for patching

    C. To lower the costs of vulnerability management

    D. To improve network performance

59. Which activity ensures all implemented security controls are working as intended and vulnerabilities have been properly remediated?

    A. Rescanning

    B. Verification

    C. Applying additional patches

    D. Network segmentation

60. What is the primary use of a web application firewall (WAF) for monitoring?

    A. To encrypt network traffic

    B. To prevent unauthorized access to the network

    C. To monitor and filter HTTP traffic to and from a web application

    D. To monitor physical access to a data center

61. A company wants to monitor applications for performance issues and ensure security compliance. Which tool should be used?

    A. Database management system (DBMS)

    B. Application performance monitoring (APM)

    C. Endpoint detection and response (EDR)

    D. Public key infrastructure (PKI)

62. A security analyst must ensure alerts for unusual network activity are generated. What process should they focus on?

    A. Quarantine

    B. Alert response and remediation

    C. Alerting

    D. Archiving

63. A company needs to ensure that sensitive data does not leave its network. Which tool should it use to monitor and control data movement?

    A. NetFlow

    B. Security information and event management (SIEM)

    C. Data loss prevention (DLP)

    D. Vulnerability scanner

64. What is the role of a screened subnet in network security?

    A. To allow unrestricted access to internal resources

    B. To create an isolated network segment for sensitive servers

    C. To bypass firewall rules

    D. To enable direct connections between all devices

65. When configuring a firewall, which protocol should be blocked to prevent unauthorized remote access to servers?

    A. Simple Mail Transfer Protocol (SMTP)

    B. File Transfer Protocol (FTP)

    C. Secure Shell (SSH)

    D. Domain Name System (DNS)

66. A security team notices a trend of repeated login attempts from a single IP address. Which Intrusion detection system (IDS)/Intrusion prevention system (IPS) feature would help them detect this type of activity?

    A. Signature-based detection

    B. Anomaly-based detection

    C. Blocking rules

    D. Encryption protocols

67. What is a common outcome of a gap analysis in security management?

    A. A detailed risk management plan

    B. A list of areas where security improvements are needed

    C. A newly designed user access control system

    D. A comprehensive incident response team

68. What is the main advantage of using an Intrusion detection system (IDS) with a signature-based detection system?

    A. It detects zero-day attacks effectively

    B. It has a low false positive rate when identifying known threats

    C. No updates are required to recognize new threats

    D. It can block traffic automatically without administrator intervention

69. The security team wants to harden all remote communications between computers on the network. Which protocol is considered insecure because it transmits data in plaintext?

    A. SSH

    B. HTTPS

    C. Telnet

    D. FTPS

70. How does URL scanning enhance the security provided by a web filter?

    A. By checking URLs against a list of known good websites

    B. By blocking all URLs that are not explicitly allowed

    C. By analyzing the content of a URL to detect malicious behavior

    D. By allowing all traffic to pass without inspection

71. What is the primary function of Group Policy in a Windows environment?

    A. To control network traffic between devices

    B. To manage and configure user and computer settings centrally

    C. To encrypt all files on a device

    D. To provide a backup solution for user data

72. Which of the following is a key feature of SELinux?

    A. It provides a graphical user interface for managing permissions.

    B. It enforces mandatory access control (MAC) on processes and files.

    C. It automatically updates all software packages.

    D. It is used exclusively for managing network security.

73. Which port is typically used by HTTPS to secure web traffic?

    A. Port 21

    B. Port 443

    C. Port 80

    D. Port 23

74. A turnstile has been installed at an entry point within a company. Which of the following types of controls is this?

    A. Physical

    B. Detective

    C. Corrective

    D. Technical

75. What is the primary purpose of using Transport Layer Security (TLS) in network communications?

    A. To compress data before transmission

    B. To encrypt data and ensure secure communication

    C. To authenticate user credentials

    D. To block unauthorized access to the network

76. In a zero-trust architecture, what type of authentication is the most commonly emphasized?

    A. Single-factor authentication

    B. Multi-factor authentication

    C. Password-based authentication

    D. Location-based authentication

77. What is the primary purpose of the Sender Policy Framework (SPF) in email security?

    A. To encrypt the contents of emails

    B. To authenticate the sender's email address

    C. To provide a digital signature for email messages

    D. To check the reputation of the email sender

78. What is a crucial benefit of implementing DomainKeys Identified Mail (DKIM)?

    A. It provides email encryption for confidentiality.

    B. It digitally signs emails to verify the sender's domain.

    C. It filters spam emails based on content.

    D. It blocks emails from unknown senders.

79. What is the main advantage to a company when implementing policy-driven access control?

    A. It enforces security policies consistently across the network.

    B. It only allows access to users based on their physical location.

    C. It uses biometric data for authentication.

    D. It automatically updates security patches.

80. Which of the following is a key benefit of implementing file integrity monitoring in an enterprise environment?

    A. Reducing the size of files on disk

    B. Monitoring changes to critical system files

    C. Automating the creation of user accounts

    D. Improving network bandwidth usage

81. Which of the following best describes a fail-closed mechanism in a security infrastructure?

    A. All network services are available to users even if a security device fails to ensure continuous operation

    B. If a security device fails, the system will restrict access to the network or resource, reducing the risk of unauthorized access

    C. User access is granted based on the device's operational status, regardless of security device failure

    D. The system automatically reboots to restore operations if a failure occurs in a security device

82. When planning for disaster recovery, a security administrator must ensure the technological infrastructure can handle the company's critical applications. What aspect of capacity planning does this primarily involve?

    A. People

    B. Data sensitivity

    C. Technology

    D. Geographic location

83. A security team wants to prevent employees from copying sensitive data to USB drives. Which Data loss prevention (DLP) feature should they configure to achieve this?

   A. Monitoring web browsing activity

   B. Restricting file transfers to specific email domains

   C. Blocking or encrypting data transfers to USB devices

   D. Allowing only trusted applications to run

84. In a Network access control (NAC) setup, what is the role of a remediation server?

   A. To log all network activity

   B. To provide updates and patches for non-compliant computers

   C. To enforce policies on compliant computers

   D. To manage Virtual private network (VPN) connections

85. A security team wants to enforce password complexity across all company computers. Which tool should they use?

   A. SELinux

   B. Group Policy

   C. Antivirus software

   D. Firewall

The answers to this mock exam are provided in the Solutions chapter on page **132**.

3

CompTIA Security+ SY0-701 Mock Exam 3

1. To allow secure remote access to the company network, which port should the firewall permit traffic on?

   A. Port 21

   B. Port 22

   C. Port 23

   D. Port 25

2. A security consultant is teaching employees how to identify phishing attempts. Which of the following is a common indicator of a phishing email?

   A. The email is sent from an internal company address

   B. The email requests urgent action and contains suspicious links

   C. The email is from a recognized vendor with a professional tone

   D. The email contains attachments with known file types such as .pdf or .docx

3. How does video surveillance contribute to physical security?

   A. By providing real-time monitoring and recording of activity for later review

   B. By replacing the need for physical security guards

   C. By securing network communications between buildings

   D. By serving as an emergency communication system

4. A security team at a large company wants to evaluate the security posture of a potential vendor before engaging in a business relationship. Which technique would most effectively identify security vulnerabilities within the vendor's systems?

    A. Supply chain analysis

    B. Independent assessments

    C. Penetration testing

    D. Right-to-audit clause

5. An organization uses a platform where security contractors are incentivized to find vulnerabilities. What is this type of program called?

    A. Penetration testing

    B. Bug bounty program

    C. Vulnerability scan

    D. Package monitoring

6. How does zero trust handle access control compared to traditional security models?

    A. Provides access based on network perimeter defenses

    B. Grants access based on user roles only

    C. Continuously evaluates and verifies access requests

    D. Trusts all internal network traffic by default

7. A security analyst is investigating unusual behavior on a company server. Which log type should be checked to review user login events and system-level changes?

    A. Network logs

    B. Application logs

    C. OS-specific security logs

    D. Intrusion detection system (IDS)/Intrusion prevention system (IPS) logs

8. A company has installed a CCTV camera that will not be monitored. Which of the following types of controls describes this setup?

    A. Detective

    B. Deterrent

    C. Physical

    D. Preventive

9. What is the primary role of the data plane in a network?

    A. To manage network routing and control traffic flow

    B. To handle and forward user data packets based on routing decisions

    C. To configure network devices and establish network policies

    D. To monitor and analyze network traffic for security incidents

10. Which AAA component tracks user activities and resource usage?

    A. Authentication

    B. Authorization

    C. Accounting

    D. Auditing

11. Which type of log would a security team review to investigate unauthorized access attempts from external sources?

    A. Application logs

    B. Firewall logs

    C. Endpoint logs

    D. OS-specific security logs

12. Company personnel must provide a photo ID and enter the data center facility through a gate barrier. Which of the following best describes this form of security control?

    A. Physical

    B. Managerial

    C. Technical

    D. Operational

13. In a serverless architecture, where applications run on a cloud provider's infrastructure without being managed by servers, what is a key security implication?

    A. Enhanced control over underlying server configurations

    B. Reduced responsibility for managing and patching operating systems

    C. Increased complexity in data encryption and key management

    D. Simplified access control for managing physical hardware

14. What is the primary purpose of creating secured zones within a network?

    A. To increase the number of network devices connected

    B. To segregate and protect sensitive data by isolating it from less secure areas

    C. To monitor and log all network activity in real-time

    D. To simplify the user authentication process

15. What is the primary purpose of identifying the root cause during an incident investigation?

    A. To determine which systems were affected

    B. To eliminate the fundamental issue that led to the incident and prevent recurrence

    C. To document the incident for compliance purposes

    D. To assess the financial impact of the incident

16. What is the primary function of a hash algorithm in maintaining data integrity?

    A. Encrypting data to prevent unauthorized access

    B. Generating a unique value that represents the original data

    C. Providing a backup in case of data loss

    D. Ensuring data availability during system failures

17. How does risk tolerance affect an organization's approach to vulnerability management?

    A. It determines the frequency of vulnerability scans.

    B. It affects the number of employees needed for security.

    C. It guides decisions on which vulnerabilities to prioritize for remediation.

    D. It influences the design of security policies.

18. What is the primary use of a honey file in a security strategy?

    A. To encrypt sensitive information in storage

    B. To attract and detect unauthorized access attempts to specific files

    C. To manage file versions and backups

    D. To ensure filesystem integrity and consistency

19. Which vulnerability identification method involves hiring an external company to simulate attacks on the organization's network?

   A. Bug bounty program
   B. Third-party assessment
   C. Penetration testing
   D. Vulnerability scan

20. When deploying a new software solution, which consideration is crucial for ease of deployment?

   A. The complexity of the application's user interface
   B. The frequency of software updates and patches
   C. The number of software dependencies and system requirements
   D. Automating available deployment tools and predefined configurations

21. A security team needs to perform a gap analysis. Which tool is often used for this purpose?

   A. Security information and event management
   B. Risk assessment matrix
   C. Benchmarking framework or checklist
   D. Antivirus software

22. During which phase of incident response are logs and evidence collected to understand the scope of an incident?

   A. Preparation
   B. Detection
   C. Analysis
   D. Recovery

23. A security consultant needs to harden the security of an organization's cloud infrastructure. Which of the following hardening techniques would be most relevant?

   A. Implementing regular software updates
   B. Enabling encryption and access controls
   C. Configuring local firewalls
   D. Disabling unused ports on network switches

24. Which of the following is an effective hardening technique to prevent unauthorized access by restricting unused communication methods on a server?

    A. Encryption

    B. Installation of endpoint protection

    C. Disabling ports/protocols

    D. Host-based firewall

25. A large company fails to comply with data protection regulations, resulting in a breach. What is the most likely consequence of non-compliance?

    A. Reputational damage

    B. Loss of license

    C. Fines

    D. Contractual impacts

26. An administrator must ensure that all mail from company clients remains confidential. Which secure protocol is used to encrypt emails?

    A. SMTP

    B. S/MIME

    C. IMAP

    D. HTTP

27. A security team at a large company is undergoing a formal review to ensure they meet industry regulations and internal security policies. What is the main purpose of this audit?

    A. Evaluate employee productivity

    B. Ensure compliance with regulations and policies

    C. Identify business growth opportunities

    D. Create new security policies

28. Which of the following best describes the role of company stakeholders in security operations?

    A. They are the only group responsible for implementing security policies.

    B. They provide input and approval for security decisions that impact business operations.

    C. They are not involved in security operations.

    D. They handle day-to-day security monitoring and incident response.

29. A large company undergoes a review to verify that it complies with industry-specific laws and regulations. What is this process called?

    A. Self-assessment

    B. Independent third-party audit

    C. Regulatory examination

    D. Internal audit

30. What is the purpose of the company conducting a Business impact analysis (BIA) before changing security operations?

    A. To assess the potential effects of changes on business continuity and operations

    B. To determine how quickly a change can be implemented

    C. To reduce the cost of implementing security measures

    D. To increase the speed of decision-making processes

31. What is the main reason for conducting a tabletop exercise in incident response?

    A. To test the effectiveness of automated security tools

    B. To practice and review the incident response plan in a controlled, discussion-based environment

    C. To implement new security patches and updates

    D. To perform a real-time simulation of a security breach

32. What is the primary purpose of key escrow in a Public key infrastructure (PKI) system?

    A. To provide a backup of all public keys in case of loss

    B. To generate encryption keys for secure communication

    C. To distribute public keys to all network users

    D. To store copies of private keys securely, allowing authorized recovery in case of key loss

33. A security analyst wants users to be able to secure their files on the network. They have decided to implement Windows Encrypting File System (EFS). When is file-level encryption most beneficial?

    A. When you need to encrypt the entire disk drive

    B. When encrypting data in transit over a network

    C. When you need to protect specific sensitive files while leaving other files accessible

    D. When encrypting all network communications in a VPN

34. In a large enterprise, which type of Intrusion detection system (IDS) would be best suited to monitor traffic and detect attacks within the internal network?

    A. Host-based IDS

    B. Network-based IDS

    C. Wireless IDS

    D. Signature-based IDS

35. A company server is being used to store encryption keys. What is the role of this key management system (KMS) in an encryption strategy?

    A. To encrypt data at rest on hard drives

    B. To manage, distribute, and store encryption keys securely across the organization

    C. To create backup copies of all encryption keys in plaintext

    D. To perform real-time encryption of network traffic

36. An organization has data that, if lost or tampered with, would severely impact operations and could result in significant financial loss. What is the best classification for this data?

    A. Public

    B. Critical

    C. Restricted

    D. Private

37. What is the primary goal of the preparation phase in incident response?

    A. To identify and analyze potential threats and vulnerabilities

    B. To ensure that all incident response team members are trained and equipped

    C. To recover from the impact of an incident

    D. To contain the spread of the incident

38. Which intrusion detection system (IDS)/intrusion prevention system (IPS) detection method will likely generate false positives due to deviations from normal network behavior?

    A. Signature-based detection

    B. Anomaly-based detection

    C. Protocol-based detection

    D. Heuristic detection

39. Which mobile solution allows employees to select from a company-approved list of devices and use them for work purposes?

    A. Bring your own device (BYOD)

    B. Mobile device management (MDM)

    C. Corporate-owned, personally enabled (COPE)

    D. Choose your own device (CYOD)

40. Which metric would an organization use to measure how much damage a specific vulnerability could cause?

    A. Risk tolerance

    B. Exposure factor

    C. False positive rate

    D. Common Vulnerability Scoring System (CVSS) base score

41. How does tokenization differ from encryption in terms of data protection?

    A. Tokenization alters the original data to make it unreadable, while encryption replaces data with random tokens.

    B. Encryption is used for data in transit, while tokenization is only for data at rest.

    C. Tokenization can be reversed to reveal the original data, while encryption cannot.

    D. Encryption secures data by transforming it with an algorithm, while tokenization replaces sensitive data with a token that is stored separately.

42. Which authentication protocol should a company use to provide secure and scalable authentication services across its network?

    A. Internet Protocol Security (IPSec)

    B. Simple Authentication and Security Layer (SASL)

    C. Lightweight Directory Access Protocol (LDAP)

    D. Extensible Authentication Protocol (EAP)

43. Data masking needs to meet an organization's compliance requirements. Which is the most likely requirement?

    A. Storing all data in plaintext for easy access

    B. Protecting personal data in non-production environments, such as during software testing

    C. Ensuring that all data is encrypted before transmission

    D. Creating multiple backups of sensitive data for disaster recovery

44. The security administrator relies on a root of trust (RoT) to set up a secure network infrastructure. What is the role of the RoT in a cryptographic system?

    A. To act as the foundational trust anchor that validates all digital certificates within a public key infrastructure (PKI)

    B. To store encrypted user passwords securely

    C. To manage and distribute encryption keys across the network

    D. To handle all network traffic encryption and decryption processes

45. A company is concerned about complying with legal requirements that dictate where data must be stored based on the data's geographic origin. What concept is the company focusing on?

    A. Geolocation

    B. Data sovereignty

    C. Data in use

    D. Data at rest

46. A group of individuals working together to commit cybercrime for financial gain is best described as which type of threat actor?

    A. Organized crime

    B. Nation-state

    C. Insider threat

    D. Hacktivist

47. A security consultant notices that an employee has accessed confidential data outside of business hours, which is unusual for their role. How would this behavior be categorized?

    A. Routine behavior

    B. Unintentional access

    C. Unexpected behavior

    D. Risky behavior

48. Employees use unauthorized personal devices and cloud services to bypass corporate IT policies. What is this an example of?

    A. Insider threat

    B. Shadow IT

    C. Unskilled attacker

    D. Nation-state

49. Attackers use social engineering to trick employees into disclosing sensitive information over the phone. What is this attack vector?

    A. File-based attack

    B. Image-based attack

    C. Voice call attack

    D. Removable device

50. Who is primarily responsible for establishing policies and ensuring that data is used and managed according to those policies within an organization?

    A. Data custodian

    B. Data owner

    C. Data processor

    D. Security administrator

51. An organization experiences a breach because an employee unknowingly installed malicious software from a seemingly legitimate image file received via email. What is this attack an example of?

    A. File-based attack

    B. Unsupported systems and applications

    C. Vulnerable software

    D. Image-based attack

52. A security administrator discovers that employees have received text messages with malicious links pretending to be from the company's IT department. What is this attack an example of?

    A. Phishing

    B. Vishing

    C. Smishing

    D. Impersonation

53. An attacker poses as the CEO, sending a fraudulent email to the finance department requesting a wire transfer. What is this type of attack known as?

    A. Pretexting

    B. Business email compromise

    C. Vishing

    D. Watering hole

54. What is the purpose of a legal hold in the context of digital forensics?

    A. To ensure that all digital evidence is encrypted before analysis

    B. To prevent the alteration or destruction of relevant data and evidence

    C. To automatically back up data to a secure location

    D. To conduct a real-time analysis of network traffic

55. A security administrator finds that a company's website has been targeted by attackers who created a fake website that closely resembles the original but with a slight misspelling in the domain name. What is this attack called?

    A. Typosquatting

    B. Brand impersonation

    C. Phishing

    D. Watering hole

56. Which of the following is a key principle of the chain of custody in digital forensics?

    A. Ensuring that data is deleted after analysis.

    B. Documenting every person who handles the evidence and every action taken.

    C. Encrypting evidence to prevent unauthorized access.

    D. Removing evidence from the original location for analysis.

57. A security consultant finds that a company's hardware devices run outdated software without updates or support. What type of vulnerability is this an example of?

    A. Firmware

    B. End-of-life

    C. Legacy

    D. Resource reuse

58. During a security assessment, the consultant discovers that an attacker could break out of the guest operating system and interact with the host system. What is this type of vulnerability called?

    A. Legacy

    B. Resource reuse

    C. Virtual machine escape

    D. Firmware

59. A consultant finds that old network devices still in use are no longer receiving security patches from the manufacturer. What type of vulnerability is this?

    A. End-of-life

    B. Zero-day

    C. Virtual machine escape

    D. Firmware

60. During an investigation, the security consultant discovers a piece of malware that appears to perform a legitimate function but secretly records keystrokes and sends them to an attacker. What type of malware is this most likely to be?

    A. Keylogger

    B. Rootkit

    C. Logic bomb

    D. Worm

61. During a security assessment, the consultant discovers that an unauthorized individual has copied the information from an employee's access badge to gain entry into restricted areas. What type of malicious activity does this suggest?

    A. Brute force

    B. RFID cloning

    C. Environmental attack

    D. Keylogger

62. Which risk management strategy involves purchasing insurance to handle the financial impact of a potential security breach?

    A. Accept

    B. Avoid

    C. Transfer

    D. Mitigate

63. During an investigation, the security consultant discovers that an attacker is sending spoofed requests to a server, causing it to respond to a victim's IP address with a flood of data. What type of attack does this describe?

    A. Reflected attack

    B. Wireless attack

    C. Credential replay attack

    D. DNS attack

64. Which risk analysis method uses numerical data, such as potential financial loss and likelihood of occurrence, to evaluate risk?

    A. Qualitative risk analysis

    B. Quantitative risk analysis

    C. Probability-based risk analysis

    D. Impact-based risk analysis

65. Which policy defines the rules and guidelines for employees' use of company systems and resources, including user behavior and prohibited actions?

    A. Business continuity plan

    B. Incident response plan

    C. Acceptable use policy (AUP)

    D. Disaster recovery plan

66. During a security audit, the administrator finds that attackers can access restricted directories on a server by manipulating URL paths. What type of attack does this describe?

    A. Replay attack

    B. Buffer overflow

    C. Directory traversal

    D. Request forgery

67. A company's security team ensures compliance with industry regulations by regularly assessing its security practices and documenting the results. What process is this?

    A. Due diligence

    B. Attestation and acknowledgment

    C. Internal automation

    D. Supply chain analysis

68. During a cryptographic analysis, the security team finds that two different inputs produced the same hash value, undermining the integrity of a hashing algorithm. What type of cryptographic attack is this?

    A. Birthday attack

    B. Downgrade attack

    C. Collision attack

    D. Side-channel attack

69. An attacker uses a tool to try every possible combination of characters to guess a user's password, regardless of account lockout policies. What type of attack is this?

    A. Password spraying

    B. Brute-force attack

    C. Dictionary attack

    D. Credential stuffing

70. A security administrator observes that the same user account is logged in from two different geographic locations simultaneously, which is impossible given the travel time between them. What is this an example of?

    A. Out-of-cycle logging

    B. Concurrent session usage

    C. Impossible travel

    D. Missing logs

71. To protect sensitive data from being accessed by external threats, a company physically separates its most critical systems from any network connection, including the internet. What is this technique called?

    A. Demilitarized zone (DMZ)

    B. Virtual local area network (VLAN)

    C. Air-gap

    D. Subnetting

72. An administrator wants to block all email traffic on the firewall. Which protocol and port should be specified in the firewall rule?

    A. Allow HTTP on port 80

    B. Deny DNS on port 53

    C. Allow FTP on port 21

    D. Deny SMTP on port 25

73. Which of the following is a key benefit of using an application allow list as a mitigation technique?

    A. It blocks all network traffic by default.

    B. It ensures only pre-approved applications can run, reducing the risk of malware.

    C. It allows applications to run except for those on a block list.

    D. It automatically updates with the latest software patches.

74. What is the purpose of configuring a firewall with specific rules for different types of network traffic?

    A. To reduce network latency

    B. To control and secure network communications

    C. To increase network throughput

    D. To enhance the speed of the internet connection

75. A security team at a large company needs to ensure that a vendor will meet specific performance and uptime expectations for a cloud service. Which type of agreement should they establish to formalize these expectations?

    A. Memorandum of agreement (MOA)

    B. Service-level agreement (SLA)

    C. Non-disclosure agreement (NDA)

    D. Master service agreement (MSA)

76. Which data source would a security team use to proactively identify security weaknesses in the company's network before exploiting them?

    A. Dashboards

    B. Vulnerability scans

    C. Packet captures

    D. Automated reports

77. When using a microservices architecture, where applications are divided into loosely coupled services, what is the main security challenge?

    A. Increased difficulty in scaling services independently

    B. Enhanced monitoring and logging across the entire application

    C. Complexity in ensuring secure communication between microservices

    D. Reduced need for application-level encryption

78. Which consideration is most important when planning for scalability in a cloud architecture?

    A. Choosing a single server with high processing power

    B. Using a stateless design and auto-scaling groups to handle varying loads

    C. Ensuring that all components are tightly integrated to avoid scaling issues

    D. Limiting the number of users to reduce the need for scaling

79. Which data type is a company's proprietary algorithms and patented technologies considered to be?

    A. Intellectual property

    B. Regulated

    C. Financial information

    D. Human-readable

80. During a tabletop exercise, which of the following is typically discussed?

    A. Real-time network traffic and anomalies

    B. The theoretical response to a hypothetical incident scenario

    C. Detailed technical configurations of network devices

    D. Current security software and hardware performance metrics

81. A security administrator uses software to scramble data into a different form that can only be interpreted by someone with the correct key. What is this process called?

    A. Segmentation

    B. Masking

    C. Hashing

    D. Obfuscation

82. In which phase should an organization perform an after-incident review to identify what went wrong and how to improve future responses?

    A. Preparation

    B. Eradication

    C. Lessons Learned

    D. Containment

83. A firewall is configured with a default rule that blocks all incoming traffic. What is this type of rule commonly known as?

    A. Allow list

    B. Deny list

    C. Default deny

    D. Default allow

84. A security analyst monitors network traffic and needs to identify the exact contents of suspicious packets. Which data source would be most helpful?

    A. Dashboards

    B. Vulnerability scans

    C. Packet captures

    D. Automated reports

85. Which capability is enhanced by implementing extended detection and response (XDR) over traditional Endpoint detection and response (EDR)?

    A. Centralized control over all user passwords

    B. Comprehensive threat detection across multiple environments, including networks, servers, and endpoints

    C. Automatic software updates for all company devices

    D. Basic antivirus protection for workstations

The answers to this mock exam are provided in the Solutions chapter on page **154**.

4

CompTIA Security+ SY0-701 Mock Exam 4

1. While developing a security strategy, a security administrator considers how data is handled when applications are actively processing it. What is this type of data called?

    A. Data at rest

    B. Data sovereignty

    C. Data in use

    D. Data in transit

2. The security team has been called into a company to perform digital forensics. What is the primary goal during the Acquisition phase?

    A. To analyse and interpret the data to understand the impact of the incident

    B. To securely collect and create a bit-by-bit copy of the original digital evidence

    C. To prepare a detailed report of the incident response

    D. To preserve evidence by storing it in a secure facility

3. An employee reports a suspicious email that requests personal information. What is the first step a security consultant should recommend the employee take when responding to such an email?

    A. Immediately forward the email to colleagues to increase their awareness.

    B. Delete the email without notifying anyone.

    C. Report the email to the company's security team or help desk.

    D. Click on the links to investigate the sender's intent.

4. Which of the following focuses on ensuring that the company can continue operating critical functions when faced with a significant disruption?

    A. Information security policy

    B. Change management policy

    C. Business continuity plan

    D. Acceptable use policy (AUP)

5. What is the primary function of a honeytoken in security?

    A. To encrypt data in transit

    B. To act as a decoy token that alerts administrators to unauthorized access or tampering

    C. To provide real-time security updates to users

    D. To manage user authentication across multiple systems

6. What is one of the primary roles of security guards in physical security?

    A. To monitor network traffic for suspicious activity

    B. To provide a human presence that can deter unauthorized access and respond to incidents

    C. To configure and maintain access control systems

    D. To perform regular audits of security logs

7. Which method is the most effective for ensuring that data on a decommissioned solid-state drive (SSD) is completely unrecoverable?

    A. Degaussing the SSD

    B. Using secure erase commands specific to SSDs

    C. Performing a quick format

    D. Reinstalling the operating system

8. A recent audit made a significant finding regarding deploying a particular encryption standard in a web application for business communication. The company's technical restrictions prevent it from upgrading the encryption standard. Which kind of control should be applied to reduce the risk in this scenario?

    A. Physical

    B. Detective

    C. Preventive

    D. Compensating

9. Which of the following is a typical security concern related to the data plane?

   A. Unauthorized changes to routing protocols

   B. Data interception and modification during transmission

   C. Misconfiguration of network policies

   D. Unauthorized access to network configuration settings

10. Which authorization model uses a combination of attributes to determine access permissions?

   A. Role-based access control (RBAC)

   B. Discretionary access control (DAC)

   C. Attribute-based access control (ABAC)

   D. Mandatory access control (MAC)

11. An IT manager has to create a policy to enable secure access to the research and development department computers. Which type of security control is the manager using?

   A. Compensating

   B. Managerial

   C. Operational

   D. Technical

12. Which data type includes contracts, agreements, and other legal documentation that must be protected to ensure compliance and confidentiality?

   A. Trade secret

   B. Legal information

   C. Intellectual property

   D. Non-human readable

13. Which of the following methods is typically used to implement adaptive identity?

   A. Applying static IP address assignments to all users

   B. Utilizing behavioral analytics to adjust access permissions dynamically

   C. Limiting access to only those with physical security badges

   D. Configuring fixed access rights for all employees

14. Which of the following strategies is most effective for ensuring the high availability of a critical system?

    A.   Implementing strong password policies

    B.   Performing regular data backups

    C.   Using redundant systems and failover solutions

    D.   Encrypting all sensitive data

15. An administrator notices that a server's CPU and memory usage have unexpectedly spiked, leading to degraded performance and slow response times. What does this behavior suggest?

    A.   Resource consumption

    B.   Resource inaccessibility

    C.   Out-of-cycle logging

    D.   Missing logs

16. What is the role of micro-segmentation in a zero-trust environment?

    A.   Encrypting data at rest

    B.   Isolating network segments to limit lateral movement

    C.   Providing single sign-on (SSO) capabilities

    D.   Ensuring endpoint protection

17. The CEO asks the security team how a gap analysis differs from a vulnerability assessment. What is the best answer?

    A.   Gap analysis compares current practices to standards, while vulnerability assessments identify system weaknesses.

    B.   Vulnerability assessments compare current security measures to industry standards.

    C.   Gap analysis is a type of vulnerability assessment.

    D.   Vulnerability assessments are conducted to develop security policies.

18. What is the main advantage of using a screened subnet (DMZ) in a network architecture?

    A.   It increases internal network bandwidth

    B.   It provides extra layers of security for public-facing services

    C.   It allows unrestricted access to all internal resources

    D.   It simplifies network configuration by removing all firewalls

19. Which of the following is the best solution for providing long-term power during an extended outage and maintaining the operation of a company's critical infrastructure?

    A. Battery backups

    B. Uninterruptible power supply (UPS)

    C. Portable power bank

    D. Generator

20. An administrator must ensure that only authorized personnel can access a high-value server. What is the most likely security measure?

    A. Data encryption

    B. Access control

    C. Asset ownership

    D. Network monitoring

21. Which protocol is commonly used with single sign-on (SSO) to authenticate users using a single set of credentials across multiple applications?

    A. Lightweight Directory Access Protocol (LDAP)

    B. Open Authorization (OAuth)

    C. Security Assertion Markup Language (SAML)

    D. Simple Mail Transfer Protocol (SMTP)

22. What is the primary purpose of Open Authorization (OAuth) in a single sign-on (SSO) implementation?

    A. To provide authentication across multiple domains

    B. To grant third-party applications limited access to user resources without sharing credentials

    C. To manage user identities in a centralized directory

    D. To enable user account synchronization across different services

23. Which access control model allows users to decide who can access their files or resources?

    A. Mandatory access control (MAC)

    B. Discretionary access control (DAC)

    C. Role-based access control (RBAC)

    D. Rule-based access control

24. When assigning ownership of a software asset, what is the owner's primary role?

    A. To update the software regularly

    B. To perform security audits

    C. To manage the asset's life cycle and decide on security access

    D. To monitor and manage network traffic

25. To ensure that a vendor maintains security standards over time, a company includes a clause in its contract that allows it to verify the vendor's security practices. What is this most likely called?

    A. Penetration testing clause

    B. Right-to-audit clause

    C. Evidence of vulnerability scanning clause

    D. Supply chain verification clause

26. Which access control model grants or denies access based on predefined rules, such as network security policies?

    A. Role-based access control (RBAC)

    B. Discretionary access control (DAC)

    C. Rule-based access control

    D. Attribute-based access control (ABAC)

27. A company must implement a firewall rule allowing only outgoing emails from its mail server. Which protocol and port should be allowed?

    A. Simple Mail Transfer Protocol (SMTP) on port 25

    B. Post Office Protocol version 3 (POP3) on port 110

    C. Internet Message Access Protocol (IMAP) on port 143

    D. Hypertext Transfer Protocol (HTTP) on port 80

28. Which of the following is the primary purpose of an independent third-party audit for a company's security program?

    A. To identify cost-saving opportunities in IT budgets

    B. To provide an unbiased, objective review of security controls and practices

    C. To approve the security team's compliance reports

    D. To review employee access management practices internally

29. Which of the following is an example of something you have in multi-factor authentication?

    A. Password

    B. Security key

    C. Fingerprint scan

    D. Personal identification number (PIN)

30. A security administrator must securely connect to a remote server within the internal network. Which is the best protocol to use?

    A. Telnet

    B. SSH

    C. FTP

    D. HTTP

31. A company must ensure that its internal web servers are only accessible over a secure connection. Which protocol and port should be allowed through the firewall?

    A. HTTP on port 80

    B. HTTPS on port 443

    C. FTP on port 21

    D. Telnet on port 23

32. How is a public key typically distributed in a public key infrastructure (PKI) environment?

    A. It is sent directly to the recipient via an encrypted email

    B. It is stored in a secure hardware module that is accessible only to the key owner

    C. It is published in a public directory or sent with a digital certificate

    D. It is encrypted using the private key before distribution

33. To streamline compliance monitoring, a company automates the collection of security logs and generates reports that track adherence to regulatory requirements. What type of compliance monitoring does this represent?

    A. External attestation

    B. Internal automation

    C. Acknowledgement process

    D. Due care

34. Which encryption method is primarily used to secure data during transmission over the internet?

   A. Full-disk encryption

   B. File-level encryption

   C. Transport Layer Security (TLS)

   D. PHP for database storage

35. What is the primary purpose of a secure enclave in modern computing devices?

   A. To isolate sensitive computations and encryption processes from the central operating system

   B. To store large amounts of data securely

   C. To manage network encryption keys in real-time

   D. To perform software updates automatically

36. A security analyst is tasked with enhancing the security of stored passwords in the company's database. What should the analyst implement to prevent attackers from easily cracking passwords using pre-computed rainbow tables?

   A. Encrypt all passwords using a symmetric key

   B. Use salting to add a unique value to each password before hashing

   C. Implement digital signatures for password storage

   D. Store passwords in plain text but with restricted access

37. A company's security administrator must ensure that emails sent from the CEO's office are authentic and have not been altered. Which technology should the analyst implement?

   A. Digital signatures

   B. Salting

   C. Key stretching

   D. Blockchain

38. A security administrator must obtain a new Secure Sockets Layer (SSL)/Transport Layer Security (TLS) certificate for the organization's website. What is the first step in this process?

   A. Generate a certificate signing request (CSR) and submit it to a certificate authority (CA)

   B. Download the certificate revocation list (CRL)

   C. Configure the Online Certificate Status Protocol (OCSP)

   D. Create a wildcard certificate for the entire domain

39. Which type of threat actor is most likely to be involved in cyber espionage targeting national defense systems or intellectual property?

    A. Nation-state
    B. Hacktivist
    C. Unskilled attacker
    D. Shadow IT

40. What is a common motivation for hacktivists when conducting cyberattacks?

    A. Financial gain
    B. Political or social change
    C. Espionage
    D. Personal vendetta

41. An attacker creates a fake website that mimics a popular social media platform to steal user credentials. What is the best example of this attack?

    A. Pretexting
    B. Brand impersonation
    C. Watering hole
    D. Smishing

42. A security administrator identifies a campaign where attackers spread false information on social media to damage the reputation of a competitor. What is this type of threat best known as?

    A. Misinformation
    B. Disinformation
    C. Pretexting
    D. Impersonation

43. An attacker contacts a company's help desk, imitating an employee who has forgotten their password, to attempt to access the network. What is this tactic most likely called?

    A. Vishing
    B. Pretexting
    C. Business email compromise
    D. Smishing

44. An attacker leaves malicious links on websites frequently visited by the employees of a targeted organization. What is this type of attack known as?

   A. Watering hole

   B. Phishing

   C. Typosquatting

   D. Impersonation

45. An attacker uses phone calls to impersonate a bank representative to steal personal information from victims. What is the most likely attack vector?

   A. Phishing

   B. Smishing

   C. Vishing

   D. Pretexting

46. A security consultant is concerned about the risks associated with devices that operate on outdated, unsupported operating systems. Which category does this fall under?

   A. Virtual machine escape

   B. Resource reuse

   C. Legacy

   D. Firmware

47. An organization uses several old machines for critical operations that the vendor no longer supports. What is this type of vulnerability best described as?

   A. Firmware

   B. End of life

   C. Virtual machine escape

   D. Resource reuse

48. A security consultant finds malware that spreads across the network by exploiting vulnerabilities without user interaction. What type of malicious software is this?

   A. Spyware

   B. Trojan

   C. Worm

   D. Virus

49. A security consultant finds that the company's data center is at risk due to extreme temperatures and humidity levels, which could potentially damage the equipment. What type of malicious activity or risk does this scenario describe?

   A. Environmental

   B. Brute force

   C. RFID cloning

   D. Social engineering

50. A security consultant identifies that multiple DNS servers are being used to amplify traffic sent to the company's web servers, resulting in overwhelming data. What type of attack does this indicate?

   A. On-path attack

   B. DNS attack

   C. Amplified attack

   D. Malicious code attack

51. While monitoring network activity, the consultant notices that an attacker intercepts and alters communications between two parties without their knowledge. What type of attack is this most likely to be?

   A. On-path attack

   B. Wireless attack

   C. Credential replay attack

   D. Distributed denial of service (DDoS)

52. A company's security team identifies that an attacker has intercepted and reused a valid authentication session to access a system. What type of attack is this most likely to be?

   A. Privilege escalation

   B. Buffer overflow

   C. Replay attack

   D. Injection

53. An attacker leverages a flaw in a hashing algorithm that reduces the difficulty of generating hashes whose inputs produce the same hash value. What type of attack is most likely happening?

    A. Collision attack

    B. Replay attack

    C. Man-in-the-middle (MiTM) attack

    D. Downgrade attack

54. Which of the following best describes an attacker attempting to log in using a list of common passwords against multiple user accounts in a system?

    A. Rainbow table attack

    B. Credential stuffing

    C. Brute-force attack

    D. Password spraying

55. During a security audit, a system administrator finds that certain websites are no longer accessible to employees, and some online services malfunction. What could this indicate?

    A. Blocked content

    B. Resource consumption

    C. Account lockout

    D. Published/documented information

56. A security consultant suggests placing publicly accessible servers such as web and email servers on separate networks sitting between the private internal network and the internet. What is this network segment commonly called?

    A. Virtual local area network (VLAN)

    B. Air gap

    C. Demilitarized zone (DMZ)

    D. Intrusion detection system (IDS)

57. To enhance security, a company restricts the ability to read, write, or execute files to specific users or groups. What is this practice an example of?

    A. Multi-factor authentication (MFA)

    B. Firewall access control list (ACL)

    C. Permissions

    D. Intrusion prevention system (IPS)

58. A company wants to prevent known malicious applications from executing on its systems while allowing all other software. Which approach should the security consultant suggest?

    A. Implementing a block list

    B. Using a firewall

    C. Deploying a virtual private network (VPN)

    D. Configuring a honeypot

59. What is the main drawback of relying solely on a block list for application security?

    A. It can lead to an excessive number of false positives.

    B. It may allow new or unknown malicious software to run.

    C. It blocks all traffic by default, causing disruption.

    D. It is difficult to manage in a small environment.

60. What is the primary security risk associated with using legacy applications that are no longer supported or updated?

    A. They may have enhanced performance due to years of optimization.

    B. They are more resistant to modern security threats.

    C. They often have known vulnerabilities that cannot be patched.

    D. They provide better integration with new systems.

61. To enhance the security of a server, a consultant suggests implementing a host-based intrusion prevention system (HIPS). What is the primary function of a HIPS?

    A. Encrypt data stored on the server

    B. Prevent unauthorized physical access to the server

    C. Monitor and block suspicious activities and potential intrusions

    D. Manage user access controls and permissions

62. A security consultant advises changing default passwords on all devices within the network. What is the primary reason for this recommendation?

    A. Default passwords are often easily guessable and known to attackers

    B. Default passwords are typically encrypted by default

    C. Default passwords are managed by endpoint protection software

    D. Default passwords help in maintaining compliance with security policies

63. What distinguishes a simulation from a tabletop exercise in incident response testing?

   A. Simulations involve a hands-on, practical approach to responding to an incident, while tabletop exercises are discussion-based.

   B. Simulations are not as detailed or as realistic as tabletop exercises.

   C. Tabletop exercises focus on real-time response actions, while simulations are used for theoretical planning.

   D. Simulations do not involve team participation, whereas tabletop exercises require team collaboration.

64. Which of the following actions is part of the Preservation phase in digital forensics?

   A. Rebuilding affected systems to restore normal operations

   B. Ensuring that evidence is stored in a way that prevents modification or tampering

   C. Documenting the results of the forensic analysis in a report

   D. Conducting interviews with users involved in the incident

65. In a virtualized environment, where multiple virtual machines (VMs) run on the same physical hardware, what is a key security risk that needs to be managed?

   A. Increased physical security requirements for the data center

   B. Potential for VM escape, where a compromised VM could affect the host or other VMs

   C. Simplified data backup procedures

   D. Guaranteed isolation between VMs by default

66. A company has called in a forensic analyst to perform E-Discovery. What is E-Discovery primarily concerned with?

   A. The recovery of deleted files from hard drives

   B. Identifying, collecting, and reviewing electronic data for legal proceedings

   C. Encrypting sensitive data during transmission

   D. Monitoring network traffic for unusual activity

67. A security administrator needs to ensure that information that is freely available and does not require special protection is correctly categorized. What classification should this data have?

   A. Confidential

   B. Sensitive

   C. Restricted

   D. Public

68. A security administrator wants to enforce data privacy by restricting access to specific datasets based on different countries. What technique are they using?

    A. Geographic restrictions

    B. Hashing

    C. Masking

    D. Permission restrictions

69. What should a security administrator do during the Analysis phase to effectively handle an incident?

    A. Deploy patches to fix vulnerabilities

    B. Determine the scope, impact, and nature of the incident

    C. Communicate with stakeholders about the incident

    D. Update the organization's security policies and procedures

70. Which practices are essential when hardening an industrial control system (ICS) or supervisory control and data acquisition (SCADA) system?

    A. Regularly updating the firmware

    B. Enforcing strong password policies

    C. Isolating the ICS/SCADA network from other networks

    D. Installing antivirus software on all devices

71. To ensure the security of IoT devices within an enterprise, which of the following hardening measures is most effective?

    A. Enabling default user accounts

    B. Disabling automatic updates

    C. Changing default credentials and implementing network segmentation

    D. Increasing device screen brightness

72. What technology should be implemented when a company wants to secure mobile devices and manage their configuration remotely?

    A. Connection methods

    B. Mobile device management (MDM)

    C. Deployment models

    D. Corporate-owned, personally enabled (COPE)

73. Which cryptographic protocol is typically used when implementing a wireless network security solution that includes strong encryption and integrity checking?

   A. Advanced Encryption Standard (AES)

   B. Rivest Cipher 4 (RC4)

   C. Data Encryption Standard (DES)

   D. Secure Hash Algorithm (SHA)

74. A security consultant is implementing a mechanism to ensure that data entered into a web application is checked and filtered for validity before processing. What is this process called?

   A. Code signing

   B. Secure cookies

   C. Input validation

   D. Static code analysis

75. To enhance the security of session management in a web application, which technique should prevent cookies from being accessed by unauthorized scripts?

   A. Code signing

   B. Input validation

   C. Secure cookies

   D. Static code analysis

76. What classification level should be given to financial records that must be protected from unauthorized access but are still required for business operations?

   A. Public

   B. Restricted

   C. Confidential

   D. Sensitive

77. During a routine audit, a security administrator discovers several unauthorized devices connected to the network. Which asset management practice could help prevent this issue in the future?

   A. Implementing a patch management policy

   B. Regularly updating antivirus software

   C. Maintaining a comprehensive asset inventory

   D. Encrypting all network communications

78. What is the critical difference between data sanitization and data destruction?

    A. Sanitization permanently removes data, while destruction renders hardware unusable.

    B. Sanitization is faster than destruction.

    C. Destruction is used for software, while sanitization is used for hardware.

    D. Destruction temporarily removes data, while sanitization permanently removes it.

79. A security administrator must decommission a server with sensitive data. Before physically disposing of the server, what steps should be taken?

    A. Reboot the server to ensure that all processes are terminated

    B. Run a secure data sanitization process on the hard drives

    C. Reformat the server's operating system

    D. Change the server's IP address

80. What must be considered to ensure compliance when implementing a data retention policy?

    A. The color of the hardware casing

    B. Regulatory requirements for data storage and deletion

    C. The number of users accessing the data

    D. The geographic location of the company's headquarters

81. What is the primary function of a signature in an intrusion detection system (IDS)/intrusion prevention system (IPS)?

    A. To encrypt sensitive data before transmission

    B. To define patterns of known threats and vulnerabilities

    C. To create rules for blocking outbound traffic

    D. To optimize network bandwidth usage

82. In a web filtering solution, what is the function of block rules?

    A. To allow access to all websites except those explicitly blocked

    B. To block all traffic by default and permit only allowed sites

    C. To block access to websites based on specific criteria

    D. To enable unrestricted access during non-business hours

83. Which of the following is an example of using automation for resource provisioning?

    A. Manual hardware installation

    B. Automated virtual machine deployment

    C. Manual configuration of network settings

    D. Manual software updates

84. A security consultant identifies a risk of attackers exploiting improperly handled or cleared memory in a virtual environment. What is this type of vulnerability called?

    A. Resource reuse

    B. Firmware

    C. End of life

    D. Legacy

85. Which of the following is an example of something you know in multi-factor authentication?

    A. Security key

    B. Fingerprint scan

    C. Password

    D. Smartcard

The answers to this mock exam are provided in the Solutions chapter on page **177**.

CompTIA Security+ SY0-701
Mock Exam 5

1. An investigation reveals that a user process exploited a vulnerability to gain access to higher-level system files than intended. What type of attack does this indicate?

   A. Privilege escalation

   B. Cross-site forgery

   C. Buffer overflow

   D. Directory traversal

2. A company requests proof from a third-party vendor that it regularly reviews its security policies and procedures. What type of documentation would most likely satisfy this requirement?

   A. Departmental quarterly reviews

   B. Right-to-audit clause

   C. Supply chain analysis reports

   D. Penetration testing results

3. An employee downloads a file infected with malware from a suspicious email link. What type of behavior would this be classified as?

   A. Defensive behavior

   B. Intentional violation

   C. Unexpected behavior

   D. Unintentional behavior

4. What is the primary purpose of installing bollards before a building's entrance?

    A. To enhance aesthetic appeal

    B. To monitor foot traffic into the building

    C. To act as a backup lighting system

    D. To prevent unauthorized vehicle access

5. What is the process of documenting and tracking the ownership and status of hardware assets within an organization most commonly known as?

    A. Incident response

    B. Asset management

    C. Data encryption

    D. Threat modeling

6. What is the key benefit of regularly updating a company's software inventory?

    A. Ensuring compliance with software licenses

    B. Increasing the speed of network connections

    C. Reducing the power consumption of devices

    D. Preventing hardware failures

7. Following an incident in which the company lost data, what type of control will be used to establish how the incident happened?

    A. Technical

    B. Detective

    C. Corrective

    D. Administrative

8. Due to non-compliance with regulatory standards, a company loses the right to operate in certain sectors. What consequence of non-compliance does this represent?

    A. Contractual impacts

    B. Loss of license

    C. Reputational damage

    D. Fines

9. Why might a company purchase cyber insurance as part of its vulnerability management strategy?

    A. To reduce the number of vulnerability scans

    B. To financially protect against potential losses from a security breach

    C. To avoid having to apply patches

    D. To improve the effectiveness of compensating controls

10. Which log data type would a security analyst use to track communications between devices monitored on internal and external traffic patterns?

    A. Network logs

    B. Application logs

    C. OS-specific security logs

    D. Intrusion prevention system (IPS)/Intrusion detection system (IDS) logs

11. The security team has been asked to provide the appropriate security control for various risks. Which of the following is an example of a directive security control?

    A. Security training programs for employees

    B. Intrusion detection systems (IDSs)

    C. Firewalls

    D. Data encryption

12. Which of the following controls serve as an example of an MFA method for verifying user identity?

    A. Username and password

    B. Password and PIN

    C. Password and a one-time code sent to a mobile device

    D. Password alone

13. A company wants to verify that a software application has not been tampered with and is from a trusted source. Which security measure should it use?

    A. Secure cookies

    B. Input validation

    C. Static code analysis

    D. Code signing

14. Which of the following scenarios best illustrates a potential conflict between confidentiality and availability?

   A. Implementing encryption algorithms that slow down system performance

   B. Using digital signatures to verify data authenticity

   C. Backing up data to multiple locations for disaster recovery

   D. Enforcing strict access controls that speed up user access to resources

15. Anomaly-based detection in an IDS/IPS is designed to identify which type of network behaviour?

   A. Behaviour that matches known attack patterns

   B. Normal behaviour based on established baselines

   C. Suspicious behaviour that deviates from standard patterns

   D. Behaviour associated with specific IP addresses

16. What is the primary benefit of using a Security information and event management (SIEM) tool in a large company?

   A. It provides a secure tunnel for remote access

   B. It filters spam emails

   C. It aggregates and analyzes events across the network for alerts and reporting

   D. It manages user identities and access rights

17. A security consultant needs to perform a gap analysis exercise. Which of the following is a typical step in performing a gap analysis?

   A. Developing an incident response plan

   B. Comparing current security measures with industry standards or regulations

   C. Implementing encryption across all data systems

   D. Conducting a vulnerability assessment of the network

18. Reviewing the company's resilience and recovery plans, a security administrator determines that the current infrastructure does not support the required load during peak disaster recovery scenarios. What is the administrator likely focusing on?

   A. Capacity planning

   B. Incident response

   C. Data encryption

   D. Access control

19. When a security consultant must ensure that application code adheres to security best practices and does not have hidden vulnerabilities, which practice should they implement?

    A. Code signing

    B. Input validation

    C. Static code analysis

    D. Secure cookies

20. Which of the following best describes the primary function of the control plane in a network?

    A. To handle user data traffic between network devices

    B. To manage and route traffic based on network policies and routing protocols

    C. To encrypt and decrypt data packets as they travel through the network

    D. To provide physical security measures for network hardware

21. What does adaptive identity management primarily aim to achieve in a network security context?

    A. To enforce rigid user access policies

    B. To adapt access controls based on real-time risk assessments

    C. To monitor network traffic for unauthorized access

    D. To provide a static set of permissions for all users

22. During a security review, a consultant identifies several users with weak passwords, which attackers could easily exploit. How should this type of behavior be described?

    A. Unexpected behavior

    B. Risky behavior

    C. Unintentional behavior

    D. Malicious behavior

23. Which method is most commonly used to protect a private key within a Public key infrastructure (PKI) system?

    A. Storing it on a publicly accessible server

    B. Encrypting it with a strong passphrase or storing it in a hardware security module (HSM)

    C. Sharing it with trusted third parties

    D. Distributing it along with the public key

24. Which statement accurately differentiates asymmetric from symmetric encryption?

    A. Asymmetric encryption uses a single key for both encryption and decryption

    B. Symmetric encryption is generally faster than asymmetric encryption

    C. Symmetric encryption is used for digital signatures, while asymmetric is used for bulk data encryption

    D. Asymmetric encryption is always used for full-disk encryption

25. An administrator is asked to safely store the organization's encryption keys. How does a trusted platform module (TPM) differ from a hardware security module (HSM)?

    A. TPMs are software-based, while HSMs are hardware-based

    B. TPMs are integrated into devices as chips, while HSMs are external devices

    C. TPMs manage cloud-based encryption keys, while HSMs handle local keys only

    D. TPMs perform real-time encryption, while HSMs only store keys

26. What is the purpose of key-stretching techniques such as PBKDF2 and bcrypt?

    A. To shorten encryption keys for faster processing

    B. To enhance password security by increasing the time required to perform brute-force attacks

    C. To increase the length of a password to meet security requirements

    D. To generate public-private key pairs for encryption

27. A security contractor working for an organization is tasked with ensuring that all financial transactions are transparent and cannot be tampered with after being recorded. The contractor suggests using blockchain technology. Which feature of blockchain best supports this requirement?

    A. The use of symmetric encryption to secure transactions

    B. The creation of a public ledger where all transactions are visible and immutable

    C. The implementation of digital signatures for each transaction

    D. The addition of salting to each transaction to prevent data breaches

28. A security analyst needs to secure multiple subdomains within the organization's domain. Which type of certificate would be most appropriate?

    A. Self-signed certificate

    B. Wildcard certificate

    C. Extended validation (EV) certificate

    D. Code-signing certificate

29. Which of the following best describes a threat actor that unintentionally exposes the organization to risk through unauthorized IT activities?

    A. Hacktivist

    B. Nation-state

    C. Shadow IT

    D. Organized crime

30. An organized crime group will most likely target which of the following?

    A. Government secrets

    B. Personal social media accounts

    C. Financial institutions

    D. Protest organizations

31. In hardening a router, which action is crucial to enhance its security?

    A. Setting up virtual LANs (VLANs)

    B. Installing anti-malware software

    C. Configuring strong access controls and disabling web interfaces

    D. Regularly defragmenting the router's storage

32. A security administrator notices a sudden increase in emails asking employees to verify their credentials by clicking a link. The emails are designed to look like legitimate company communications. What is this an example of?

    A. Business email compromise

    B. Phishing

    C. Brand impersonation

    D. Pretexting

33. An attacker sends out emails pretending to be from a well-known company, urging recipients to update their account information on a fake website. What is the best example of this?

    A. Phishing

    B. Smishing

    C. Typosquatting

    D. Brand impersonation

34. What is the main objective of the containment phase in incident response?

    A. To prevent the incident from affecting other systems and networks

    B. To remove the root cause of the incident from the network

    C. To restore affected systems to normal operation

    D. To review and improve the incident response plan

35. An attacker uses fake caller ID information to impersonate a customer support representative, convincing victims to reveal sensitive information. What is this technique known as?

    A. Vishing

    B. Impersonation

    C. Smishing

    D. Watering hole

36. A company must verify its compliance with specific industry regulations to a government agency. The agency assigns auditors to assess the company's adherence to these rules. What is this type of audit known as?

    A. Third-party assessment

    B. Regulatory examination

    C. Self-assessment

    D. Departmental audit

37. A security consultant finds that attackers could exploit vulnerabilities in the low-level software that manages an organization's device hardware. What is this code known as?

    A. Firmware

    B. Hardware

    C. Mean time to repair (MTTR)

    D. Ransomware

38. An organization faces security risks because its virtual machines may inadvertently cause memory to be used again, leading to potential data leaks. What vulnerability does this describe?

    A. Firmware

    B. Virtual machine sprawl

    C. Mean time between failures (MTBF)

    D. Resource reuse

39. A security consultant discovers that several devices' outdated firmware versions are no longer receiving updates. What is this risk known as?

    A. Annualized loss expectancy (ALE)

    B. End of life

    C. Cross-site request forgery (CSRF)

    D. SQL injection (SQLi)

40. While monitoring a company's systems, the security consultant detects hidden malware that gives attackers administrative control over the system, effectively hiding its presence. What type of malware is this likely to be?

    A. Rootkit

    B. Bloatware

    C. Logic bomb

    D. Spyware

41. A security team detects interference with wireless communication signals around the company's premises, which could potentially disrupt network availability. What type of activity could this indicate?

    A. Brute force

    B. RFID cloning

    C. Environmental

    D. SQL injection

42. A company decides to implement additional controls, such as encryption and access control, to lower the risk of data breaches. Which risk management strategy is this?

    A. Accept

    B. Avoid

    C. Transfer

    D. Mitigate

43. A security consultant discovers that attackers have captured and reused an employee's login to access the company's systems without authorization. What type of malicious activity does this indicate?

    A. DNS attack

    B. Malicious code attack

    C. Credential replay attack

    D. Amplified attack

44. To enhance security and reduce the risk of internal threats, a company implements network segmentation by creating multiple VLANs. Which of the following best describes the primary benefit of using VLANs?

    A. Provides redundancy for critical systems

    B. Isolates network traffic based on organizational units or functions

    C. Allows unrestricted access to the internet for all employees

    D. Facilitates easy physical access to network devices

45. A security consultant ensures that only the finance team can access the company's financial records. Which access control method would be most appropriate for this scenario?

    A. Access control list (ACL) configured to allow only the finance team's role

    B. Disabling all network shares

    C. Implementing network segmentation

    D. Granting full control permissions to all employees

46. Which mitigation technique involves specifying a list of trusted applications allowed to run on a company's systems?

    A. Block list

    B. Content filtering

    C. Application allow list

    D. Data loss prevention (DLP)

47. A company has decommissioned its old applications to mitigate security risks. What should be a key consideration during the decommissioning process?

    A. Ensuring the legacy applications are backed up in a separate cloud service

    B. Making sure all data is securely migrated or erased

    C. Keeping the applications running in a separate network segment

    D. Updating the legacy applications to the latest version

48. A consultant is setting up a host-based firewall on a company's workstations. What is the main purpose of this firewall?

   A. To encrypt data during transmission

   B. To monitor and prevent unauthorized access to and from the workstation

   C. To remove unnecessary software from the workstation

   D. To provide an additional layer of protection by managing user permissions

49. What is a primary security challenge when integrating internet of things (IoT) devices into a company's network?

   A. IoT devices are always automatically updated with the latest security patches.

   B. IoT devices often lack robust security features and can be a weak point for network attacks.

   C. IoT devices have built-in encryption that secures all network traffic.

   D. IoT devices provide enhanced control over network traffic and data flow.

50. When investigating a suspected insider threat, which log would likely provide the most relevant information regarding actions performed on workstations?

   A. Firewall logs

   B. Endpoint logs

   C. Metadata

   D. Network logs

51. A security administrator assesses the security posture of an industrial control system (ICS) used to manage critical infrastructure. What is a primary security concern with ICSs/SCADA systems?

   A. They are typically protected by consumer-grade antivirus software.

   B. They often use proprietary protocols and legacy systems that may need more modern security features.

   C. They are generally updated automatically with the latest security patches.

   D. They are isolated from network connections and do not require network security measures.

52. Which strategy best supports risk transference in cloud computing?

   A. Implementing local backups and disaster recovery plans

   B. Using a cloud service provider with comprehensive security certifications and insurance coverage

   C. Maintaining an in-house IT team to handle all security incidents

   D. Avoiding cloud services to eliminate third-party risks

53. Which factor is critical to ease of recovery for a company recovering from a major data loss incident?

    A. Regularly scheduled backups with tested recovery procedures

    B. The speed of the internet connection

    C. The number of physical security measures in place

    D. The complexity of the network architecture

54. What is the primary difference between active and passive security monitoring in a network security context?

    A. Active monitoring involves collecting data without interacting with the network, while passive monitoring interacts with the network to gather data.

    B. Active monitoring involves directly interacting with the network or systems to detect and respond to threats, while passive monitoring collects data without altering network traffic.

    C. Passive monitoring involves making real-time changes to the network configuration, while active monitoring only logs network traffic without any intervention.

    D. Active monitoring is used for historical data analysis, while passive monitoring is used for real-time threat detection.

55. Which of the following is an example of active security measures in a network environment?

    A. An intrusion detection system (IDS) that only logs suspicious activities without taking action

    B. A firewall that blocks unauthorized access based on predefined rules

    C. A network traffic analyzer that passively observes and records traffic patterns

    D. A system that generates periodic reports on network activity without real-time interaction

56. Which protocol is used to secure communication over IP networks by providing confidentiality, integrity, and authentication?

    A. Hypertext Transfer Protocol (HTTP)

    B. Internet Protocol Security (IPSec)

    C. File Transfer Protocol (FTP)

    D. Simple Network Management Protocol (SNMP)

57. What is the main advantage of a software-defined wide area network (SD-WAN) compared to traditional WAN solutions?

    A. Using cloud-based technologies, SD-WAN offers centralized management and enhanced security features

    B. SD-WAN provides better physical security for data centers than traditional WAN solutions

    C. SD-WAN focuses on encrypting data at rest within enterprise storage systems

    D. SD-WAN is designed to manage and control local area network (LAN) traffic only

58. A company requires a backup site that can be made operational quickly but only needs to be fully equipped sometimes. This site has some hardware installed and is partially configured. What type of site is this most likely to be?

    A. Hot site

    B. Cold site

    C. Warm site

    D. Geographic dispersion

59. An organization must protect its data centers across many sites to minimize the risk of data loss and downtime due to severe weather conditions. What is this most likely called?

    A. Warm site

    B. Cold site

    C. Hot site

    D. Geographic dispersion

60. A security administrator wants to test the response of employees and systems to a hypothetical cyberattack. This test should mimic a real-world scenario as closely as possible. Which testing method is most appropriate?

    A. Tabletop exercise

    B. Failover

    C. Simulation

    D. Parallel processing

61. To validate the effectiveness of the disaster recovery plan, a security administrator runs critical applications on both the primary and backup systems simultaneously. What type of testing is this?

    A. Simulation

    B. Tabletop exercise

    C. Parallel processing

    D. Failover

62. What measure should a security administrator implement to ensure the security of sensitive data during the backup process?

    A. Replication

    B. Frequency adjustment

    C. Encryption

    D. Onsite storage

63. A company requires real-time data backup to ensure minimal data loss during a failure. Which backup strategy is best suited for this need?

    A. Full backup

    B. Incremental backup

    C. Replication

    D. Snapshot

64. During a power outage. Which device should be installed to provide immediate, short-term power to these systems?

    A. Diesel generator

    B. Solar panels

    C. Uninterruptible power supply (UPS)

    D. Power strip

65. Which connection method is most commonly used to ensure that mobile devices connect securely to the corporate network?

    A. Cellular

    B. Bluetooth

    C. Wi-Fi

    D. Mobile application management (MAM)

66. A company's data management policy requires classifying all assets. Which classifications would be appropriate for data that could cause significant damage if disclosed?

    A. Public

    B. Restricted

    C. Unrestricted

    D. Internal

67. An administrator assigns a team to manage the security and updates of a critical application. What is this assignment an example of?

    A. Role-based access control

    B. Application patching

    C. Ownership assignment

    D. Data classification

68. What is a critical consideration when selecting a method for data destruction?

    A. The size of the hard drive

    B. The sensitivity of the data and the ability to recover data

    C. The age of the hardware

    D. The operating system in use

69. A company is replacing old laptops with new ones. What should the security administrator do to decommission the old laptops securely?

    A. Sell the laptops without making any changes

    B. Perform a standard file deletion

    C. Sanitize the hard drives by overwriting them with random data

    D. Reinstall the operating system

70. Which of the following is a data destruction method that physically alters the storage media to make data recovery impossible?

    A. Disk encryption

    B. Data wiping

    C. Shredding

    D. Data backup

71. What is the purpose of obtaining a certificate of destruction when decommissioning hardware?

    A. To ensure the hardware is under warranty

    B. To provide documentation that data has been securely destroyed

    C. To prove that the hardware was expensive

    D. To track the number of devices decommissioned

72. What is the purpose of package monitoring in vulnerability management?

    A. To identify vulnerabilities in software packages within organizations

    B. To monitor network traffic for potential threats

    C. To assess the physical security of server rooms

    D. To update operating systems

73. A company participates in a community that shares information about vulnerabilities and threats. What type of identification method is this?

    A. Static analysis

    B. Information-sharing organization

    C. Penetration testing

    D. Dynamic analysis

74. Which of the following is an example of using Open-source intelligence (OSINT)for vulnerability identification?

    A. Scanning the internal network for known vulnerabilities

    B. Hiring a third-party firm for a security assessment

    C. Gathering data from public sources about new vulnerabilities

    D. Running a bug bounty program

75. Which of the following describes a situation where a security measure fails to detect a genuine threat?

    A. False positive

    B. False negative

    C. True positive

    D. True negative

76. Why is it important for an organization to classify vulnerabilities?

    A. To ensure all systems are running the latest software versions
    B. To organize vulnerabilities based on their potential impact and exploitability
    C. To limit the number of employees with access to sensitive data
    D. To reduce the cost of security tools

77. An administrator needs to prioritize patching based on vulnerability severity. Which tool would be most helpful?

    A. Risk assessment matrix
    B. Common Vulnerability Scoring System (CVSS)
    C. Firewall logs
    D. Encryption software

78. An administrator has applied patches and updated controls but wants to ensure ongoing security. What is the most likely next step in the vulnerability management process?

    A. Reporting the remediation actions to stakeholders
    B. Conducting an audit to verify compliance and effectiveness
    C. Segregating the patched systems into different network segments
    D. Acquiring cyber insurance

79. An attacker unintentionally spreads incorrect information in a company's internal communication channels, leading to employee confusion. What is the best description of this attack?

    A. Misinformation
    B. Disinformation
    C. Phishing
    D. Impersonation

80. What is the main reason for performing a vulnerability scan after patching a system?

    A. To identify new vulnerabilities that were introduced by the patch
    B. To check whether the system needs to be segmented
    C. To create a report for senior management
    D. To check the effectiveness of resolving the identified vulnerabilities

81. When a vulnerability cannot be immediately patched, which of the following is the best course of action?

    A. Ignore the vulnerability until a patch is available

    B. Apply compensating controls to reduce the risk

    C. Purchase additional insurance coverage

    D. Perform an audit of the affected systems

82. Why is auditing an essential part of the vulnerability management process?

    A. It identifies new vulnerabilities after patch deployment

    B. It checks the remediation process to ensure compliance and effectiveness

    C. It replaces the need for rescanning systems

    D. It assists in creating a report for regulatory authorities

83. A company employee reports unusual activity on their wireless network, including rogue access points that mirror the company's network. What type of attack might the security consultant suspect?

    A. DNS attack

    B. Evil twin attack

    C. Credential replay attack

    D. Malicious code attack

84. Which of the following is essential for monitoring system performance and ensuring optimal resource utilization?

    A. Hypervisor

    B. Load balancer

    C. System resource monitoring tool

    D. Domain controller

85. Which protocol provides a secure mechanism for controlling authentication and authorization between two parties, such as a user and a service provider?

    A. Lightweight Directory Access Protocol (LDAP)

    B. Security Assertion Markup Language (SAML)

    C. Hypertext Transfer Protocol (HTTP)

    D. Post Office Protocol (POP3)

The answers to this mock exam are provided in the Solutions chapter on page **198**.

CompTIA Security+ SY0-701 Mock Exam 6

1. Which technology allows users to log in once and gain access to many applications and services without the need to re-authenticate?

    A. Lightweight Directory Access Protocol (LDAP)

    B. Open Authorization (OAuth)

    C. Transport Layer Security (TLS)

    D. Security Assertion Markup Language (SAML)

2. When setting up a firewall, which rule, when applied, will prevent unauthorized access to the company's email server from external sources?

    A. Allow traffic on port 443

    B. Deny traffic on port 25

    C. Allow traffic on port 21

    D. Deny traffic on port 22

3. A security team needs to monitor the network for signs of malicious activity. Which tool can provide real-time monitoring and alerting based on predefined rules?

    A. Intrusion detection system (IDS)

    B. Data loss prevention (DLP)

    C. Application firewall

    D. Secure Sockets Layer (SSL)

4. A security consultant trains staff on what to do when they receive a phishing email. Which action is most appropriate when encountering a suspicious email?

    A. Respond to the sender asking for more information

    B. Open attachments to confirm whether the email is legitimate

    C. Mark the email as spam and delete it

    D. Report the email to the security team and avoid interacting with its contents

5. What is a common function of access badges in a secure facility?

    A. To log employee work hours automatically

    B. To provide multi-factor authentication for network access

    C. To grant or restrict physical access to specific areas within the facility

    D. To identify personal property within the building

6. Two organizations are working together on a project and need to define the scope of their partnership, but without binding legal obligations. Which agreement is best suited for this purpose?

    A. Business partnership agreement (BPA)

    B. Memorandum of understanding (MOU)

    C. Statement of work (SOW)

    D. Non-disclosure agreement (NDA)

7. The security manager wants to perform a gap analysis on several company servers. Who should typically be involved in this process?

    A. Only the IT department

    B. Only external auditors

    C. Key stakeholders from various departments, including IT, security, and management

    D. Only the compliance team

8. What is a common method for authenticating multiple users in a large organization?

    A. Single sign-on (SSO)

    B. Manual verification

    C. Shared credentials

    D. Role-based access lists

9. Which firewall rule should be implemented to block file-sharing services from being used on the network?

    A. Block traffic on port 22

    B. Block traffic on port 80

    C. Block traffic on port 445

    D. Block traffic on port 53

10. In the context of the CIA triad, what is the primary goal of using HTTPS for web applications?

    A. Ensuring data confidentiality

    B. Ensuring data availability

    C. Ensuring data integrity

    D. Ensuring system redundancy

11. What should an organization do after applying patches and rescanning to mitigate vulnerabilities?

    A. Report remaining vulnerabilities and mitigation strategies to stakeholders

    B. Immediately apply older patches

    C. Remove all compensating controls

    D. Increase insurance coverage

12. What is the purpose of rescanning in the validation of remediation?

    A. To audit the security controls implemented

    B. To ensure that the previously detected vulnerabilities have been successfully patched or mitigated

    C. To verify user compliance with security policies

    D. To apply older patches if needed

13. What role does the identity provider (IdP) play in a Single Sign-On (SSO) implementation using Security Assertion Markup Language (SAML)?

    A. It provides a database of user credentials.

    B. It authenticates the user and provides an assertion to the service provider.

    C. It manages the user's session across multiple applications.

    D. It grants access permissions to resources based on user roles.

14. How does policy-driven access control differ from traditional access control methods?

    A. It provides access based on predefined rules rather than static permissions.

    B. It requires manual configuration for each access request.

    C. It eliminates the need for user authentication.

    D. It relies solely on physical security measures.

15. Which policy explicitly outlines the steps a company will take to respond to security incidents, such as data breaches or cyberattacks?

    A. Business continuity plan

    B. Incident response plan

    C. Disaster recovery plan

    D. Change management policy

16. What is the primary purpose of analyzing false positives in vulnerability management?

    A. To improve the accuracy of detection tools

    B. To reduce the number of updates required

    C. To increase the company's risk tolerance

    D. To classify vulnerabilities more effectively

17. Which of the following factors can impact the performance of the data plane?

    A. Configuration of network routing protocols

    B. Encryption and decryption of data packets

    C. Updates to network security policies

    D. Physical security of network devices

18. Which of the following is a key step in implementing a zero-trust security model?

    A. Establishing a robust network perimeter

    B. Trusting all devices once authenticated

    C. Continuously monitoring and logging network activity

    D. Simplifying access controls for ease of use

19. What is a key advantage of passive security monitoring over active monitoring?

    A. Passive monitoring can provide real-time alerts and automated responses to security incidents.

    B. Passive monitoring doesn't alter network traffic or impact system performance, making it less intrusive.

    C. Active monitoring has lower costs due to less need for complex hardware and software solutions.

    D. Passive monitoring is more effective at preventing attacks by actively defending against them.

20. In which scenario would key escrow be particularly beneficial?

    A. When ensuring that encrypted data can be recovered even if an employee leaves the company and their private key is lost

    B. When a company needs to distribute public keys to all employees

    C. When the company wants to make private keys accessible to all staff members

    D. When avoiding the need to issue digital certificates

21. Which method is commonly used to securely exchange encryption keys over an insecure channel?

    A. Symmetric key exchange

    B. Plaintext transmission

    C. Transport Layer Security (TLS) without any encryption

    D. Public key infrastructure (PKI)

22. What access control model would be most suitable for an organization where employees need to access files based on their department's groups?

    A. Attribute-based access control (ABAC)

    B. Role-based access control (RBAC)

    C. Locationary access control

    D. Mandatory access control (MAC)

23. How does a secure enclave enhance security if an organization means to perform key exchange?

    A. By generating encryption keys that are accessible by all applications on the device

    B. By securely generating and storing encryption keys within an isolated environment inaccessible to the main operating system

    C. By providing a cloud-based environment for key exchange

    D. By allowing remote access to encryption keys for ease of use

24. Which of the following data classification levels is typically used for internal emails and internal documents that do not contain sensitive information?

    A. Restricted

    B. Public

    C. Confidential

    D. Internal

25. What is the role of a public ledger in blockchain technology?

    A. To maintain a centralized database of all users

    B. To encrypt transactions for secure communication

    C. To provide a transparent and immutable record of all transactions

    D. To store private keys for blockchain participants

26. A company's security analyst is evaluating the use of blockchain to ensure the transparency and integrity of financial transactions. What feature of blockchain is most important for maintaining a transparent and tamper-proof record?

    A. Salting each transaction

    B. Using a public ledger to record all transactions

    C. Implementing key stretching for transaction data

    D. Encrypting the entire blockchain with a private key

27. An IT administrator realizes that several certificates within the organization are about to expire. What should be done to ensure continued secure communications?

    A. Create a new certificate signing request (CSR) for each expiring certificate.

    B. Add the expiring certificates to the certificate revocation list (CRL).

    C. Disable Online Certificate Status Protocol (OCSP) to prevent issues with expired certificates.

    D. Transition to using only wildcard certificates to prevent expiration issues.

28. Which threat actor is most likely to be an insider threat with knowledge of internal systems and processes?

    A. Nation-state

    B. Unskilled attacker

    C. Hacktivist

    D. Employee

29. Employees' use of unauthorized software and devices can create vulnerabilities in an organization's security. What is this practice commonly associated with?

    A. Nation-state

    B. Organized crime

    C. Shadow IT

    D. Insider threat

30. A security team conducts an internal review of its practices without external oversight. What type of assessment is it performing?

    A. Compliance audit

    B. Self-assessment

    C. External audit

    D. Third-party assessment

31. A security consultant is concerned about the potential for attackers to exploit third-party relationships to gain access to a company's network. Which of the following represents the most significant risk in this scenario?

    A. Open service ports

    B. Managed service providers

    C. Default credentials

    D. Company employees

32. During a security audit, a consultant discovers that a critical database server is accessible via an open port that is not required for operation. What is the primary concern associated with this finding?

    A. Default credentials

    B. Vulnerable software

    C. Open service ports

    D. Insider threats

33. A security consultant identifies that a vendor used by the company has weak security practices, potentially exposing the company to risk. What is this type of risk best categorized as?

    A. Default credentials

    B. Vendor-related threat

    C. Phishing attack

    D. Watering hole attack

34. A company's security consultant finds that many network devices still use their factory default usernames and passwords. What is the most likely attack vector associated with this oversight?

    A. Managed service providers

    B. Suppliers

    C. Open service ports

    D. Default credentials

35. During a security review, the consultant determines that a critical application runs on an outdated platform that can no longer be updated. What is this platform categorized as?

    A. Legacy

    B. Cloud

    C. On-premises

    D. Resource overuse

36. A security team is using a tool that measures the potential impact of a vulnerability on a system. What is this tool likely measuring?

    A. Risk tolerance

    B. Vulnerability classification

    C. Exposure factor

    D. False negative rate

37. In a firewall, which port should be blocked to prevent Telnet access to network devices?

    A. Port 80

    B. Port 23

    C. Port 443

    D. Port 110

38. A security administrator discovers that an application running in the cloud is vulnerable due to improper access controls, allowing unauthorized users to access sensitive data. What is the most likely vulnerability?

    A. Misconfiguration

    B. Zero-day

    C. Cryptographic

    D. Jailbreaking

39. During a security review, the administrator identifies a risk where attackers could exploit a flaw in a mobile device's operating system that the vendor has not yet discovered. What is this type of vulnerability called?

    A. Sideloading

    B. Zero-day

    C. Cloud-specific

    D. Supply chain

40. An organization's mobile devices are found to be vulnerable due to users installing apps from unauthorized sources, potentially exposing the devices to malware. What is this process known as?

    A. Automated Information System (AIS)

    B. Sideloading

    C. Recovery Time Objective (RTO)

    D. Vendor diversity

41. A security administrator is concerned about the potential risks posed by third-party software providers who may introduce vulnerabilities into the organization's network. What type of vulnerability is this most likely to be?

    A. Cloud-specific

    B. Cryptographic

    C. Supply chain

    D. Full Disk Encryption (FDE)

42. Which monitoring tool can help identify unauthorized changes to system files and configurations?

    A. Configuration management database (CMDB)

    B. File integrity monitoring (FIM)

    C. Virtual local area network (VLAN)

    D. Content delivery network (CDN)

43. The security team identifies that an employee has modified their company-issued smartphone to bypass security restrictions, allowing unauthorized apps to be installed. What is this practice best known as?

    A. Zero-day

    B. Cross-Site Scripting (XSS)

    C. Application allow list

    D. Jailbreaking

44. A company is at risk because of weak encryption protocols used in its communications, making it susceptible to data breaches. What type of vulnerability does this describe?

    A. Cryptographic

    B. Public cloud

    C. Mobile devices

    D. Sideloading

45. When configuring an access control list (ACL) on a router, a security consultant specifies rules that allow traffic from certain IP addresses while blocking others. What is the primary purpose of using ACLs in this context?

    A. To log all incoming and outgoing traffic

    B. To control and restrict access to network resources

    C. To provide end-to-end encryption

    D. To automatically detect and block malware

46. A security consultant recommends using both an application allow list and a block list for a more comprehensive security strategy. What is the primary reason for this approach?

    A. To ensure that only the block list is effective against known threats

    B. To provide flexibility in allowing necessary applications while blocking known threats

    C. To enable end-to-end encryption for all network traffic

    D. To simplify network segmentation

47. When decommissioning legacy servers, what is the most important step to ensure that no sensitive data is exposed?

    A. Shutting down the servers and removing them from the network

    B. Performing a factory reset and wiping the disks

    C. Encrypting the data stored on the servers

    D. Disconnecting the servers from the internet

48. Which risk management strategy is used when a company decides not to engage in an activity, such as not storing sensitive customer data, to eliminate the associated risks?

    A. Transfer

    B. Accept

    C. Avoid

    D. Mitigate

49. What is a significant security consideration when implementing a real-time operating system (RTOS) in a critical application?

    A. RTOS environments are typically designed with extensive user interfaces for easy configuration.

    B. RTOS environments often have minimal support for advanced security features and may require additional hardening.

    C. RTOS environments automatically encrypt all data transmitted across the network.

    D. RTOS environments generally support multiple operating systems simultaneously, reducing complexity.

50. After a data breach caused by non-compliance with security protocols, a company's failure appears in the media, leading to the loss of customers and business partners. What is this a likely consequence of?

    A. Reputational damage

    B. Contractual impacts

    C. Fines

    D. Loss of license

51. In a system utilizing embedded systems, what is a key security challenge that needs to be addressed?

    A. Embedded systems often have ample resources for complex security protocols.

    B. Embedded systems usually feature user-friendly management interfaces with strong security controls.

    C. Embedded systems may have limited resources and lack robust security mechanisms, making them vulnerable to attacks.

    D. Embedded systems automatically integrate with other systems without additional security configurations.

52. How does patch availability affect the security posture of a cloud-based architecture?

    A. Patches are automatically applied by the cloud provider with no need for user intervention.

    B. The availability of patches depends on the cloud provider's update schedule and policy.

    C. Patch availability is irrelevant in a cloud environment.

    D. Patches are less frequent in cloud environments compared to on-premises systems.

53. Which situation exemplifies the inability to patch as a concern?

    A. An application running on a modern, actively supported operating system

    B. A legacy system with outdated software that no longer receives updates or support

    C. A cloud service provider offering frequent security updates

    D. A new application designed with built-in patch management features

54. When considering the power and computing needs for a new data center, which factor is most relevant?

    A. The availability of office space for employees

    B. The design of the data center's aesthetics

    C. The geographic location of the data center

    D. The capacity and redundancy of power supplies and cooling systems.

55. What is the primary purpose of a jump server in a secure network architecture?

    A. To provide encrypted communications between endpoints on a public network

    B. To allow secure access to servers' administrative interfaces in a restricted network segment

    C. To balance the load of incoming traffic across multiple servers

    D. To act as a gateway for monitoring and blocking malicious traffic

56. How does a proxy server enhance security for an organization's network?

    A. By encrypting data in transit between users and the internet

    B. By directly blocking malicious network traffic based on content filters

    C. By serving as an intermediary that filters, caches, and logs requests between users and the internet

    D. By providing real-time analysis of network traffic for threat detection

57. Secure access service edge (SASE) combines network and security functions. What is a key benefit of implementing SASE?

    A. It integrates wide area network (WAN) capabilities with comprehensive security features to deliver secure, optimized access to cloud and on-premises resources.

    B. It provides enhanced physical security measures for data centers.

    C. It focuses solely on endpoint protection and antivirus capabilities.

    D. It specializes in managing user authentication for remote access.

58. What type of secure communication access is characterized by creating a private network over a public internet connection?

    A. Virtual private network (VPN)

    B. Cloud access security broker (CASB)

    C. Network access control (NAC)

    D. Intrusion detection system (IDS)

59. A security administrator is responsible for protecting data related to the company's earnings, transactions, and budgets. What type of data is this?

    A. Financial information

    B. Intellectual property

    C. Trade secret

    D. Human-readable

60. What is the primary purpose of directive security controls in a security management framework?

    A. To monitor and record security events

    B. To ensure compliance with security policies and procedures

    C. To provide physical barriers to unauthorized access

    D. To detect and respond to security threats in real-time

61. What type of data can be easily interpreted by humans without requiring decoding or transformation?

    A. Regulated

    B. Human-readable

    C. Non-human-readable

    D. Legal information

62. Which data classification should be used for personal information about employees protected by privacy laws and should not be disclosed without consent?

    A. Public

    B. Restricted

    C. Private

    D. Unrestricted

63. A company's intellectual property and trade secrets are highly valuable and should be protected against unauthorized access. What is the most appropriate data classification for this information?

    A. Public

    B. Secure

    C. Open

    D. Restricted

64. A security administrator must ensure that data stored on a cloud service complies with regional data storage and access laws. Which consideration is most relevant in this context?

    A. Data in use

    B. Data sovereignty

    C. Data at rest

    D. Geolocation

65. To enhance security, an organization uses GPS technology to track the location of its devices and data storage facilities. What concept does this practice involve?

    A. Data sovereignty

    B. Data in transit

    C. Geolocation

    D. Data in use

66. To secure sensitive data, the administrator replaces some parts of their critical data with a random value, especially in test environments. Which technique is being applied?

    A. Tokenization

    B. Masking

    C. Encryption

    D. Segmentation

67. What method divides a network into smaller, more isolated segments to improve control over data access?

    A. Segmentation

    B. Hashing

    C. Tokenization

    D. Obfuscation

68. Which connection method best suits a mobile device to ensure data security outside the corporate network?

    A. Bluetooth

    B. Cellular

    C. Wi-Fi

    D. Mobile device management (MDM)

69. In asset management, why is it important to classify data according to sensitivity and confidentiality?

    A. To ensure compliance with software licenses

    B. To manage network traffic efficiently

    C. To apply appropriate security controls

    D. To simplify asset inventory

70. A security administrator is tasked with documenting all software versions installed across the company's computers. Which practice is being implemented?

    A. Network segmentation

    B. Asset tracking

    C. Access control

    D. Incident response

71. What is the primary purpose of using automated tools for finding all the workstations in a large organization?

    A. To reduce the cost of purchasing new hardware

    B. To ensure hardware compatibility with new software

    C. To accurately track and manage all hardware assets

    D. To improve employee productivity

72. A security administrator needs to ensure the company keeps its data long enough to comply with compliance laws. Which action should they take?

    A. Implement data encryption

    B. Develop and enforce a data retention policy

    C. Upgrade all hardware every year

    D. Deploy a network firewall

73. A company has decommissioned an old server. The security administrator wants to ensure the data is permanently removed. Which method is the best approach?

    A. Format the server's hard drives

    B. Use a secure erase tool to overwrite all data

    C. Delete all user accounts

    D. Remove the server from the network

74. When should an organization conduct a third-party assessment for its vulnerability management program?

    A. To gather real-time threat data from external sources

    B. When identifying vulnerabilities in externally developed software

    C. To perform daily network vulnerability scans

    D. When monitoring software packages for updates

75. Why would administrators use static analysis tools in their vulnerability management process?

    A. To simulate potential attacks on a live system

    B. To examine code for vulnerabilities before deployment

    C. To subscribe to external threat feeds

    D. To monitor network traffic for anomalies

76. When a security team is working through the Chain of Custody process, what should they do each time evidence is transferred?

    A. Encrypt the electronic evidence to secure it.

    B. Notify all users and stakeholders about the evidence transfer.

    C. Perform a full system backup before the transfer.

    D. Update the chain of custody documentation to reflect the transfer.

77. A digital forensic team has asked for a company's computer to be put under Legal Hold. What is the most likely reason for this?

    A. It is used to limit access to sensitive areas of the network.

    B. It ensures that all potential evidence is preserved and protected from deletion or alteration.

    C. It involves taking legal action against individuals involved in the incident.

    D. It facilitates the recovery of lost or deleted data.

78. When should an organization conduct a third-party assessment as part of its vulnerability management program?

    A. To gather real-time threat data from external sources

    B. When identifying vulnerabilities in externally developed software

    C. To perform daily network vulnerability scans

    D. When monitoring software packages for updates

79. A security consultant identifies the Root Cause of a security incident. What is the next critical step in the incident response process?

    A. Conducting a financial impact analysis of the incident

    B. Implementing Corrective Actions to address and resolve the root cause

    C. Notifying external regulatory bodies about the incident

    D. Reassessing the company's security policies and procedures

80. A security administrator is compiling a report for management after completing a vulnerability remediation process. What information should this report include?

    A. The cost of the remediation actions taken

    B. Effectiveness of patches and other controls, including remaining risks

    C. A detailed description of each vulnerability detected

    D. The names of the employees responsible for each system

81. What should be done next after segmenting a network to mitigate a vulnerability?

    A. Rescan the network to ensure segmentation was properly implemented

    B. Disable compensating controls

    C. Reinstall the operating system on all affected systems

    D. Purchase cyber insurance for the isolated segments

82. A company has completed vulnerability remediation and needs to ensure all steps are followed correctly. What is the best method to validate the remediation process?

    A. Use audit logs to review applied patches and their effectiveness

    B. Search the workstations for malware

    C. Apply further compensating controls

    D. Decrease insurance coverage

83. What access control method restricts access based on the time of day or other temporal constraints?

    A. Mandatory access control (MAC)

    B. Rule-based access control (RBAC)

    C. Attribute-based access control (ABAC)

    D. Discretionary access control (DAC)

84. What is the primary purpose of conducting a gap analysis in a security context?

    A. To identify and document the differences between current security practices and the desired security goals

    B. To create new security policies from scratch

    C. To increase the physical security of the organization's facilities

    D. To manage and allocate the security budget

85. What type of control occurs when an administrator changes rules on a host firewall?

    A. Administrative

    B. Technical

    C. Detective

    D. Alternative

The answers to this mock exam are provided in the Solutions chapter on page **222**.

Solutions

CompTIA Security+ SY0-701 Mock Exam 1

1. The correct answer is **C**. To ensure internal database servers are not accessible from the public internet, the firewall rule should be configured to deny all incoming traffic to the database servers.

    A is incorrect. Allowing all incoming traffic would expose the database servers to the public internet, contrary to the goal of preventing external access.

    B is incorrect. Denying all outbound traffic would not address the issue of incoming access. It controls what can leave the network but does not affect incoming connections.

    D is incorrect. Port 80 is used for HTTP traffic and would not specifically address the need to block access to database servers.

2. The correct answer is **A**. A centralized proxy handles web filtering and policy enforcement at the network level, which means users do not need to configure web filtering settings on their devices.

    B is incorrect. A centralized proxy does not inherently encrypt web traffic.

    C is incorrect. A centralized proxy does not replace the need for antivirus software.

    D is incorrect. A centralized proxy can reduce bandwidth consumption by filtering and caching content rather than increasing it.

3. The correct answer is **B**. An access control vestibule, or "mantrap," is a small, secure area between two interlocking doors where individuals can be held until their identity and authorization are confirmed.

    A is incorrect. Mantraps are designed to control access for people, not vehicles.

    C is incorrect. While access attempts could be monitored, the primary function of a mantrap is to control physical entry.

    D is incorrect. Mantraps are not designed for emergency exits.

4. The correct answer is **C**. An intrusion detection system (IDS) is a detective control because it monitors network traffic for suspicious activity and alerts administrators to potential security incidents. It doesn't prevent or correct incidents but identifies them.

    A is incorrect. Corrective controls address and fix issues after they occur.

    B is incorrect. Physical controls involve tangible security measures not related to network monitoring.

    D is incorrect. Managerial controls involve policies and procedures, not technical detection mechanisms like an IDS.

5. The correct answer is **B**. Directive controls focus on influencing and guiding user behavior to comply with security policies, while preventive controls aim to stop security incidents before they happen.

    A is incorrect. This statement incorrectly reverses the roles of directive and preventive controls.

    C is incorrect. Real-time alerts are characteristic of detection controls.

    D is incorrect. Protecting data and focusing on compliance are roles of different control types.

6. The correct answer is **B**. Least privilege ensures that systems have the lowest level of access necessary to operate, reducing the risk of unwanted access within the network. This core principle aligns closely with the Zero Trust model.

    A is incorrect. "Trust but verify" implies that initial trust has been granted and verification is used periodically. Zero Trust does not rely on inherent trust but assumes all network components could be compromised, requiring continuous verification.

    C is incorrect. Implicit trust within the network means assuming that internal network traffic is safe, contrary to the Zero Trust model. Zero Trust assumes no implicit trust and verifies every request as if it originates from an open network.

    D is incorrect. Access based on location implies that trust is granted depending on a user's or device's geographical or network location. Zero Trust does not consider location as a factor for granting access and instead focuses on independently verifying each access request.

7. The correct answer is **B**. The primary difference between an IPS and an IDS is that an IPS can actively block or prevent malicious traffic. At the same time, an IDS only detects and alerts potential threats without taking direct action.

    A is incorrect. This describes the function of an IDS, not an IPS.

    C is incorrect. IPS and IDS can operate automatically, though they may require configuration and tuning.

    D is incorrect. An IPS is designed to monitor both inbound and outbound traffic and can act on malicious activity in either direction.

8. The correct answer is **B**. Threat scope reduction improves security by minimizing the attack surface through network segmentation and isolation, limiting potential entry points for attackers.

   A is incorrect. Expanding the attack surface increases risk, contrary to the goal of threat scope reduction.

   C is incorrect. Increasing open ports does not reduce the attack surface but potentially increases exposure.

   D is incorrect. Encryption enhances security, but the issue of reducing the attack surface needs to be addressed directly.

9. The correct answer is **B**. The main purpose of a honeypot is to create a decoy environment that attracts attackers. It allows IT security to monitor and analyze attackers' methods and tools. This information helps improve overall network security by understanding attack patterns.

   A is incorrect. Increasing network bandwidth involves expanding the capacity of a network to handle more data. A honeypot serves a different purpose; it focuses on security and monitoring, not network performance improvements.

   C is incorrect. Providing backups involves creating copies of essential data to prevent loss in case of failure or attack. A honeypot is not a backup solution; it is used for detecting and analyzing attacks.

   D is incorrect. Enforcing access control policies involves managing and restricting who can access specific resources based on predefined rules. A honeypot does not enforce access controls but is designed to lure and monitor attackers.

10. The correct answer is **B**. Signature-based detection is the method IDSs/IPSs use to identify known attack patterns. It compares network traffic or system activity to a local database of signatures or patterns.

    A is incorrect. Anomaly-based detection identifies deviations from normal behavior. It does not explicitly rely on known attack patterns but looks for unusual patterns that might indicate a new or unknown type of attack.

    C is incorrect. Heuristic detection involves analyzing traffic behavior to match threats based on behavior rather than known signatures.

    D is incorrect. Behavioral analysis focuses on understanding how a system or network behaves under normal and abnormal conditions.

11. The correct answer is **A**. Conducting a gap analysis is essential for identifying and documenting the differences between current security practices and desired goals. By comparing existing security measures against industry standards or regulations, a gap analysis highlights discrepancies and areas where security practices fall short of required or desired levels.

    B is incorrect. Vulnerability scans show us some vulnerabilities on certain devices, but we need to compare all our findings with the desired security standards.

    C is incorrect. Implementing encryption is a specific security measure aimed at protecting data. While encryption might address gaps identified during the analysis, the purpose of the gap analysis itself is not.

    D is incorrect. Conducting a vulnerability assessment involves finding and addressing weaknesses within the network. Although related, it is a different process from a gap analysis.

12. The correct answer is **C**. An insider threat refers to an employee or others who have access to an organization's information or systems and intentionally use that access to cause harm.

    A is incorrect. Shadow IT refers to using unauthorized hardware, software, or cloud services within an organization, typically by employees unaware of the risks.

    B is incorrect. Nation-state actors are typically government-sponsored groups that engage in cyber espionage, sabotage, or other forms of cyber warfare.

    D is incorrect. Organized crime groups are typically involved in illicit activities such as fraud, extortion, and theft, often for financial gain.

13. The correct answer is **B**. The primary purpose of using ACLs in a firewall is to specify rules that control network traffic flow. ACLs define which traffic is allowed or denied based on various criteria, such as ports and protocols.

    A is incorrect. While ACLs can indirectly impact network performance by controlling traffic, their primary purpose is not to increase network speed but to enforce access control policies.

    B is incorrect. ACLs are not used to monitor network performance. Network performance monitoring typically involves tools and techniques that are separate from ACLs.

    D is incorrect. ACLs are not designed to store encryption keys.

14. The correct answer is **B**. A file-based attack involves the delivery of malicious payloads through files, such as email attachments, and the attackers use attachments to compromise the email system.

    A is incorrect. An image-based attack involves embedding malicious code within image files, such as JPEGs or PNGs.

    C is incorrect. A voice call attack involves using phone calls to extract information or deceive individuals.

    D is incorrect. While the attack involves an email system, the specific method used is through malicious file attachments.

15. The correct answer is **B**. Vulnerable software refers to applications or systems with security flaws that attackers can exploit.

   A is incorrect. Unsupported systems and applications refer to software or systems no longer supported by their vendors and can contribute to vulnerabilities.

   C is incorrect. A removable device attack involves using devices such as USB drives to deliver malware or compromise systems.

   D is incorrect. A message-based attack involves malicious content delivered via messages, such as phishing emails.

16. The correct answer is **C**. A message-based attack involves malicious content delivered through messages, such as phishing emails. In this case, phishing emails with malicious links are designed to steal login credentials.

   A is incorrect. An image-based attack involves embedding malicious code or payloads within image files.

   B is incorrect. A file-based attack involves delivering malicious payloads through files, such as attachments.

   D is incorrect. A voice call attack involves using phone calls to extract information or deceive individuals, such as in social engineering or vishing.

17. The correct answer is **A**. Buffer overflows happen when an excess of data is written to a memory buffer, leading to crashes or code execution. It is not the same as memory injection.

   B is incorrect. Cross-site scripting (XSS) is a vulnerability where attackers input malicious Javascript into client web pages.

   C is incorrect. XML injection is a type of attack where malicious XML code is injected into an application that processes XML data.

   D is incorrect. SQL injection is a technique in which attackers inject malicious SQL statements into a query to manipulate a database.

18. The correct answer is **D**. Cross-site scripting (XSS) is a vulnerability where a web application fails to properly validate input, allowing attackers to inject JavaScript which executes in the browsers of users who view the affected web page.

   A is incorrect. Buffer overflow involves writing more data to a buffer than it can hold, potentially leading to system crashes or code execution.

   B is incorrect. Race conditions occur when the timing of events leads to unintended behavior in a system.

   C is incorrect. Memory injection involves injecting malicious code into an application's memory to execute it.

19. The correct answer is **C**. SQL injection (SQLi) involves injecting malicious SQL statements into input fields to manipulate or access a database in unauthorized ways.

   A is incorrect. Memory injection involves injecting malicious code into the memory space of an application, not SQL queries.

   B is incorrect. Buffer overflow occurs when data exceeds a buffer's capacity, potentially causing crashes or code execution.

   D is incorrect. Cross-site scripting (XSS) is an attack where input scripts are injected into HTML pages and executed in users' browsers.

20. The correct answer is **B**. Buffer overflow occurs when more data is written to a buffer than it can hold, potentially leading to system crashes or the execution of malicious code.

   A is incorrect. Race conditions involve timing issues where the outcome depends on the sequence of events.

   C is incorrect. Cross-site scripting (XSS) involves injecting malicious scripts into web pages viewed by users.

   D is incorrect. SQL injection involves injecting malicious SQL statements into a query to manipulate a database.

21. The correct answer is **C**. HTTP traffic is found on port 80 and HTTPS traffic on port 443. By allowing traffic on these ports, the firewall rule restricts incoming traffic to only HTTP and HTTPS.

   A is incorrect. Port 25 is used for SMTP (Simple Mail Transfer Protocol), and port 110 is used for POP3 (Post Office Protocol version 3).

   B is incorrect. Port 53 is used for DNS (Domain Name System) queries, and port 123 is used for NTP (Network Time Protocol).

   D is incorrect. Port 21 is used for FTP (File Transfer Protocol), and port 22 is used for SSH (Secure Shell).

22. The correct answer is **C**. Ransomware is malicious software performing encryption of files on computers and demanding payment for a decryption key to restore access.

   A is incorrect. A virus is malicious code that attaches itself to legitimate programs and can replicate itself, but it does not typically encrypt files or demand payment for access.

   B is incorrect. A Trojan is malicious software that disguises itself as a legitimate program.

   D is incorrect. Bloatware refers to software that manufacturers pre-install on devices. It often consumes excessive resources without providing significant value to the user.

23. The correct answer is **D**. A brute-force attack involves the use of various permutations of passwords to gain unauthorized access. An unusual number of failed login attempts within a short period indicates a brute-force attack, where the attacker tries multiple credentials until successful.

    A is incorrect. An environmental attack refers to threats from environmental factors such as natural disasters, power failures, or temperature changes that can damage physical or digital assets.

    B is incorrect. RFID cloning involves copying the data from a radio frequency identification (RFID) tag to create a duplicate.

    C is incorrect. Phishing is a social engineering attack in which an attacker might impersonate a trustworthy entity to deceive individuals into revealing sensitive information.

24. The correct answer is **B**. An injection attack occurs when an attacker exploits an application's vulnerability to insert arbitrary commands or code into a program that the program executes, particularly within input fields. This is SQL injection.

    A is incorrect. A buffer overflow attack occurs when an attacker sends excess data to a memory buffer, causing it to overflow with data into adjacent memory.

    C is incorrect. Privilege escalation is an attack in which the attacker gains higher access levels or privileges than they are authorized, allowing them to perform unauthorized actions on a system.

    D is incorrect. Directory traversal is an attack that exploits insufficient security checks to access files and directories outside the intended directory.

25. The correct answer is **B**. A downgrade attack occurs when an attacker forces a system or application to revert to a less secure version of a protocol or cryptographic algorithm. By forcing outdated and less secure protocols, attackers can exploit vulnerabilities that may not be present in the more secure versions.

    A is incorrect. A birthday attack is a cryptographic attack that exploits the birthday paradox. It is typically used to find hash collisions (where two inputs produce the same hash output).

    C is incorrect. A collision attack aims to find two different inputs that hash to the same value. This attack is typically relevant to cryptographic hashing functions and does not involve the forced use of less secure cryptographic protocols.

    D is incorrect. A replay attack involves intercepting and replaying valid data transmission to trick a system into unauthorized actions.

26. The correct answer is **C**. Password spraying is an attack where the attacker attempts to log in to many different login accounts using common passwords over an extended period.

    A is incorrect. A brute-force attack involves trying multiple combinations of complex characters to try and crack a password, usually in a short period. This attack is characterized by systematically trialing all possible passwords until the correct one is found.

    B is incorrect. A dictionary attack attempts to gain unauthorized access using a pre-compiled list of common passwords (a "dictionary"). The attacker tries each password in the dictionary against a user's account.

    D is incorrect. A rainbow table attack is a cryptographic attack that attempts to recover plaintext passwords from hashed password databases using precomputed hash-value tables.

27. The correct answer is **B**. A web filter's primary purpose is to block access to websites that are deemed unauthorized, harmful, or malicious.

    A is incorrect. While web filters may sometimes improve loading times by blocking unwanted content, their primary function is not to speed up web page loading but to control website access.

    C is incorrect. Encrypting outbound traffic is typically handled by encryption protocols and VPNs, not web filters.

    D is incorrect. Managing user credentials is a function of identity and access management (IAM) systems, not web filters.

28. The correct answer is **B**. Account lockout occurs when a user account is automatically deactivated after a predefined number of failed login attempts as a security measure to prevent unauthorized access.

    A is incorrect. Concurrent session usage refers to having multiple simultaneous active sessions for a single user account, which could indicate account sharing or compromise.

    C is incorrect. Impossible travel refers to a situation in which a user's login attempts are detected from geographically distant locations quickly, indicating a potential compromise or misuse of credentials.

    D is incorrect. Resource consumption typically refers to the overuse or depletion of system resources, such as CPU, memory, or network bandwidth, which can potentially cause service disruptions.

29. The correct answer is **B**. An access control list (ACL) is a set of rules used to control network traffic and specify which users or systems can access a particular resource based on various criteria, such as IP addresses, protocols, or ports.

    A is incorrect. Role-based access control (RBAC) assigns user permissions based on the job they perform in the organization. It focuses on users' job functions rather than specific IP addresses or protocols.

    C is incorrect. Mandatory access control (MAC) is a strict access control method in which the operating system enforces access policies based on security labels assigned to all users and resources.

    D is incorrect. Discretionary access control (DAC) allows resource owners to decide who can access them. Access is typically controlled based on user identity and not specific to IP addresses or protocols.

30. The correct answer is **A**. An application-allow list (or whitelist) is a security approach that only permits pre-approved and trusted applications to run on a system or network. This method effectively prevents unauthorized or malicious applications from executing.

    B is incorrect. Firewall rules are designed to control network traffic based on predetermined security criteria, such as IP addresses and ports.

    C is incorrect. A block list (or blacklist) identifies specific applications, websites, or IP addresses that are prohibited from accessing a system or network.

    D is incorrect. Antivirus scanning is a reactive security measure that detects and removes malware or viruses based on known signatures.

31. The correct answer is **D**. Decommissioning outdated and unsupported hardware and replacing it with modern hardware is the most effective way to reduce the risk associated with legacy servers.

    A is incorrect. Applying security patches is crucial for maintaining security, but patches are no longer available if the hardware is outdated and no longer supported by the vendor.

    B is incorrect. Increasing physical security can help protect against physical threats but does not address the inherent security risks associated with outdated and unsupported hardware.

    C is incorrect. Using outdated hardware in a test environment might limit risk exposure, but it does not eliminate the vulnerabilities inherent in the hardware.

32. The correct answer is **C**. Endpoint protection software is designed to detect, block, and respond to malware and other malicious threats on individual devices. This is a key benefit as it helps prevent infections and security breaches on endpoints.

    A is incorrect. Endpoint protection software does not impact network bandwidth. Its primary purpose is to safeguard individual devices from threats, not to affect network performance.

    B is incorrect. Endpoint protection software typically focuses on detecting and preventing malware and other security threats on individual devices. Other security measures, such as VPNs or specific encryption protocols, generally handle encryption for data in transit.

    D is incorrect. Endpoint protection software is not designed to manage user access or simplify access controls. Access control systems or identity management solutions usually handle user access management.

33. The correct answer is **B**. In a public cloud environment, the provider manages the underlying infrastructure, reducing the company's responsibility for hardware maintenance and infrastructure management.

    A is incorrect. In a public cloud environment, the physical security of hardware is managed by the cloud provider, not the company.

    C is incorrect. While a company may control its software configurations, it does not entirely control the underlying hardware or infrastructure in a public cloud environment.

    D is incorrect. Public cloud environments can reduce the complexity of managing internal network security, as cloud providers often offer advanced security features and services.

34. The correct answer is **A**. In a decentralized architecture, each independent system must be managed and configured separately, which can make it difficult to maintain consistent security policies and configurations across all systems.

    B is incorrect. In a decentralized architecture, no central authority manages data access and encryption uniformly across all systems.

    C is incorrect. Decentralized architectures can complicate scaling and expanding the infrastructure due to the need to coordinate and integrate multiple independent systems.

    D is incorrect. Decentralized systems often face unified logging and monitoring challenges because each system may operate independently, making it difficult to aggregate and analyze logs and monitoring data across all systems.

35. The correct answer is **B**. Availability in a cloud-based architecture is indeed influenced by the provider's SLA, which specifies the uptime guarantees, and the redundancy measures implemented to ensure continuity of service.

    A is incorrect. No cloud provider can guarantee 100% uptime due to the potential for unforeseen issues such as hardware failures, network outages, or other disruptions.

    C is incorrect. In a cloud-based architecture, while the internal IT team has some control over configurations and management, the overall availability is significantly influenced by the cloud provider's infrastructure, SLAs, and the redundancy measures they implement.

    D is incorrect. Availability is critical in cloud services, even though cloud environments offer flexibility and scalability.

36. The correct answer is **C**. Deploying a multi-region architecture with failover capabilities is crucial for ensuring resilience. This approach spreads resources across multiple geographic regions, allowing the application to continue operating even if one region experiences issues or outages.

    A is incorrect. While high-capacity storage is important for handling large volumes of data, it does not inherently ensure resilience.

    B is incorrect. Relying on a single data center, even with extensive security controls, does not provide adequate resilience.

    D is incorrect. Minimizing backup systems is not advisable for resilience. Backup systems are crucial for data recovery in case of failures or data loss.

37. The correct answer is **C**. Minimizing the number of exposed services and interfaces is crucial for managing the attack surface. Reducing the number of potential entry points decreases attackers' opportunities to exploit vulnerabilities.

    A is incorrect. While limiting the number of physical devices can reduce potential points of failure and management overhead, it does not directly address the attack surface.

    B is incorrect. Placing all devices in a single security zone increases risk by creating a large, homogeneous area that can be targeted if compromised.

    D is incorrect. Increasing physical security is important for protecting against unauthorized physical access and tampering, but it does not directly address the network attack surface.

38. The correct answer is **C**. This is crucial for secure network design. Placing devices according to their function within defined security zones helps to enforce access controls, segment the network, and limit exposure to potential threats.

    A is incorrect. While cost is an important budgeting consideration, other factors determine secure device placement.

    B is incorrect. Although ease of access for administrators is important for maintenance and management, it should not be prioritized over security concerns.

    D is incorrect. Although reducing cabling can improve aesthetics and manageability, it should not precede security concerns.

39. The correct answer is **B**. This approach is crucial for ensuring continued operations during failures. Redundant systems and failover mechanisms are designed to provide backup resources and capabilities if primary systems fail, thereby maintaining functionality and minimizing downtime.

    A is incorrect. Single points of failure are detrimental to network reliability and availability.

    C is incorrect. Not using backup systems increases risk and vulnerability. Backups are essential for data recovery and the continuity of operations in case of a system failure or data loss.

    D is incorrect. Centralizing critical systems in a single location can increase risk because a failure or disaster affecting that location could compromise all vital systems.

40. The correct answer is **A**. The primary function of remote access solutions is to allow users to securely access corporate resources, applications, and data from locations outside the corporate network.

    B is incorrect. Monitoring and controlling network traffic based on security rules is typically the function of firewalls or intrusion prevention systems (IPSs), not remote access solutions.

    C is incorrect. Endpoint protection systems or mobile device management (MDM) solutions generally manage and enforce security policies on endpoint devices.

    D is incorrect. Encrypting data stored on disk drives is a function of data encryption solutions or disk encryption tools, not remote access solutions.

41. The correct answer is **C**. Data that is regulated by the government, such as through the GDPR or HIPAA, is categorized as regulated data.

    A is incorrect. Intellectual property refers to company-designed products or inventions.

    B is incorrect. Trade secrets are confidential business information that provides a competitive edge.

    D is incorrect. Human-readable data means data that can be understood by people, as opposed to encrypted or encoded data.

42. The correct answer is **D**. Confidential data is information that, if disclosed without authorization, could seriously harm the organization's reputation and operations. This classification requires stringent controls to ensure its protection and restrict access to authorized individuals only.

    A is incorrect. Public data is intended for general access and does not require significant protection as it is not sensitive.

    B is incorrect. Restricted data is typically sensitive and limited in access but may not necessarily cause severe damage if disclosed.

    C is incorrect. While critical data is highly sensitive and crucial to the organization's operations, it is not a standard classification term used in many data classification schemes.

43. The correct answer is **C**. Data at rest refers to data stored on a physical medium and not actively being used or transmitted. Implementing encryption for files stored on servers protects explicit data at rest from unauthorized access.

    A is incorrect. Data in use refers to data actively accessed, processed, or manipulated by applications or users.

    B is incorrect. Data in transit refers to data actively moving across a network or between devices.

    D is incorrect. Data sovereignty is data that is subject to the laws of the country in which it is stored.

44. The correct answer is **B**. Obfuscation makes data clear and unintelligible to unauthorized users. This technique masks data, making it difficult for unintended users to interpret or reverse-engineer the original information.

    A is incorrect. Hashing is a process that converts data into a string of characters, typically a hash value. It is primarily used for verifying data integrity, such as ensuring that data has not been altered.

    C is incorrect. Certification verifies that an individual, system, or organization meets specific standards or criteria. It is not related to the process of masking data.

    D is incorrect. Encryption converts data into a coded format that only the correct decryption key can decode. While encryption protects data by making it unreadable to unauthorized users, it is different from obfuscation.

45. The correct answer is **C**. Encryption is a method of converting data into an unreadable cipher text that requires a matching decryption key.

    A is incorrect. Masking involves obscuring specific parts of data to prevent unauthorized access to sensitive information.

    B is incorrect. Hashing is a process that converts data into a fixed-size string of characters, typically a hash value.

    D is incorrect. Tokenization replaces sensitive data with unique identifiers or tokens with no meaningful value.

46. The correct answer is **B**. Staffing levels pertain to the number and availability of personnel required to manage and operate the disaster recovery site during an emergency.

    A is incorrect. Network bandwidth is the amount of data that can be transmitted over a network at any time.

    C is incorrect. Data replication involves copying data from one location to another to ensure data availability and consistency.

    D is incorrect. Power supply is critical for keeping the site operational by ensuring systems remain powered during a disaster. However, it does not address the need for adequate human resources to manage and operate the site.

47. The correct answer is **B**. The primary function of an IDS is to watch network traffic for signs of suspicious activity and potential security breaches.

    A is incorrect. An IDS does not block traffic; it only detects and alerts potential threats.

    C is incorrect. Encrypting network communications is the role of encryption technologies and protocols, not an IDS.

    D is incorrect. Managing user authentication is handled by authentication systems and services, such as Single Sign-On (SSO) or Active Directory, not by an IDS.

48. The correct answer is **B**. A tabletop exercise is a discussion-based session where team members review and discuss their roles during an incident using a simulated scenario.

    A is incorrect. Failover testing involves switching operations from a primary to a backup system to ensure continuity.

    C is incorrect. Parallel processing testing involves running a new system alongside the old one to verify that both produce the same results.

    D is incorrect. Simulation testing involves creating a real-world scenario to test the incident response plan's effectiveness in a more realistic environment.

49. The correct answer is **B**. Storing backups offsite means keeping them at a different physical location from the main office. This method provides a vital safeguard against physical disasters at the main office.

    A is incorrect. Storing backups onsite means keeping them in the exact location as the original data. While this may offer faster access and recovery times, it does not protect against physical disasters.

    C is incorrect. Backing data to a local drive means storing it on a device connected to the leading network.

    D is incorrect. Storing backups "cloud only" means the data is stored online in a cloud service provider's data center. A combination of offsite physical backups and cloud backups is often recommended.

50. The correct answer is **D**. Establishing security baselines for servers is the first step in ensuring they adhere to the company's security standards. A security baseline defines the minimum security requirements, configurations, and settings that must be applied to the servers.

    A is incorrect. For security purposes, it is not recommended to deploy servers with default settings. Default settings often include common passwords, open ports, and unnecessary services that can be exploited.

    B is incorrect. While conducting regular vulnerability scans is an important part of maintaining security, there are other steps to ensure that new servers meet security standards.

    C is incorrect. Maintaining security updates is crucial for ongoing security management, but it comes after the initial setup.

51. The correct answer is **B**. The Deploy step involves applying the defined security baselines to systems as they are deployed. This ensures that new systems are configured in line with the organization's security standards from the moment they are introduced into the environment.

    A is incorrect. The Establish step involves creating and defining the security baselines, not applying them.

    C is incorrect. The Maintain step involves ongoing management and updating security baselines after deploying systems.

    D is incorrect. The Review step involves periodically evaluating the security baselines and their effectiveness, not applying them.

52. The correct answer is **B**. BYOD stands for bring your own device. This policy allows employees to use their personal devices for work purposes.

    A is incorrect. COPE stands for corporate-owned, personally enabled. This policy involves the company providing devices to employees that they can use for both work and personal activities.

    C is incorrect. CYOD stands for choose your own device. This policy allows employees to choose from a selection of company-approved devices.

    D is incorrect. Mobile device management (MDM) refers to software solutions used to monitor, manage, and secure employees' mobile devices.

53. The correct answer is **C**. WPA3 is the latest and most secure encryption standard for Wi-Fi networks. It provides enhanced security over WPA2, including more robust encryption algorithms, protection against brute-force attacks, and improved security protocols for open networks.

    A is incorrect. WPA2 is a substantial encryption standard widely used for many years. However, it is now a lower standard.

    B is incorrect. WEP is an outdated and insecure encryption protocol for Wi-Fi networks. It is vulnerable to numerous security attacks and should not be used to protect any network.

    D is incorrect. EAP is not an encryption protocol but an authentication framework that uses certificates to secure the authentication procedure.

54. The correct answer is **B**. Digital certificates are commonly used to authenticate systems or devices, ensuring that they are legitimate and trusted entities in the network.

    A is incorrect. VPN credentials are used for authenticating users to access a VPN, they are not specifically used for authenticating systems or devices within a network.

    C is incorrect. Security questions are typically used for user account recovery rather than system authentication.

    D is incorrect. Biometric data is used for personal authentication rather than system authentication.

55. The correct answer is **A**. Static code analysis examines code for vulnerabilities, bugs, and coding errors without actually executing the program.

    B is incorrect. Dynamic code analysis involves analyzing the code's behavior during execution. This technique helps identify runtime vulnerabilities and issues such as memory leaks or runtime exceptions.

    C is incorrect. Penetration testing assesses a company's security posture by testing it against a simulated malicious adversary.

    D is incorrect. Code signing is a security process that involves digitally signing code to verify its authenticity and integrity.

56. The correct answer is **A**. Configuration management involves managing and maintaining the settings and configurations of hardware and software systems.

    B is incorrect. BYOD, or bring your own device, is where employees use their personal mobile devices for the business environment.

    C is incorrect. Data encryption is a process for securing data by converting it into code to prevent unauthorized access.

    D is incorrect. Incident response involves handling and managing the aftermath of a security breach or attack.

57. The correct answer is **C**. The confidential classification is used for sensitive information that requires protection from unauthorized access. This label is appropriate for documents containing sensitive company information not intended for public or unrestricted access.

    A is incorrect. The public classification is used for information that is available to anyone and does not contain sensitive or confidential data.

    B is incorrect. The restricted classification is used for highly sensitive information intended for a specific group of individuals or departments.

    D is incorrect. The internal classification typically refers to information meant for use within the organization but is not necessarily sensitive.

58. The correct answer is **A**. Inventory management involves tracking and maintaining an updated list of an organization's hardware and software assets. This process ensures that the organization accurately records all devices and their status.

    B is incorrect. Software licensing refers to managing and complying with software usage rights and licenses, not tracking hardware devices.

    C is incorrect. Data encryption converts data into a secure format to prevent unauthorized access.

    D is incorrect. Vulnerability scanning involves identifying and assessing security vulnerabilities within systems and applications.

59. The correct answer is **D**. Physically destroying hard drives is the most secure method of ensuring that sensitive data cannot be recovered. This involves methods such as shredding or crushing, which render the drive completely unusable and the data irretrievable.

    A is incorrect. Formatting the hard drives removes the filesystem but does not erase the data. Even after formatting, data can often be recovered with specialized tools.

    B is incorrect. It is secure but might not be the most foolproof method compared to physical destruction.

    C is incorrect. Encrypting hard drives protects data while they are in use but does not prevent data recovery if the drive is retired.

60. The correct answer is **B**. The primary goal of data sanitization is to ensure that all data on the hardware is thoroughly removed, making it impossible to recover. This is crucial for protecting sensitive information when hardware is decommissioned.

    A is incorrect. Data sanitization does not aim to improve performance but to securely remove data. Enhancing performance is unrelated to the sanitization process.

    C is incorrect. Data sanitization does not involve upgrading hardware.

    D is incorrect. While compliance with software licenses is essential, it is not the goal of data sanitization.

61. The correct answer is **C**. Data certification involves verifying and certifying that a piece of hardware has been sanitized according to industry standards.

    A is incorrect. Data encryption is a process used to protect data by converting it into a secure format. It does not involve certifying the sanitization of hardware.

    B is incorrect. Data destruction refers to completely removing data from a storage medium, but it does not include certifying that the process meets industry standards.

    D is incorrect. Data retention refers to the policies and practices for storing and managing data for a specific period.

62. The correct answer is **B**. Vulnerability scanning involves identifying known vulnerabilities in the network by comparing the network's configuration and software against a database of known vulnerabilities.

    A is incorrect. Penetration testing involves exploiting vulnerabilities to assess the system's security.

    C is incorrect. A bug bounty program incentivizes external researchers to find and report vulnerabilities, often including exploitation.

    D is incorrect. Dynamic analysis involves testing a running application for vulnerabilities and may include exploiting some vulnerabilities to assess their impact.

63. The correct answer is **B**. Static analysis involves analyzing the source code, bytecode, or binaries without executing the code. It aims to identify potential security vulnerabilities based on the code's structure and patterns.

    A is incorrect. Dynamic analysis involves testing a running application for vulnerabilities by executing the code and observing its behavior.

    C is incorrect. Vulnerability scanning involves detecting known vulnerabilities by scanning the network or application.

    D is incorrect. A bug bounty program involves external researchers identifying and reporting vulnerabilities, often through active testing and exploitation.

64. The correct answer is **C**. A false positive occurs when a scan incorrectly reports the presence of a vulnerability that does not exist.

    A is incorrect. A false negative occurs when a vulnerability exists but is not detected by the scan.

    B is incorrect. A true positive occurs when the scan correctly identifies a vulnerability and does exist.

    D is incorrect. A true negative occurs when a scan correctly identifies that a vulnerability does not exist.

65. The correct answer is **B**. The data plane executes the routing decisions made by the control plane. It is responsible for handling the actual user data traffic based on the routing information provided by the control plane.

    A is incorrect. The control plane makes routing decisions, while the data plane handles data transmission, not vice versa.

    C is incorrect. Encryption and decryption are not specific tasks of control plane and data plane interaction.

    D is incorrect. The control plane and data plane interact closely but do not operate independently.

66. The correct answer is **D**. An acceptable use policy is a preventive control because it sets guidelines and rules to prevent misuse of mobile devices and ensure that employees follow secure practices, thereby reducing the likelihood of security incidents.

    A is incorrect. Detective controls identify and alert on policy violations but don't prevent them.

    B is incorrect. Compensating controls provide alternative controls when primary controls are not feasible; they are not directly related to setting usage guidelines.

    C is incorrect. Corrective controls address and fix issues after they occur and are not focused on preventing misuse.

67. The correct answer is **C**. A false negative occurs when a security scan does not detect a vulnerability that does exist in a system.

    A is incorrect. A true positive occurs when a security scan correctly identifies a vulnerability that does exist.

    B is incorrect. A false positive occurs when a security scan incorrectly reports a non-existent vulnerability.

    D is incorrect. A true negative occurs when a security scan correctly identifies that a vulnerability does not exist.

68. The correct answer is **B**. Applying patches is a direct action to address the identified vulnerabilities, as a first step.

    A is incorrect. Rescanning is important to verify whether vulnerabilities still exist after remediation efforts, but not the first step.

    C is incorrect. Although cyber insurance is important for risk management and financial protection, it does not directly address the vulnerabilities.

    D is incorrect. Reporting vulnerabilities to senior management is important for raising awareness and making decisions, but it does not directly address or remediate the vulnerabilities.

69. The correct answer is **C**. Rescanning the systems after applying patches is a direct method to verify that the vulnerabilities have been effectively mitigated.

    A is incorrect. While applying compensating controls can enhance security, it does not directly verify that the specific vulnerabilities addressed by the patches have been mitigated.

    B is incorrect. Network segregation can help limit the impact of potential issues, but it does not verify that the patches have successfully addressed the vulnerabilities.

    D is incorrect. Purchasing insurance is a measure for managing residual risk, but it does not directly verify the effectiveness of the patches applied.

70. The correct answer is **A**. Rescanning the systems is the most direct method to validate that the applied patches have resolved the identified vulnerabilities.

    B is incorrect. While network segregation can enhance security by isolating systems, it does not verify whether the patches have successfully addressed the vulnerabilities.

    C is incorrect. Compensating controls might be necessary if vulnerabilities remain or if patching is ineffective.

    D is incorrect. Reporting the patch application to senior management is an important communication task but does not validate whether the patches have effectively resolved the vulnerabilities.

71. The correct answer is **D**. SNMP is a protocol for managing and monitoring network devices, including servers. It provides information on various device performance and health aspects, such as CPU usage, memory utilization, and network traffic.

    A is incorrect. An IDS detects and responds to suspicious activities and potential threats within a network but is not specifically designed to monitor server health and performance.

    B is incorrect. NAC primarily controls and enforces policies regarding visiting devices that connect to the network.

    C is incorrect. SIEM systems collect, analyze, and manage security-related data and events across the network.

72. The correct answer is **B**. SIEM systems are explicitly designed to collect, aggregate, and analyze log data from various systems and applications across the network.

    A is incorrect. A VPN creates an encrypted connection over an insecure network, such as the internet.

    C is incorrect. A firewall controls network traffic flow based on predefined security rules and policies.

    D is incorrect. A WAF is designed to protect web applications by filtering and monitoring HTTP traffic between them and the internet.

73. The correct answer is **B**. Log aggregation involves collecting and consolidating logs from various devices into a centralized point.

    A is incorrect. Scanning examines systems, networks, or applications for vulnerabilities or security issues.

    C is incorrect. Alert tuning is adjusting the thresholds and parameters for generating alerts to minimize false positives and ensure that alerts are relevant and actionable.

    D is incorrect. Archiving involves storing logs and other data for long-term retention.

74. The correct answer is **D**. Scanning refers to actively probing networks and systems to detect vulnerabilities, misconfigurations, and weaknesses.

   A is incorrect. Alerting refers to notifying administrators about detected issues or anomalies in the system.

   B is incorrect. Quarantine involves isolating infected or potentially harmful components from the rest of the network to prevent further spread or damage.

   C is incorrect. Reporting involves documenting and communicating findings, such as vulnerabilities or incidents.

75. The correct answer is **B**. SCAP is a set of specifications that provides a standardized approach for automated compliance and vulnerability management. It evaluates systems against security benchmarks and ensures they meet specific security standards.

   A is incorrect. A vulnerability scanner is used to identify vulnerabilities within systems and networks but does not explicitly automate the assessment of security compliance against security benchmarks.

   C is incorrect. DLP tools are designed to prevent data breaches and loss by monitoring and controlling data access and movement.

   D is incorrect. NetFlow is a network protocol for collecting and monitoring network traffic data.

76. The correct answer is **B**. Hacktivists are individuals or groups that use hacking techniques to promote political, social, or ideological causes.

   A is incorrect. Organized crime groups are typically motivated by financial gain and commit fraud, extortion, and theft.

   C is incorrect. Nation-state actors are usually government-sponsored and conduct cyberattacks to achieve strategic objectives, such as espionage, intelligence gathering, or sabotage.

   D is incorrect. Shadow IT refers to the unauthorized use of technology within an organization, often by employees seeking convenience or efficiency.

77. The correct answer is **A**. NetFlow is a network protocol used for monitoring network traffic and collecting data about the flow of network packets. It operates by analyzing data collected from network devices without requiring software installed on each device.

   B is incorrect. While a security information and event management (SIEM) system can collect and analyze data from various sources, it typically requires installation or configuration on endpoints to gather logs and events from those devices.

   C is incorrect. Data loss prevention tools are used to protect data due to leakage.

   D is incorrect. Vulnerability scanners are designed to identify vulnerabilities in specific systems and usually require installation or configuration on the target systems to perform scans.

78. The correct answer is **C**. A VLAN is a technique for segmenting network traffic logically rather than physically, which allows for better management and enhanced security. By placing critical servers on separate VLANs, unauthorized access from the main corporate network can be prevented, effectively isolating those servers from other network traffic.

   A is incorrect. An air gap refers to a security measure in which a system or network is physically isolated from other systems or networks.

   B is incorrect. A DMZ (demilitarized zone) is a perimeter network that separates an organization's internal network from untrusted external networks, such as the internet.

   D is incorrect. A proxy server acts as an intermediary between a user and the internet, often used to improve security and manage network traffic.

79. The correct answer is **B**. File integrity monitoring (FIM) is primarily used to detect unauthorized changes to files and ensure that they have not been tampered with or altered without proper authorization.

   A is incorrect. Encrypting files for confidentiality is not the primary purpose of FIM.

   C is incorrect. Backing up files is not related to monitoring file integrity.

   D is incorrect. File integrity monitoring does not optimize file storage or management; it focuses on the integrity of the files.

80. The correct answer is **B**. To prevent sensitive information from being sent outside the company through email, the DLP solution should scan and inspect email attachments for sensitive data. This feature helps detect and prevent the transmission of confidential information.

   A is incorrect. Monitoring network bandwidth does not prevent data loss.

   C is incorrect. Blocking all outgoing emails is not practical for business operations.

   D is incorrect. Encrypting inbound emails protects data in transit but does not prevent outbound data loss.

81. The correct answer is **B**. A quarantine network isolates non-compliant computers from the rest of the network to prevent potential security risks until those computers are remediated.

   A is incorrect. A guest network, not a quarantine network, is used for guest users.

   C is incorrect. Bandwidth management is not the purpose of a quarantine network.

   D is incorrect. Quarantine networks do not create secure channels for sensitive data but isolate non-compliant devices.

82. The correct answer is **B**. EDR solutions are designed to monitor and detect suspicious activity on endpoints such as workstations and servers, providing detailed visibility and analysis of threats.

    A is incorrect. Managing network traffic based on predefined rules is typically a function of a firewall, not EDR.

    C is incorrect. Enforcing access control policies is generally done by the IAM system.

    D is incorrect. Providing backup and recovery services is not the primary function of EDR solutions.

83. he correct answer is **C**. A hot site is a fully operational offsite data center equipped with all the necessary hardware, software, and data, allowing it to take over operations immediately in the case of a primary site failure.

    A is incorrect. A cold site is a backup location that has yet to be used. It typically provides only the basic infrastructure and utilities but needs more hardware and data to run business operations instantly. Setting up a cold site takes significant time to become operational after a failure.

    B is incorrect. A warm site is partially equipped and ready to use but requires some setup and configuration to be fully operational.

    D is incorrect. Geographic dispersion refers to spreading data centers or resources across different locations to reduce the risk of regional disasters.

84. The correct answer is **B**. A distributed denial-of-service (DDoS) attack involves multiple systems, often part of a botnet, sending a large volume of traffic to a targeted server to overwhelm its resources and make it unavailable to legitimate users.

    A is incorrect. A reflected attack typically refers to a specific type of denial-of-service attack in which the attacker sends requests to a server with a spoofed IP address (the victim's IP).

    C is incorrect. A wireless attack targets vulnerabilities in wireless networks, such as Wi-Fi. These attacks may involve intercepting data or unauthorized access but do not typically involve a high volume of traffic directed toward a web server from multiple IP addresses.

    D is incorrect. A credential replay attack involves an attacker capturing and replaying valid credentials to gain unauthorized access.

85. The correct answer is **C**. Nation-state actors are typically government-sponsored groups with access to substantial resources, including advanced tools, highly skilled personnel, and intelligence capabilities.

    A is incorrect. Hacktivists are typically motivated by ideological or political reasons. They may have some technical skills but generally lack substantial resources and deep expertise.

    B is incorrect. Insider threats involve individuals within an organization who may have access to sensitive information or systems.

    D is incorrect. Unskilled attackers, or "script kiddies," lack the advanced knowledge, skills, and resources required to carry out complex attacks on critical infrastructure.

CompTIA Security+ SY0-701 Mock Exam 2

1. The correct answer is **B**. Agent-based web filtering involves installing software (an agent) on each user's device. This agent enforces web filtering policies directly on the device, even when not connected to the corporate network.

    A is incorrect. Although agent-based web filtering can communicate with a centralized server for policy updates or reporting, the filtering is handled locally on the user's device.

    C is incorrect. Agent-based web filtering can work for users on the network or remotely.

    D is incorrect. Agent-based web filtering can support URL scanning as part of its filtering capabilities.

2. The correct answer is B. Integrating IDS/IPS systems with an SIEM solution provides centralized analysis of security events and alerts, allowing faster and more effective real-time threat detection.

    A is incorrect. Does not directly affect the manual configuration of firewall rules. Firewall management requires separate processes.

    C is incorrect. Network traffic encryption is handled by secure protocols, not by IDS/IPS or SIEM integration.

    D is incorrect. IDS/IPS and SIEM systems focus on logical and network security, not physical security measures.

3. The correct answer is **B**. A common use case for an intrusion prevention system is to block traffic from IP addresses linked to known malicious activities, such as those flagged for hosting malware, launching attacks, or performing brute force login attempts.

    A is incorrect. Allowing all traffic during business hours would defeat the purpose of an IPS of preventing unauthorized or harmful traffic from entering the network.

    C is incorrect. IPS systems are not responsible for encrypting data in transit.

    D is incorrect. Allowing unrestricted access to all external websites would compromise network security and go against the purpose of an IPS.

4. The correct answer is **C**. Automating security operations significantly saves time by enabling quicker responses to security incidents and more efficient task completion.

    A is incorrect. Automation is designed to reduce the need for manual reviews by handling repetitive and time-consuming tasks.

    B is incorrect. Automation is implemented to increase efficiency, not reduce it.

    D is incorrect. Automation generally reduces the risk of human error by performing tasks based on predefined rules and scripts, which minimizes the potential for mistakes associated with manual processes.

5. The correct answer is **C**. Fencing serves as a physical barrier to deter unauthorized entry and enhance the security of the premises.

    A is incorrect. While fencing can be decorative, its primary purpose is security.

    B is incorrect. Fencing may support surveillance equipment, but its primary role is to create a barrier.

    D is incorrect. Fencing is not primarily used to guide visitors.

6. The correct answer is **B**. Segmentation involves dividing a network into smaller, isolated segments or zones, each with its security controls, which limits the spread of vulnerabilities and attacks within the network.

    A is incorrect. Patching applies updates or fixes to software or systems to address known vulnerabilities.

    C is incorrect. Rescanning refers to re-running vulnerability scans after making changes to the system to ensure vulnerabilities have been properly addressed.

    D is incorrect. Reporting involves documenting vulnerabilities and remediation efforts to track progress or meet compliance requirements.

7. The correct answer is **C**. Encryption converts data into a coded format that can only be read by someone with the appropriate decryption key. This process ensures unauthorized users cannot access the data, thus maintaining its confidentiality.

    A is incorrect. Digital signatures ensure the authenticity and integrity of a message or document, ensuring it has not been altered. However, they do not primarily ensure the confidentiality of data.

    B is incorrect. Hashing creates a unique fixed-size string from data to verify its integrity. It does not conceal the data content and thus does not ensure confidentiality.

    D is incorrect. Redundancy involves duplicating critical components or data to ensure availability and reliability, not confidentiality. Redundancy ensures systems remain operational but does not protect data from unauthorized access.

8. The correct answer is **B**. A common security concern related to the control plane is compromising routing protocols, which can lead to incorrect routing decisions and potential network attacks or inefficiencies.

    A is incorrect. Unauthorized access to user data while in transit is more related to the data plane.

    C is incorrect. Data leakage through unencrypted channels pertains to data security, not to the control plane.

    D is incorrect. Physical security of network hardware is a concern related to physical security measures.

9. The correct answer is **B**. Role-Based Access Control (RBAC) assigns access permissions based on users' roles within an organization, simplifying permission management.

    A is incorrect. Discretionary Access Control (DAC) allows users to control access to their resources rather than assigning roles.

    C is incorrect. Mandatory Access Control (MAC) uses labels and classifications to control access based on policies set by the system, not user roles.

    D is incorrect. Attribute-Based Access Control (ABAC) uses attributes for access decisions rather than predefined roles.

10. The correct answer is **A**. A honeynet is a network of interconnected honeypots that mimic a complex network to attract and analyze more sophisticated attacks. A honeynet provides a broader view of attack techniques than a single honeypot.

    B is incorrect. A honeynet is not limited to monitoring network traffic; it actively interacts with attackers through its simulated environment. Unlike passive monitoring, which does not involve direct interaction, its primary function is to attract and engage attackers.

    C is incorrect. A honeynet is not a firewall but a collection of honeypots designed to simulate a network environment to attract attackers. Firewalls control and filter network traffic to protect against unauthorized access, which is different from the purpose of a honeynet.

    D is incorrect. A honeynet typically involves multiple honeypots rather than just one. A single honeypot might simulate different vulnerabilities, but a honeynet aims to create a more complex and realistic network environment using several honeypots.

11. The correct answer is **C**. Reviewing server logs is a detective control because it involves monitoring and analyzing logs to identify any unusual or suspicious activity, which helps detect potential security incidents.

    A is incorrect. Corrective actions fix issues after they occur and do not involve monitoring for issues.

    B is incorrect. Preventive actions aim to stop incidents from happening and are not focused on monitoring.

    D is incorrect. Deterrent actions discourage potential threats through the presence of controls but do not involve active monitoring and review.

12. The correct answer is **C**. Archiving involves the secure and organized storage of logs and historical data for long-term retention. This practice helps ensure compliance with legal and regulatory requirements by keeping records for future analysis.

    A is incorrect. Alert tuning involves adjusting and refining alert settings to reduce false positives and ensure that alerts are relevant and actionable.

    B is incorrect. Scanning identifies systems' or networks' vulnerabilities, threats, or weaknesses.

    D is incorrect. Quarantine is a security measure that isolates potentially harmful files or systems to prevent the spread of malware or other threats.

13. The correct answer is **B**. User provisioning scripts are commonly used to generate new user accounts in large organizations. These scripts help ensure consistency and efficiency by automating repetitive tasks such as setting up user accounts, assigning roles, and configuring permissions.

    A is incorrect. Manual entry involves creating user accounts by hand, which is time-consuming and prone to human error.

    C is incorrect. Security group updates relate to access control within the organization but do not directly address the automation of new user accounts.

    D is incorrect. Ticket creation refers to generating support or service requests, often used in IT service management.

14. The correct answer is **B**. Fine-tuning the sensitivity of anomaly detection helps reduce false positives by ensuring that the system only alerts on deviations that indicate a security threat.

    A is incorrect. Increasing the number of signatures can improve the detection of known threats but may also increase the likelihood of false positives.

    C is incorrect. Allowing all outbound traffic does not directly reduce false positives.

    D is incorrect. Blocking all incoming traffic is a security policy, not a tuning method for reducing false positives.

15. The correct answer is **A**. Signature-based IDS relies on predefined patterns to detect threats. It cannot identify new or unknown threats, leaving the system vulnerable to zero-day attacks.

    B is incorrect. IDS generates alerts based on matching traffic against its signatures, not for every packet.

    C is incorrect. An IDS does not transmit excessive data over the network. Instead, it analyses traffic already passing through the network.

    D is incorrect. Unlike IPS, which actively blocks threats, IDS is passive and does not block traffic.

16. The correct answer is **C**. Secure File Transfer Protocol (SFTP) is designed for secure file transfer over the internet. It encrypts both the commands and the data being transferred, providing confidentiality and integrity during the file transfer process. SFTP is built on SSH (Secure Shell), ensuring the transfer is secure against eavesdropping and tampering.

    A is incorrect. FTP (File Transfer Protocol) transfers files over the internet without encryption.

    B is incorrect. HTTP (Hypertext Transfer Protocol) transfers web pages and other web-related content and is not specifically for secure file transfers.

    D is incorrect. Telnet is a protocol for remote access to network devices and servers, not file transfer.

17. The correct answer is **A**. Reputation-based filtering evaluates websites' trustworthiness based on their reputation scores, which are determined by factors such as reports of malicious activity or past behavior.

    B is incorrect. A high visitor count does not guarantee a website's safety or trustworthiness. Malicious sites can still attract significant traffic.

    C is incorrect. Logging is not the primary purpose of reputation-based filtering. Logging does not actively block malicious sites.

    D is incorrect. Traffic encryption is managed by secure communication protocols like HTTPS or VPNs, not by reputation-based filtering.

18. The correct answer is **D**. A centralized proxy inspects all web traffic as an intermediary between users and the internet. It can analyse and filter traffic for malicious content, enforce security policies, and log activity.

    A is incorrect. Agent-based filtering does not inspect all web traffic in real-time at a centralized point.

    B is incorrect. URL scanning evaluates the reputation or safety of specific URLs but does not provide comprehensive inspection of all web traffic or content.

    C is incorrect. Block rules can prevent access to known malicious sites or content, but they are static and lack the inspection capabilities of a proxy.

19. The correct answer is **C**. SELinux implements the Mandatory Access Control (MAC. model, which restricts access to resources based on predefined policies set by administrators.

    A is incorrect. In DAC, resource owners control access permissions. SELinux does not follow this model.

    B is incorrect. RBAC focuses on granting access based on a user's role, which is less rigid than MAC.

    D is incorrect. ABAC uses attributes (department, location) to determine access. SELinux is not designed around this model.

20. The correct answer is **B**. Role-Based Access Control (RBAC) assigns permissions based on the user's organizational role.

    A is incorrect. MAC uses fixed policies to control access, not user roles.

    C is incorrect. ABAC uses attributes to determine access, not roles.

    D is incorrect. DAC is based on user discretion rather than predefined roles.

21. The correct answer is **A**. Shredding is a secure method for disposing of sensitive documents. It ensures that the information is physically destroyed and cannot be reconstructed.

    B is incorrect. Recycling does not guarantee the destruction of sensitive documents. Papers could be accessed during the recycling process.

    C is incorrect. Filing involves storing documents, not disposing of them.

    D is incorrect. Emailing sensitive documents increases the risk of unauthorized access, especially if the emails are intercepted.

22. The correct answer is **A**. Security Information and Event Management (SIEM) systems are centralized platforms for collecting logs and events from multiple sources across an enterprise network.

    B is incorrect. Simple Network Management Protocol (SNMP) traps are notifications sent from network devices to management systems to report status changes or issues.

    C is incorrect. Security Content Automation Protocol (SCAP) is a suite of standards for automating the assessment of security configurations and vulnerabilities.

    D is incorrect. Data Loss Prevention (DLP) tools are designed to prevent unauthorized access, sharing, or loss of sensitive data.

23. The correct answer is **B**. Secure Sockets Layer (SSL) and its successor Transport Layer Security (TLS) primarily operate over the Transmission Control Protocol (TCP).

    A is incorrect. User Datagram Protocol (UDP) is connectionless and does not provide the reliability required for SSL/TLS encryption.

    C is incorrect. Internet Control Message Protocol (ICMP) is used to send diagnostic and error messages, not secure data transmissions.

    D is incorrect. File Transfer Protocol (FTP) transfers files but does not secure data

24. The correct answer is **B**. Performing regular audits verifies that all necessary data is retained for compliance purposes and that no sensitive information is improperly disposed of.

    A is incorrect. Reviewing the software inventory list does not address compliance with data retention policies during decommissioning.

    C is incorrect. Physical security does not directly ensure compliance with data retention policies.

    D is incorrect. Modifying user permissions is a general security measure but does not help ensure that data retention policies are followed.

25. The correct answer is **C**. An on-premises architecture provides the organization with complete control over physical and network security measures, which is a significant advantage regarding data security. The organization can directly manage all aspects of security, including physical access to servers, network configurations, firewalls, and other security devices.

    A is incorrect. On-premises infrastructure increases the organization's data privacy and compliance responsibility.

    B is incorrect. Simplified integration with third-party applications is typically a benefit of cloud environments, not on-premises infrastructure.

    D is incorrect. Greater flexibility in scaling resources is usually a key advantage of a public cloud model due to its ability to dynamically allocate resources on demand.

26. The correct answer is **B**. Secure/Multipurpose Internet Mail Extensions (S/MIME) is a protocol used to encrypt emails and provide digital signing for message integrity and authentication. It ensures secure communication by encrypting the content and verifying the sender's identity.

    A is incorrect. (SMTP) Simple Mail Transfer Protocol is for sending emails but does not inherently provide encryption.

    C is incorrect. Internet Message Access Protocol (IMAP) is used to retrieve and manage emails on a server. It does not encrypt email content.

    D is incorrect. Hypertext Transfer Protocol (HTTP) transfers data over the web and is not specifically designed for email communication.

27. The correct answer is **A**. The total cost of ownership (TCO) is crucial when comparing on-premises and cloud solutions. This includes all costs due to purchasing and maintaining hardware, software, and other infrastructure components, as well as ongoing maintenance and support.

    B is incorrect. While the geographic location of data centers can impact latency, data residency requirements, and compliance, it does not directly impact the core cost comparison between on-premises and cloud solutions.

    C is incorrect. When choosing between on-premises and cloud solutions, the type of data encryption primarily affects security and performance, not the direct cost.

    D is incorrect. Network bandwidth affects performance and connectivity, not the primary cost factor in deciding between on-premises and cloud solutions.

28. The correct answer is **B**. CDNs and edge computing solutions are critical for applications that require responsiveness because they help reduce latency by bringing content and computation closer to the end user.

    A is incorrect. Using a centralized database can hinder responsiveness, mainly if users are globally distributed.

    C is incorrect. Relying solely on server-side processing does not account for the benefits of distributing processing closer to the user.

    D is incorrect. Limiting the number of application servers could lead to server overload, negatively impacting responsiveness.

29. The correct answer is **A**. A fail-open mechanism in network security ensures that systems and services continue to operate normally even if a security device fails.

    B is incorrect. In a fail-closed scenario, systems and services are designed to shut down or block all traffic in the event of a security device failure to prevent potential unauthorized access or breaches.

    C is incorrect. Disabling user accounts in response to a failure is not typically related to the concept of fail-open, which focuses on maintaining system operation despite security device failures rather than account management.

    D is incorrect. Encryption of network traffic is a separate security measure that can be implemented regardless of whether a fail-open or fail-closed approach is used.

30. The correct answer is **D**. Complexity ensures that passwords include a mix of different character types (uppercase, lowercase, numbers, and symbols).

    A is incorrect. Length refers to the number of characters in the password.

    B is incorrect. Reuse refers to whether a password can be used multiple times.

    C is incorrect. Expiration refers to how often a password should be changed.

31. The correct answer is **A**. A fail-open security design means that if a security device or system fails, the network or service remains operational and provides access.

    B is incorrect. A fail-open design does not inherently increase the complexity of managing and monitoring security policies.

    C is incorrect. A fail-open design is generally chosen to reduce costs and complexity associated with failover mechanisms and redundancy.

    D is incorrect. A fail-open design is designed to minimize service interruptions and downtime.

32. The correct answer is **A**. Tunneling is a technique for securing communication between two endpoints by encapsulating the data sent within another protocol. This encapsulation allows data to be securely transmitted over a network, such as the internet, even if the underlying network infrastructure is not secure.

    B is incorrect. Filtering and blocking malicious traffic based on predefined security rules is the primary function of firewalls, not tunneling.

    C is incorrect. Monitoring network traffic for suspicious activities and alerting administrators is the role of Intrusion Detection Systems (IDS) or Intrusion Prevention Systems (IPS), not tunneling.

    D is incorrect. Access control systems, such as those implemented with Active Directory or network access control (NAC) systems, typically manage and control access to network resources based on user permissions.

33. The correct answer is **B**. A trade secret refers to confidential business information that provides a company with a competitive advantage and is often protected through legal means such as non-disclosure agreements (NDAs).

    A is incorrect. Financial information refers to data related to the company's revenue, expenses, and other monetary details.

    C is incorrect. Legal information encompasses documents or data for any legal matters, such as contracts or compliance.

    D is incorrect. "Non-human-readable" refers to data formatted in a way humans cannot easily interpret, such as machine code or encrypted files.

34. The correct answer is **B**. Just-in-Time (JIT) permissions are used to grant temporary access to critical systems only when needed, reducing the risk associated with permanent access.

    A is incorrect. JIT permissions are temporary, not permanent.

    C is incorrect. Password storage is handled by password vaulting.

    D is incorrect. Continuous logging is not the main purpose of JIT permissions.

35. The correct answer is **B**. Risk tolerance refers to the amount of risk an organization is willing to accept. This is determined by the severity of potential threats and their impact on the organization's operations, assets, and reputation.

    A is incorrect. Vulnerability scanning does not determine an organization's willingness to accept specific levels of risk.

    C is incorrect. The size of the security team does not directly define its tolerance for accepting risks.

    D is incorrect. The size of the IT infrastructure does not determine how much risk the organization is willing to accept.

36. The correct answer is **C**. TLS (Transport Layer Security) is specifically designed to protect data as it moves between two endpoints, ensuring it is encrypted and secure during transmission over the network.

    A is incorrect. Data sovereignty refers to laws and regulations regarding where data is stored and managed based on geographic location.

    B is incorrect. Data in use refers to data actively processed in memory or used by an application.

    D is incorrect. Data at rest refers to stored data, such as on a disk or in a database, not data transmitted over a network.

37. The correct answer is **B**. Tokenization replaces sensitive data (such as credit card numbers) with a non-sensitive placeholder, or "token," which can be mapped back to the original data if needed.

    A is incorrect. Obfuscation involves making data less readable or understandable, but it does not provide a method to retrieve the original data in the same way tokenization does.

    C is incorrect. Geographic restrictions limit access to data based on a user's location but do not involve replacing or masking sensitive information.

    D is incorrect. Permission restrictions control who can access specific data but do not replace or tokenize sensitive data to reduce exposure.

38. The correct answer is **C**. A password of at least 12 characters is considered a best practice to enhance security.

    A is incorrect. 6 characters is too short to be secure.

    B is incorrect. 8 characters is considered minimal and less secure than longer passwords.

    D is incorrect. While 16 characters is more secure, 12 is the recommended length.

39. The correct answer is **C**. A cold site is a backup facility that provides space but lacks the necessary IT infrastructure, hardware, or software, which means the company would need to set up and install everything from scratch, leading to a longer recovery time.

    A is incorrect. A hot site is fully equipped with all necessary hardware, software, and up-to-date data, allowing almost immediate recovery after a disaster.

    B is incorrect. A warm site includes some hardware and software, but not all. It requires less time to become operational than a cold site but still takes longer than a hot site.

    D is incorrect. Geographic dispersion distributes systems across various locations to prevent complete outages.

40. The correct answer is **C**. A failover test involves switching operations from the primary site to a backup site to ensure that the backup site can handle operations in the event of a disaster.

    A is incorrect. A simulation test involves running scenarios to evaluate the effectiveness of disaster recovery procedures without actually switching systems or operations.

    B is incorrect. A tabletop exercise is a discussion-based test where team members walk through their roles and procedures in a hypothetical disaster scenario without performing actions or switching operations.

    D is incorrect. Parallel processing refers to running operations simultaneously on multiple systems to increase performance, not to testing disaster recovery processes.

41. The correct answer is **B**. A snapshot captures a point-in-time copy of a system's data. This allows for quick restoration to the state of the data at the time the snapshot was taken, providing fast recovery options.

    A is incorrect. Replication involves creating a duplicate of data on a separate system or location, typically to ensure data availability and redundancy.

    C is incorrect. Incremental backups only save changes made since the last backup.

    D is incorrect. Differential backups capture all changes made since the last full backup.

42. The correct answer is **A**. SSH services typically use port 22. To prevent external hosts from accessing internal SSH services, the firewall rule must deny any inbound traffic targeting port 22, blocking unauthorized access attempts.

    B is incorrect. Port 21 is used for FTP (File Transfer Protocol) services, not SSH.

    C is incorrect. Port 80 is used for HTTP (web traffic). Blocking this port affects web services but does not prevent access to SSH services.

    D is incorrect. Port 443 is used for HTTPS (secure web traffic).

43. The correct answer is **C**. The maintenance phase involves ongoing activities to ensure that systems meet established security baselines over time.

    A is incorrect. Establishing refers to the initial phase where security baselines are defined and set up.

    B is incorrect. Deploying is when the defined security baselines are applied to systems during rollout.

    D is incorrect. Documenting involves recording the security baselines and configurations.

44. The correct answer is **C**. The correct sequence for managing secure baselines is to first Establish the security baselines by defining the standards, then deploy these baselines to systems, and finally maintain the baselines to ensure ongoing compliance and adjustment as necessary.

    A is incorrect. This sequence is not logical because you must establish the baselines before deploying them.

    B is incorrect. Maintenance comes after deployment; you must establish the baselines before deploying and maintaining them.

    D is incorrect. You can only deploy after establishing the security baselines.

45. The correct answer is **B**. The COPE model allows the company to own the devices while enabling employees to use them for personal activities.

    A is incorrect. In the BYOD model, employees use their own devices for work, which often gives them more control over the device but may be harder to secure and manage.

    C is incorrect. In the CYOD model, employees choose from a list of company-approved devices, which are typically company-owned.

    D is incorrect. MDM is a technology or solution for managing and securing mobile devices, but it is not a deployment model.

46. The correct answer is **A**. RADIUS is a protocol used to manage authentication, authorization, and accounting (AAA) for network access. It centralizes these functions, making it ideal for managing wireless network access and ensuring secure user authentication.

    B is incorrect. WPA3 is a security protocol designed to secure wireless networks but does not handle AAA functions.

    C is incorrect. SNMP is used for managing and monitoring network devices, not for managing user authentication.

    D is incorrect. TLS is a cryptographic protocol to secure network communications.

47. The correct answer is **B**. Code signing is a technique for verifying the integrity and authenticity of application code. By signing the code with a digital certificate, developers ensure that it has not been tampered with since it was signed.

    A is incorrect. Input validation ensures that users' data is correct and secure, but it does not protect the integrity of the application's code.

    C is incorrect. Secure cookies enhance security by ensuring that cookies are only sent over HTTPS connections.

    D is incorrect. Static code analysis examines the source code for vulnerabilities and coding issues without executing it.

48. The correct answer is **C**. Assigning clear ownership of data assets ensures that specific individuals or teams manage and safeguard the assets.

    A is incorrect. While ownership may indirectly contribute to ensuring that the responsible person manages software updates, this is not the primary benefit of assigning ownership.

    B is incorrect. Assigning ownership of data assets does not directly impact network traffic.

    D is incorrect. Data ownership is related to asset management and accountability, not directly to user authentication.

49. The correct answer is **B**. Data classified as "Public" is intended to be accessible to everyone without restrictions. It is information that can be freely shared and distributed.

    A is incorrect. "Private" data is intended to be restricted to specific individuals or groups and is not meant for general public access.

    C is incorrect. "Confidential" data is protected and intended to be accessed only by authorized individuals or groups.

    D is incorrect. "Sensitive" data requires protection due to its importance and potential impact if disclosed.

50. The correct answer is **C**. Asset enumeration involves creating an inventory of all devices and software within a corporate environment. This process helps understand what assets are present, their configuration, and their status.

    A is incorrect. Identifying software updates is related to patch management.

    B is incorrect. Monitoring user activity is related to network security and user behavior analysis.

    D is incorrect. Enforcing security policies on mobile devices is related to mobile device management.

51. The correct answer is **A**. Overwriting the data multiple times, also known as data wiping or data erasure, ensures that the data on a hard drive is unrecoverable.

    B is incorrect. Deleting files typically only removes references to the data rather than erasing it.

    C is incorrect. Reformatting the hard drives may remove the file system structure but does not necessarily erase the data itself. The data could still be recovered with specialized tools.

    D is incorrect. Disconnecting the servers from the network does not affect the data stored on the servers.

52. The correct answer is **B**. A data retention policy outlines the period for which data should be retained to comply with legal, regulatory, and business needs. It ensures that data is kept for an appropriate amount of time before being disposed of or archived.

   A is incorrect. The purpose of a data retention policy is not to delete data immediately but to establish guidelines for how long data should be kept before it can be safely deleted or archived.

   C is incorrect. Data encryption is not the primary focus of a data retention policy, which deals with the duration for which data is retained.

   D is incorrect. Data retention policies are focused on how long data is kept, not on improving data accessibility.

53. The correct answer is **C**. Physically destroying the device renders the hardware unusable, ensuring that the data stored on it is unrecoverable.

   A is incorrect. While a factory reset erases data from the device, it may not be sufficient to ensure complete data destruction.

   B is incorrect. Encrypting the device helps protect data from unauthorized access while it is in use, but it does not ensure that data cannot be recovered.

   D is incorrect. Disabling the device remotely can prevent further use but does not ensure that any residual data on the device is unrecoverable.

54. The correct answer is **A**. Dynamic analysis involves running the software or system in a live environment to observe its behavior and detect any vulnerabilities that might only emerge during execution.

   B is incorrect. Static analysis is where the code is examined without execution.

   C is incorrect. Updating vulnerable packages is part of vulnerability remediation, not dynamic analysis.

   D is incorrect. Collecting data from third-party sources relates more to threat intelligence gathering.

55. The correct answer is **C**. A threat feed is a service that provides ongoing updates on current threats, vulnerabilities, and indicators of compromise. Organizations subscribe to these feeds to stay informed about emerging risks.

   A is incorrect. Package monitoring refers to tracking software packages for updates or vulnerabilities.

   B is incorrect. OSINT involves gathering information from publicly available sources, but it is broader in scope and not limited to threat and vulnerability feeds.

   D is incorrect. Static analysis is a technique for reviewing code without executing it.

56. The correct answer is **C**. CVSS is a standardized framework used to assess the severity of security vulnerabilities. It assigns a score (typically from 0 to 10) based on various factors, such as the ease of exploitation, the potential impact on systems, and the degree of access required by the attacker.

    A is incorrect. CVSS does not assess the financial impact of a breach.

    B is incorrect. CVSS is not used to measure the effectiveness of antivirus software or any specific security solutions.

    D is incorrect. CVSS does not help determine the number of false positives in vulnerability detection.

57. The correct answer is **D**. While network traffic might be monitored for security purposes, it is not a direct factor in classifying vulnerabilities. Vulnerability classification focuses on aspects such as the potential impact, exploitability, and other vulnerability characteristics rather than general network conditions.

    A is incorrect. Potential impact is a critical factor in classifying vulnerabilities.

    B is incorrect. Exploitability refers to how easily an attacker can exploit a vulnerability. Factors such as the complexity of the attack, the privileges required, and the availability of exploit code are considered when classifying vulnerabilities.

    C is incorrect. Risk tolerance, though more specific to an organization's response, plays a role in prioritizing vulnerabilities.

58. The correct answer is **A**. Compensating controls are security measures implemented when it's not feasible to directly address a vulnerability, such as by patching or configuration changes.

    B is incorrect. Compensating controls do not replace the need for patching; they are temporary solutions used when patching isn't immediately possible.

    C is incorrect. While compensating controls might be more cost-effective in certain situations, their primary purpose is not to reduce costs but to manage risks when direct remediation isn't feasible.

    D is incorrect. Compensating controls do not enhance network performance.

59. The correct answer is **B**. Verification is the process of checking whether the security controls implemented are functioning as expected and confirming that vulnerabilities have been effectively remediated. It involves reviewing and testing the effectiveness of implemented measures to ensure they have addressed the identified security issues.

    A is incorrect. Rescanning involves running vulnerability scans again after initial remediation efforts.

    C is incorrect. Applying patches is part of the remediation process to fix vulnerabilities. However, applying additional patches alone does not guarantee that all security controls work correctly.

    D is incorrect. Network segmentation divides a network into isolated segments to limit the impact of vulnerabilities or attacks.

60. The correct answer is **C**. A web Application Firewall (WAF) monitors, filters, and analyzes HTTP/HTTPS traffic between a web application and the internet.

    A is incorrect. While encryption is essential for securing network traffic, a WAF is not designed to encrypt traffic.

    B is incorrect. A WAF is focused on protecting web applications, not the entire network. Firewalls, intrusion prevention systems (IPS), and access control mechanisms typically prevent unauthorized access to the network.

    D is incorrect. Monitoring physical access to a data center involves security measures such as surveillance cameras, access control systems, and physical security guards, not a WAF.

61. The correct answer is **B**. Application Performance Monitoring (APM) tools are specifically designed to monitor and manage application performance. They provide insights into application performance issues, such as slow response times or bottlenecks, and can also help ensure that applications meet security compliance requirements by monitoring application behavior and transactions.

    A is incorrect. A Database Management System (DBMS) manages databases, handles data storage, and performs queries.

    C is incorrect. Endpoint Detection and Response (EDR) tools monitor and find security threats on computers and mobile devices.

    D is incorrect. A Public Key Infrastructure (PKI) provides a framework for managing digital certificates and public-key encryption.

62. The correct answer is **C**. The alerting process involves configuring and managing systems to generate notifications or alerts when unusual activity is found on the network. This process ensures that security analysts are promptly informed of potential security incidents or anomalies, allowing for timely investigation and response.

    A is incorrect. Quarantine refers to isolating potentially harmful files or systems to prevent the spread of malware or other threats.

    B is incorrect. Alert response and remediation involve actions taken after an alert, such as investigating the alert, mitigating the threat, and applying fixes.

    D is incorrect. Archiving involves storing data, such as logs, for long-term retention and compliance.

63. The correct answer is **C**. Data Loss Prevention (DLP) tools are specifically designed to monitor and control the movement of sensitive data within and outside of a network. DLP solutions help prevent unauthorized access, sharing, or transfer of confidential information by monitoring data flows and enforcing policies restricting how and where sensitive data can be sent.

    A is incorrect. NetFlow is a network protocol developed by Cisco for collecting and analyzing network traffic data.

    B is incorrect. Security Information and Event Management (SIEM) systems aggregate and analyze network logs and events to detect security threats.

    D is incorrect. Vulnerability scanners are tools used to identify and assess vulnerabilities in systems, applications, and networks.

64. The correct answer is **B**. A screened subnet is a network that isolates certain servers (often web servers, email servers, etc.) from the internal network.

    A is incorrect. A screened subnet is designed to restrict access to sensitive internal resources.

    B is incorrect. A screened subnet works in conjunction with firewall rules.

    D is incorrect. A screened subnet separates certain devices (like public-facing servers) from the internal network.

65. The correct answer is **C**. SSH (Secure Shell) is a protocol for secure remote access and server management. Blocking SSH on a firewall prevents unauthorized users from accessing critical systems remotely.

    A is incorrect. Simple Mail Transfer Protocol is for sending email, not for remote server access.

    B is incorrect. FTP (File Transfer Protocol) transfers files between computers and is not for secure remote server access.

    D is incorrect. DNS (Domain Name System) resolves domain names to IP addresses and is unrelated to remote access.

66. The correct answer is **B**. Anomaly-based detection works by identifying patterns of behavior that deviate from the norm, such as many login attempts from a single IP address.

    A is incorrect. Signature-based detection looks for specific patterns or signatures of known threats.

    C is incorrect. Blocking rules are actions configured in an IDS/IPS to block specific traffic automatically based on predefined criteria.

    D is incorrect. Encryption protocols, such as SSL or TLS, secure communication by encrypting data in transit.

67. The correct answer is **B**. A gap analysis commonly results in a list of areas where security improvements are needed, which helps organizations understand the specific gaps between their current and desired states.

    A is incorrect. A detailed risk management plan involves identifying, assessing, and mitigating organizational risks.

    C is incorrect. Designing a user access control system involves creating or updating policies and technologies for managing user access. This might result from addressing gaps identified during the gap analysis, but it is not a direct outcome of the gap analysis.

    D is incorrect. A comprehensive incident response team involves assembling a group responsible for handling and responding to security incidents.

68. The correct answer is **B**. Signature-based detection systems use predefined patterns or signatures of known threats to identify malicious activities. Because the system is based on recognized attack patterns, it typically has a lower false positive rate when detecting known threats.

    A is incorrect. Signature-based detection is ineffective at detecting zero-day attacks – new and unknown threats that do not yet have a known signature.

    C is incorrect. Signature-based systems need regular updates to stay effective.

    D is incorrect. A signature-based IDS typically only detects and alerts administrators to suspicious activity based on matching known signatures.

69. The correct answer is **C**. Telnet is considered insecure because it transmits data, including login credentials, in plaintext, making it vulnerable to eavesdropping

    A is incorrect. Secure Shell (SSH) is a secure protocol that encrypts data during remote communications.

    B is incorrect. Hypertext Transfer Protocol Secure (HTTPS) encrypts web communications.

    D is incorrect. File Transfer Protocol Secure (FTPS) encrypts data during file transfers.

70. The correct answer is **C**. URL scanning enhances web security by examining the content of a URL, including scripts, links, and other elements, to detect malicious behavior. This approach identifies potentially harmful websites or phishing attempts, even if the URL seems harmless.

    A is incorrect. Checking URLs only allows access to websites on a predefined list but doesn't actively scan for malicious behavior.

    B is incorrect. Blocking all prohibited URLs is a restrictive approach but does not involve URL scanning.

    D is incorrect. Allowing all traffic to pass without inspection would significantly reduce security and negate the purpose of URL scanning and web filtering.

71. The correct answer is **B**. Group Policy in Windows is primarily for central management and configuration for users and computers, which allows administrators to enforce security policies, software installations, user permissions, and other configurations across multiple machines in an Active Directory environment.

    A is incorrect. Controlling network traffic between devices is typically the function of firewalls or network management tools, not Group Policy.

    C is incorrect. File encryption is handled by tools such as BitLocker or Encrypting File System (EFS) in a Windows environment, not Group Policy.

    D is incorrect. Group Policy is not a backup solution for user data.

72. The correct answer is **B**. SELinux (Security-Enhanced Linux) is a security architecture integrated into the Linux kernel that enforces mandatory access control (MAC). Unlike discretionary access control (DAC), where users have control over their resources, MAC ensures that security policies defined by the system administrator are enforced strictly on processes and files.

    A is incorrect. SELinux does not provide a graphical user interface (GUI) for managing permissions.

    C is incorrect. SELinux is not responsible for updating software packages.

    D is incorrect. Although SELinux can contribute to network security by controlling which processes can communicate over the network, it is more focused on enforcing access controls on processes and files than network security.

73. The correct answer is **B**. Port 443 is the standard HTTPS (Hypertext Transfer Protocol Secure) port to secure web traffic.

    A is incorrect. Port 21 is used by FTP (File Transfer Protocol) for transferring files.

    C is incorrect. Port 80 is used by HTTP (Hypertext Transfer Protocol), the standard protocol for transferring web pages without encryption.

    D is incorrect. Telnet, a protocol for remote command-line access, uses port 23.

74. The correct answer is **A**. A turnstile is a physical control because it is a tangible mechanism that regulates access to a physical space, ensuring that only authorized individuals can enter.

    B is incorrect. Detective controls detect and alert but don't physically control access.

    C is incorrect. Corrective controls fix issues after they occur but are irrelevant to access control.

    D is incorrect. Technical controls involve software or hardware, not a physical barrier such as a turnstile.

75. The correct answer is **B**. Transport Layer Security (TLS) encrypts data transmitted over the network, ensuring that communication between parties remains confidential and secure from eavesdropping, tampering, and forgery.

    A is incorrect. TLS does not handle data compression.

    C is incorrect. Although TLS ensures secure communication, it is not primarily used to authenticate user credentials.

    D is incorrect. TLS does not block unauthorized access to the network. Instead, it focuses on securing the data transmitted between clients and servers.

76. The correct answer is **B**. Multifactor authentication (MFA) involves using two or more independent credentials (e.g., something you know, something you have, and something you are) to verify identity. In zero-trust architecture, MFA enhances security by thoroughly verifying access requests, even if an initial authentication factor is compromised.

    A is incorrect. Single-factor authentication relies on one verification form, such as a password. Zero Trust emphasizes stronger security measures, which typically involve multiple layers of authentication.

    C is incorrect. Password-based authentication relies solely on a password for user verification. While passwords are a common method of authentication, Zero Trust architecture requires more robust measures, such as MFA, to enhance security beyond passwords.

    D is incorrect. Location-based authentication involves verifying a user's location as part of the access control process. While location might be considered in some security models, Zero Trust focuses more on the ID and access to users and devices through methods such as MFA rather than relying on location.

77. The correct answer is **B**. The primary purpose of the Sender Policy Framework (SPF) is to authenticate the sender's email address. SPF helps prevent email spoofing by identifying any mail servers that are authorized to send emails.

    A is incorrect. SPF does not manage email encryption. Protocols like S/MIME manage the encryption of email contents.

    C is incorrect. SPF does not provide digital signatures for email messages.

    D is incorrect. SPF does not check the reputation of the email sender. Checking the sender's reputation involves other systems or services that assess the sender's trustworthiness.

78. The correct answer is **B**. DKIM (DomainKeys Identified Mail) provides a key benefit by digitally signing emails with a cryptographic signature. It is used to verify that the email was indeed sent by an authorized sender from the domain and that the content has not been altered during transit.

    A is incorrect. DKIM does not handle email encryption.

    C is incorrect. DKIM does not filter spam emails based on content.

    D is incorrect. DKIM does not block emails from unknown senders.

79. The correct answer is **A**. Policy-Driven Access Control ensures that security policies are applied consistently to all access requests across the network, providing uniform protection.

   B is incorrect. Access based solely on physical location is not a primary function of Policy-Driven Access Control.

   C is incorrect. Biometric data is related to authentication methods rather than access control policies.

   D is incorrect. Updating security patches is a maintenance task.

80. The correct answer is **B**. FIM is beneficial for monitoring changes to critical system files, ensuring that any unauthorized modifications are detected promptly.

   A is incorrect. FIM does not reduce file sizes.

   C is incorrect. Automating user account creation is not related to FIM.

   D is incorrect. FIM does not directly affect network bandwidth usage.

81. The correct answer is **B**. A fail-closed mechanism in a security infrastructure means the system will automatically restrict access to the network or resource if a security device fails.

   A is incorrect. A fail-open mechanism allows network services to remain available to users even if a security device fails, prioritizing continuous operation over security.

   C is incorrect. A fail-closed mechanism does not grant access based on a device's operational status, regardless of security failures.

   D is incorrect. A fail-closed mechanism does not involve automatically rebooting the system to restore operations.

82. The correct answer is **C**. In disaster recovery, capacity planning involves ensuring that the technological infrastructure, such as servers, storage, and network resources, can support critical applications.

   A is incorrect. Capacity planning primarily involves ensuring the technology can support critical applications, not human resources.

   B is incorrect. Data sensitivity is more relevant to determining how to handle and protect different data types.

   D is incorrect. Location matters for redundancy and failover in disaster recovery.

83. The correct answer is **C**. To prevent employees from copying sensitive data to USB drives, DLP solutions should be configured to block or encrypt data transfers to USB devices, which prevents unauthorized data exfiltration via removable media.

   A is incorrect. Monitoring web browsing does not address USB data transfers.

   B is incorrect. Restricting file transfers to email domains is unrelated to USB use.

   D is incorrect. Allowing only trusted applications to run does not prevent data loss via USB.

84. The correct answer is **B**. A remediation server in an NAC environment provides updates, patches, and security fixes to non-compliant computers to meet the required security standards.

    A is incorrect. Logging network activity is not the primary role of a remediation server.

    C is incorrect. Enforcing policies on compliant computers is managed by NAC policies, not a remediation server.

    D is incorrect. VPN servers, not remediation servers, manage VPN connections.

85. The correct answer is **B**. Group Policy is a feature in Windows that allows administrators to enforce password complexity rules, such as minimum length, special character requirements, and expiration policies, across all computers in the organization.

    A is incorrect. Security-Enhanced Linux (SELinux) is a Linux kernel security module that manages access controls.

    C is incorrect. Antivirus software is designed to detect and remove malware but does not manage or enforce password complexity rules.

    D is incorrect. A firewall controls incoming and outgoing network traffic based on security rules but does not handle password complexity enforcement.

CompTIA Security+ SY0-701 Mock Exam 3

1. The correct answer is **B**. Port 22 is the Secure Shell protocol, used for secure remote access to networked systems, which makes it the preferred port for secure remote access.

    A is incorrect. Port 21 is used for the File Transfer Protocol (FTP), which is not secure by default.

    C is incorrect. Port 23 is used for Telnet, an older remote access protocol that transmits data in plain text.

    D is incorrect. Port 25 is used for the Simple Mail Transfer Protocol (SMTP) for sending emails.

2. The correct answer is **B**. A common tactic in phishing emails is to use urgency to trick users into making hasty actions, such as clicking on suspicious links or providing sensitive information.

    A is incorrect. Phishing emails often try to spoof or mimic legitimate internal addresses, but seeing an internal address alone is not a reliable indicator of phishing.

    C is incorrect. If the email is from a recognized vendor with no suspicious elements, it is less likely to be a phishing attempt.

    D is incorrect. Attackers may hide malware in such files, but the attachment type is not necessarily suspicious without other indicators such as unexpected content or senders.

3. The correct answer is **A**. Video surveillance systems monitor and record activities in real time, which can be reviewed later for security incidents.

    B is incorrect. Video surveillance complements, but does not replace, physical security guards.

    C is incorrect. Video surveillance is focused on physical areas rather than securing network communications.

    D is incorrect. Video surveillance is not designed as a communication system.

4. The correct answer is **C**. Penetration testing is a highly effective technique for identifying security vulnerabilities within a vendor's systems. It involves simulating real-world attacks on the vendor's systems to assess their security defenses. By testing the system's resilience against various attack vectors, the security team can gain insight into potential weaknesses and areas for improvement.

    A is incorrect. Supply chain analysis is useful for evaluating the risks associated with a vendor's broader supply chain but does not specifically focus on identifying vulnerabilities in the vendor's own systems.

    B is incorrect. Independent assessments can provide valuable insights into the vendor's overall security posture, policies, and practices, but they are generally more formal reviews rather than the active testing of vulnerabilities.

    D is incorrect. A right-to-audit clause allows a company to audit a vendor's security practices and compliance with contractual obligations. While this ensures the company can review the vendor's security controls and processes, it does not directly identify vulnerabilities like penetration testing would.

5. The correct answer is **B**. Bug bounty programs involve offering rewards or incentives to external security researchers and hackers for discovering and reporting vulnerabilities in an organization's systems.

    A is incorrect. Penetration testing involves hiring external security experts to simulate attacks and identify vulnerabilities within an organization's systems.

    C is incorrect. Vulnerability scans use automated tools to identify known vulnerabilities within a system. These scans are generally not incentivized and do not involve external researchers or reporting vulnerabilities for rewards.

    D is incorrect. Package monitoring involves tracking software packages' updates to identify potential vulnerabilities or issues.

6. The correct answer is **C**. In the zero-trust model, access is not granted based on static trust levels or network location. Zero Trust continuously evaluates and verifies every access request based on real-time factors, such as user identity, device status, and access context. This approach ensures that trust is not implicit and that every request is rigorously checked.

    A is incorrect. Traditional security models often rely on perimeter defenses to secure the network, assuming internal traffic is safe once it has passed through the firewall.

    B is incorrect. Traditional models might grant access based on user roles, but Zero Trust takes a more dynamic approach.

    D is incorrect. Zero Trust does not assume trust for internal network traffic.

7. The correct answer is **C**. OS-specific security logs provide detailed records of login attempts, authentication events, and system changes, helping identify potential unauthorized access or modifications.

    A is incorrect. Network logs capture traffic and events but do not focus on user login activities.

    B is incorrect. Application logs track activities within specific applications.

    D is incorrect. IPSs/IDSs log monitor for malicious traffic or intrusion attempts but are not used to track user login or system-level activities directly.

8. The correct answer is **B**. An unmonitored CCTV camera primarily discourages criminal activity through its presence, acting as a deterrent. It doesn't actively detect, prevent, or physically stop incidents but instead aims to prevent them by making potential wrongdoers aware that they could be watched.

    A is incorrect. A CCTV camera would only be a detective control if it was being monitored.

    C is incorrect. A CCTV camera doesn't provide physical security.

    D is incorrect. A CCTV camera doesn't actively prevent incidents.

9. The correct answer is **B**. The data plane is responsible for handling and forwarding user data packets based on the routing decisions made by the control plane. It performs the actual data transmission.

   A is incorrect. Managing routing and controlling traffic flow is the primary function of the control plane.

   C is incorrect. Configuring network devices and establishing network policies are tasks associated with network management.

   D is incorrect. Monitoring and analyzing network traffic for security incidents are typically performed by security tools and systems rather than the data plane itself.

10. The correct answer is **C**. Accounting is an AAA component that tracks and records user activities and resource usage for auditing and compliance purposes.

    A is incorrect. Authentication verifies user identity.

    B is incorrect. Authorization determines what resources a user can access.

    D is incorrect. Auditing involves reviewing and analyzing records, which are closely related to but distinct from accounting.

11. The correct answer is **B**. Firewall logs provide detailed records of all incoming and outgoing network traffic, including any attempts to access the network that were blocked or allowed.

    A is incorrect. Application logs track the activity within specific software applications but are not typically used to detect unauthorized external access.

    C is incorrect. Endpoint logs record events related to individual devices on the network and are more focused on internal system activity.

    D is incorrect. OS-specific security logs contain information about system-level security events on a specific OS.

12. The correct answer is **A**. Requiring a photo ID and using a gate barrier are physical controls because they involve tangible measures to restrict access to the data center, ensuring that only authorized personnel can enter.

    B is incorrect. Managerial controls involve policies and procedures, not physical access controls.

    C is incorrect. Technical controls involve software and hardware solutions, not physical barriers.

    D is incorrect. Operational controls involve the implementation and execution of security practices but not specifically physical access restrictions.

13. The correct answer is **B**. In a serverless architecture, the cloud provider manages the underlying infrastructure, including operating systems. The organization using serverless services has reduced responsibility for tasks such as patching and maintaining operating systems, allowing them to focus more on application-level security.

    A is incorrect. In a serverless architecture, the organization controls the underlying server configurations less because the cloud provider manages the infrastructure.

    C is incorrect. Serverless architecture does not inherently increase the complexity of encryption or key management.

    D is incorrect. In serverless architecture, organizations do not manage physical hardware, as that responsibility is entirely with the cloud provider.

14. The correct answer is **B**. Secured zones isolate sensitive areas of a network from less secure ones, helping to protect critical data and systems.

    A is incorrect. Increasing the number of connected devices does not align with the purpose of secured zones.

    C is incorrect. Monitoring and logging are related to security operations rather than secured zones.

    D is incorrect. Simplifying authentication is not the main purpose of creating secured zones.

15. The correct answer is **B**. Identifying the root cause during an incident investigation eliminates the fundamental issue that led to the incident and prevents recurrence. This helps address the underlying problem, ensuring that similar incidents don't happen in the future.

    A is incorrect. Identifying affected systems is part of the incident response process but not the primary goal of determining the root cause.

    C is incorrect. Documenting the incident is a different aspect of incident management.

    D is incorrect. Financial impact assessment is part of the incident analysis but is separate from the purpose of root cause identification.

16. The correct answer is **B**. A hash algorithm generates a unique fixed-size string (hash value) from the original data. If the data changes, the hash value changes, allowing verification that the data has not been altered.

    A is incorrect. Encrypting data is primarily used to ensure confidentiality by rendering data unreadable to unwanted users.

    C is incorrect. Providing a backup is related to data availability and recovery, ensuring that data can be restored in case of loss. It does not involve verifying the integrity of data.

    D is incorrect. Ensuring data availability involves keeping systems and data accessible during failures, often through redundancy and failover solutions. It does not relate to verifying the integrity of data.

17. The correct answer is **C**. Risk tolerance represents the level of risk an organization is willing to accept. It influences how the organization prioritizes vulnerabilities for remediation.

    A is incorrect. While risk tolerance influences overall risk management strategies, it does not directly determine the frequency of vulnerability scans.

    B is incorrect. Risk tolerance influences overall risk management but does not directly dictate the required security personnel.

    D is incorrect. Risk tolerance does play a role in shaping security policies but it is not the primary factor.

18. The correct answer is **B**. A honey file is placed in a system to lure attackers. When accessed, it indicates unauthorized activity, helping to detect and analyze potential breaches or malicious behavior.

    A is incorrect. Encrypting sensitive information in storage involves using crypto techniques to protect it from unauthorized access. A honey file, however, is not used for encryption but to detect and analyze unauthorized access attempts.

    C is incorrect. Managing file versions and backups involves tracking different versions of files and creating backup copies to prevent data loss. A honey file does not perform these functions; it is used to detect unauthorized access.

    D is incorrect. Ensuring filesystem integrity and consistency involves checking that the filesystem remains intact and correct. While important, this is not the primary purpose of a honey file.

19. The correct answer is **C**. Penetration testing involves hiring external security experts to simulate attacks on an organization's network, applications, or systems to identify and exploit vulnerabilities. This method provides a detailed assessment of security weaknesses and how real attackers could exploit them.

    A is incorrect. Bug bounty programs reward individuals (often researchers or hackers) who find and report vulnerabilities in an organization's systems.

    B is incorrect. Third-party assessment generally refers to any evaluation conducted by an external entity, which could include various types of security assessments such as audits or reviews.

    D is incorrect. Vulnerability scans use automated tools to identify known vulnerabilities within a system by scanning for specific weaknesses.

20. The correct answer is **D**. The availability of automated deployment tools and predefined configurations is a crucial factor in facilitating deployment. These tools simplify the process by using automation, thereby speeding up deployment.

    A is incorrect. While the user interface's complexity may impact end users, it does not directly affect the ease of deployment.

    B is incorrect. Although frequent updates and patches are important for security and functionality, they do not directly influence the ease of the initial deployment.

    C is incorrect. While having many dependencies and system requirements can complicate the deployment process, it is not the most crucial factor.

21. The correct answer is **C**. A benchmarking framework or checklist is commonly used for a gap analysis, as it helps compare current practices against standards.

    A is incorrect. A SIEM system collects, analyzes, and manages security events and logs. While SIEM systems are important for monitoring and detecting security incidents, they are not typically used to perform gap analysis.

    B is incorrect. A risk assessment matrix evaluates and highlights risks based on their likelihood and impact. While useful in risk management, it is not designed explicitly for gap analysis.

    D is incorrect. Antivirus software is designed to detect, prevent, and remove system malware. While critical for protecting against malicious threats, it is not used for performing gap analysis.

22. The correct answer is **C**. The Analysis phase of incident response is when logs, evidence, and other data are collected to understand the scope, cause, and impact of an incident.

    A is incorrect. The Preparation phase is focused on ensuring the cyber security team can respond to incidents but does not involve collecting evidence.

    B is incorrect. The Detection phase is about identifying whether an incident has occurred.

    D is incorrect. The Recovery phase involves restoring systems to normal operations after the incident has been resolved.

23. The correct answer is **B**. In a cloud infrastructure, encryption ensures that data is protected while at rest and in transit, and access controls manage who can access or modify cloud resources.

    A is incorrect. Regular software updates are essential for securing systems by patching vulnerabilities. They are not specific to cloud infrastructure hardening, where encryption and access controls play a more direct role in securing data and resources.

    C is incorrect. Configuring local firewalls is important for protecting internal networks and systems, although the focus is more on cloud-native security features such as network security groups, virtual firewalls, and cloud-provider-specific security settings than traditional local firewalls.

    D is incorrect. Disabling unused ports on network switches is a good practice for hardening network security in a traditional on-premises environment but is less relevant for cloud infrastructure.

24. The correct answer is **C**. Disabling unused ports and protocols is an effective hardening technique because it reduces the attack surface by restricting communication methods that are not necessary for the server's operation.

    A is incorrect. Encryption is essential for protecting data confidentiality but does not prevent unauthorized access.

    B is incorrect. While endpoint protection software helps detect and block malware, viruses, and other threats, it does not specifically focus on turning off unused ports or protocols to limit communication methods.

    D is incorrect. A host-based firewall can help control incoming and outgoing network traffic by defining rules for which ports or services can be accessed.

25. The correct answer is **C**. Fines are a common and likely consequence of not complying with data protection regulations, especially after a breach.

    A is incorrect. Reputational damage is severe but the most likely immediate consequence would be financial penalties.

    B is incorrect. Loss of license can occur but is less common than fines for non-compliance.

    D is incorrect. There could be impacts on contracts due to non-compliance, which are secondary to the immediate financial penalties.

26. The correct answer is **B**. An access control list (ACL) defines rules that control which users are allowed to access certain resources. In this case, the security consultant sets up rules based on IP addresses and protocols characteristic of ACLs.

    A is incorrect. RBAC manages permissions by assigning users to roles; each role has predefined access rights to resources.

    C is incorrect. MAC is an access control model where resource access is decided by a central authority based on security classifications.

    D is incorrect. DAC allows the resource owner to determine who can access their resources. The control is based on users' or groups' identities, but it does not involve specifying access based on IP addresses and protocols.

27. The correct answer is **B**. Regulations and policies are the main purpose of conducting a formal audit. This process helps verify that the security measures align with industry standards and internal requirements.

    A is incorrect. Evaluating employee productivity focuses on assessing workforce efficiency rather than compliance with security regulations.

    C is incorrect. Identifying business growth opportunities is not the primary focus of a security audit.

    D is incorrect. Creating new security policies may highlight areas needing policy improvement, but their primary aim is to assess existing compliance.

28. The correct answer is **B**. Stakeholders provide input and approvals for decisions that impact the business, including security operations, ensuring that these decisions align with organizational goals.

    A is incorrect. Stakeholders are not the only group responsible for implementing security policies.

    C is incorrect. Stakeholders are involved in security operations, especially at the decision-making level.

    D is incorrect. Day-to-day security monitoring and incident response are typically handled by IT teams.

29. The correct answer is **C**. A regulatory examination is when a regulatory body reviews a company to verify compliance with industry-specific laws.

    A is incorrect. Self-assessment is an internal review conducted by the organization, not an external regulatory body.

    B is incorrect. An independent third-party audit involves an external auditor but is not specifically a regulatory examination.

    D is incorrect. Internal audits refer to an organization's internal assessment of its own practices and controls.

30. The correct answer is **A**. Impact analysis helps organizations understand how changes to security operations might affect business continuity, operations, and overall risk, ensuring that potential negative impacts are minimized.

    B is incorrect. While timing is important, impact analysis focuses more on the effects of changes rather than speed.

    C is incorrect. Impact analysis is not directly concerned with cost reduction but with understanding risks and impacts.

    D is incorrect. The speed of decision-making is not the primary focus of impact analysis.

31. The correct answer is **B**. The primary purpose of conducting a tabletop exercise is to practice and review the incident response plan in a controlled, discussion-based environment.

    A is incorrect. To test the effectiveness of automated security tools is not the primary goal of a tabletop exercise.

    C is incorrect. Implementing new security patches and updates is unrelated to a tabletop exercise.

    D is incorrect. A real-time simulation of a security breach involves more active, hands-on testing, whereas a tabletop exercise is a discussion-based activity.

32. The correct answer is **D**. Key escrow involves securely storing a copy of private keys so they can be recovered by authorized personnel if the original key is lost or becomes inaccessible.

    A is incorrect. Public keys are not typically backed up in key escrow, as they can be regenerated from the private key.

    B is incorrect. Key escrow does not generate encryption keys; it stores them for recovery purposes.

    C is incorrect. Key escrow deals with private keys, not the distribution of public keys.

33. The correct answer is **C**. File-level encryption allows users to encrypt specific files, making it useful for protecting sensitive data while keeping other files unencrypted and accessible.

    A is incorrect. Full-disk encryption encrypts the entire disk, not file-level encryption.

    B is incorrect. File-level encryption is for data at rest, not in transit.

    D is incorrect. Protocols such as VPNs typically handle encrypting network communications.

34. The correct answer is **B**. A network-based IDS (NIDS) is designed to monitor and analyze network traffic across the entire network. It is well suited for detecting attacks and intrusions within the internal network by capturing and inspecting packets traveling through the network.

    A is incorrect. A host-based IDS (HIDS) is installed on individual hosts or endpoints and monitors activity on that specific device.

    C is incorrect. A wireless IDS (WIDS) monitors and secures wireless networks.

    D is incorrect. A signature-based IDS refers to detecting threats based on known attack signatures.

35. The correct answer is **B**. A KMS is responsible for the centralized management, distribution, and storage of encryption keys, ensuring they are securely handled throughout their lifecycle.

    A is incorrect. KMS manages keys; it does not directly encrypt data at rest.

    C is incorrect. KMS should not store backup keys in plaintext. They must be stored securely.

    D is incorrect. KMS does not perform real-time encryption. It manages the keys used in encryption processes.

36. The correct answer is **B**. Critical data is essential to the organization's operations. If compromised, lost, or tampered with, it would significantly impact the business, leading to severe disruptions or significant financial loss. This classification is used for data that must be protected at the highest level due to its importance to the company's survival.

    A is incorrect. Public data is information that can be freely shared without causing harm to the organization if exposed.

    C is incorrect. Restricted data is sensitive but not necessarily critical to the organization's operations.

    D is incorrect. Private data generally refers to personal information, such as employee or customer details, that must be kept confidential.

37. The correct answer is **B**. The primary goal of the Preparation phase in incident response is to ensure that all incident response team (IRT) members are trained to handle incidents effectively.

    A is incorrect. Identifying and analyzing potential threats and vulnerabilities occurs in the Identification or Detection phase.

    C is incorrect. Recovering from the impact of an incident occurs during the Recovery phase.

    D is incorrect. Containing the spread of the incident is part of the Containment phase.

38. The correct answer is **B**. Anomaly-based detection works by identifying deviations from the network's established baseline behavior. Since it relies on recognizing unusual patterns or behaviors that differ from the norm, it is prone to generating false positives when legitimate but uncommon activities occur.

    A is incorrect. Signature-based detection identifies known threats by matching patterns or signatures of known attacks.

    C is incorrect. Protocol-based detection monitors and analyzes network protocols for protocol standards and rules violations.

    D is incorrect. Heuristic detection uses rules and algorithms to identify potential threats based on behaviors or patterns likely to indicate malicious activity.

39. The correct answer is **D**. Choose your own device (CYOD) is a mobile solution in which employees are given a selection of pre-approved devices to use for work purposes.

    A is incorrect. Bring your own device (BYOD) allows personal device use by employees for work purposes.

    B is incorrect. Mobile device management (MDM) refers to the technology used to manage, secure, and enforce policies on mobile devices within an organization.

    C is incorrect. Corporate-owned, personally enabled (COPE) involves the company providing devices to employees that are primarily for corporate use but allow some personal use.

40. The correct answer is **B**. The exposure factor is a metric used to estimate the potential impact or damage a vulnerability could cause if exploited. It represents the percentage of loss or damage to an asset resulting from a successful exploit of a vulnerability.

    A is incorrect. Risk tolerance is the amount of risk a company is willing to accept to continue in its objectives.

    C is incorrect. The false positive rate measures the frequency at which a security tool incorrectly identifies a benign event as a threat.

    D is incorrect. The Common Vulnerability Scoring System (CVSS) base score provides a numeric score reflecting the severity of a vulnerability based on its characteristics.

41. The correct answer is **D**. Encryption transforms data using an algorithm and a key. Tokenization replaces sensitive data with a token that can then be re-mapped back to the original data via a separate system.

    A is incorrect. This reverses the roles of tokenization and encryption.

    B is incorrect. Depending on the implementation, both encryption and tokenization can be used for data at rest or in transit.

    C is incorrect. Tokenization and encryption can be reversed, but tokenization typically involves a mapping, whereas encryption involves decryption.

42. The correct answer is **D**. The Extensible Authentication Protocol (EAP) is a flexible authentication framework widely used for network access control and secure authentication, particularly in wireless networks and VPNs.

    A is incorrect. Internet Protocol Security (IPSec) is a protocol suite for securing IP communications by authenticating and encrypting each IP packet.

    B is incorrect. Simple Authentication and Security Layer (SASL) is an authentication framework that adds authentication support to connection-based protocols such as Internet Message Access Protocol (IMAP) and Simple Mail Transfer Protocol (SMTP).

    C is incorrect. Lightweight Directory Access Protocol (LDAP) is used for the manipulation of a site's directory services information.

43. The correct answer is **B**. Data masking is often used to protect personal or sensitive data in environments where real data is unnecessary, such as software testing or development, helping organizations comply with data protection regulations.

    A is incorrect. Storing data in plaintext is generally discouraged and not a compliance measure.

    C is incorrect. Encrypting data before transmission is not the same as data masking.

    D is incorrect. Creating backups is related to data protection but not specifically to data masking.

44. The correct answer is **A**. The root of trust is a critical component in a PKI, serving as the trust anchor that verifies the authenticity of all digital certificates in the infrastructure.

   B is incorrect. Storing encrypted passwords is not the function of a root of trust.

   C is incorrect. While the root of trust is integral to key management, its primary role is to validate certificates.

   D is incorrect. Encryption and decryption of network traffic are not handled directly by the root of trust.

45. The correct answer is **B**. Data sovereignty specifies that data is subject to the regulations of the country where it is collected or stored. Many legal frameworks mandate that certain data types, such as personal or sensitive information, must reside within specific geographic boundaries.

   A is incorrect. Geolocation refers to the identification of a device or user's physical location, often through GPS or IP address tracking.

   C is incorrect. Data in use refers to a system's active processing or accessing information.

   D is incorrect. Data at rest refers to information stored on a device or server that is not being processed or transmitted.

46. The correct answer is **A**. Organized crime groups are typically involved in coordinated activities that aim to generate financial profit through illegal means, including cybercrime.

   B is incorrect. Nation-state actors are government-sponsored groups that engage in cyber operations for strategic purposes, such as espionage, intelligence gathering, or sabotage.

   C is incorrect. Insider threats involve users in a company who misuse access to sensitive information, often due to personal grievances or coercion.

   D is incorrect. Hacktivists are motivated by political, social, or ideological causes rather than financial gain.

47. The correct answer is **C**. Unexpected behavior refers to actions that deviate from the patterns of an employee's role or responsibilities. For this employee, accessing confidential data outside of business hours is unusual, making it unexpected.

   A is incorrect. Routine behavior refers to actions that align with an employee's normal job duties and typical work patterns.

   B is incorrect. Unintentional access happens when employees accidentally access data they should not have.

   D is incorrect. Risky behavior involves actions that pose a security risk, such as using insecure methods to access sensitive data or engaging in activities that violate security policies.

48. The correct answer is **B**. Shadow IT refers to employees' use of unauthorized personal devices, software, and cloud services, often to improve productivity or convenience.

   A is incorrect. While insider threats involve individuals within an organization who intentionally or unintentionally cause harm, the scenario described is more accurately classified as shadow IT.

   C is incorrect. Unskilled attackers are external actors who use pre-made tools and scripts to exploit vulnerabilities.

   D is incorrect. Nation-state actors are sophisticated, government-sponsored groups that engage in cyber operations for strategic purposes, such as espionage or sabotage.

49. The correct answer is **C**. A voice call attack involves using phone calls to deceive or manipulate individuals into disclosing confidential information.

   A is incorrect. A file-based attack involves delivering malicious payloads through files, such as email attachments or downloads.

   B is incorrect. An image-based attack involves embedding malicious code, such as PNGs, within image files.

   D is incorrect. Removable device attacks involve physical devices to deliver malware.

50. The correct answer is **B**. The data owner establishes rules and policies to ensure data is used, managed, and accessed according to those policies.

   A is incorrect. The data custodian is responsible for the safe storage and maintenance of data.

   C is incorrect. Data processors refer to individuals or systems that process data on behalf of the data controller within a regulatory framework.

   D is incorrect. The security administrator focuses on implementing security measures and controls decided by the owner.

51. The correct answer is **D**. An image-based attack hides malicious code, such as JPEGs or PNGs, within image files. In this case, malicious software was delivered via an image file.

   A is incorrect. A file-based attack generally refers to malicious payloads delivered through various types of files. This question is more specific.

   B is incorrect. Unsupported systems and applications refer to software or systems no longer maintained or updated.

   C is incorrect. Vulnerable software refers to applications or systems with security flaws that can be exploited.

52. The correct answer is **C**. Smishing is a form of phishing that involves sending fraudulent text messages (SMSs) to try to get users to activate malicious links or give away sensitive information.

    A is incorrect. Phishing generally refers to fraudulent emails that trick users into revealing sensitive information.

    B is incorrect. Vishing (voice phishing) involves using phone calls to trick individuals into divulging personal information.

    D is incorrect. Impersonation is a tactic in which the attacker pretends to be someone else; it is a broader term that can occur in various contexts.

53. The correct answer is **B**. Business email compromise (BEC) involves using compromised or spoofed email accounts to impersonate executives or trusted individuals.

    A is incorrect. Pretexting involves creating a fabricated scenario to obtain information or perform an action.

    C is incorrect. Vishing involves using phone calls to deceive individuals into revealing sensitive information.

    D is incorrect. A watering-hole attack involves compromising a legitimate website to target specific users.

54. The correct answer is **B**. In digital forensics, the purpose of a legal hold is to prevent the alteration or destruction of relevant data and evidence. It ensures that data, which may be critical for an investigation or litigation, is preserved and not tampered with.

    A is incorrect. A legal hold does not involve encryption.

    C is incorrect. Backing up data may be part of preserving evidence, but a legal hold explicitly aims to prevent data alteration.

    D is incorrect. A legal hold is about preserving data, not analyzing it in real time.

55. The correct answer is **A**. Typosquatting involves registering domain names similar to legitimate ones, often with slight misspellings, to trick users into visiting the fake site.

    B is incorrect. Brand impersonation involves creating websites or communications that mimic a legitimate brand to deceive users.

    C is incorrect. Phishing generally refers to sending fraudulent communications via email, in order to reveal personal information.

    D is incorrect. Watering-hole attacks involve compromising a legitimate website to target regularly visiting users.

56. The correct answer is **B**. In digital forensics, the chain of custody documents every person who handles the evidence and every action taken. This ensures that the integrity of the evidence is maintained and can be verified throughout the investigation process.

   A is incorrect. Deleting data after analysis contradicts the goal of maintaining evidence integrity in forensics.

   C is incorrect. Encrypting evidence is not a principle of the chain of custody.

   D is incorrect. The chain of custody ensures that every move and handler is documented, not just the removal.

57. The correct answer is **B**. End-of-life (EOL) refers to software or hardware no longer supported by the manufacturer, meaning it does not receive updates, including security patches, making it a significant vulnerability.

   A is incorrect. Firmware refers to the low-level software that controls a device's hardware.

   C is incorrect. Legacy systems are older systems that may still be in use but are typically not the latest technology.

   D is incorrect. Resource reuse typically refers to the reuse of system resources, such as memory or storage, in a way that could expose sensitive information.

58. The correct answer is **C**. A virtual machine escape is a vulnerability that allows an attacker to break out of a virtualized environment (the guest operating system) and gain access to the underlying host system, which can lead to a significant security breach.

   A is incorrect. Legacy refers to older systems or software still in use.

   B is incorrect. Resource reuse involves the potential security risks of reusing system resources, such as memory or files.

   D is incorrect. Firmware is the low-level software controlling hardware. It is unrelated to escaping from a virtual machine to the host.

59. The correct answer is **A**. End-of-life (EOL) vulnerabilities occur when manufacturers stop providing support, updates, or security patches for devices or software.

   B is incorrect. A zero-day vulnerability refers to a flaw that is unknown to the software or hardware vendor and for which no patch or fix is available.

   C is incorrect. A virtual machine escape is a specific type of vulnerability in which an attacker can break out of a virtualized environment to access the host system.

   D is incorrect. Firmware refers to the software embedded in hardware devices.

60. The correct answer is **A**. A keylogger is a type of malware that secretly records keystrokes made by the user. Its primary purpose is to capture sensitive input such as passwords or other personal data and send it to an attacker.

    B is incorrect. A rootkit is malware designed to provide unauthorized root-level access to a system and remain hidden.

    C is incorrect. A logic bomb is malware triggered by a scheduled event or action.

    D is incorrect. A worm is malware that self-replicates and spreads across networks without user intervention. It doesn't typically perform actions such as recording keystrokes; instead, its goal is to spread quickly across systems and cause disruption.

61. The correct answer is **B**. RFID cloning refers to duplicating the data from a radio frequency identification (RFID) badge or card, often used for physical access control. Unauthorized individuals can use the cloned badge to bypass security and gain access to restricted areas.

    A is incorrect. A brute-force attack involves systematically attempting all possible combinations to crack passwords or encryption keys.

    C is incorrect. An environmental attack refers to physical threats to a system's environment, such as fires, floods, or power outages.

    D is incorrect. A keylogger is malware that captures and records keystrokes on a computer or device.

62. The correct answer is **C**. The transfer strategy involves purchasing insurance to offload the financial impact of a potential security breach to a third party.

    A is incorrect. Accepting involves acknowledging the risk and deciding to proceed without taking action to mitigate it.

    B is incorrect. Avoiding aims to eliminate risk by avoiding the actions that create it.

    D is incorrect. Mitigating involves taking steps to reduce the likelihood or impact of the risk but does not involve transferring the risk.

63. The correct answer is **A**. A reflected attack, often part of a Distributed denial of service (DDoS) attack, occurs when an attacker sends spoofed requests to a server, making it respond to the victim's IP address instead of their own. The server "reflects" the response to the victim, overwhelming the target with a flood of data.

    B is incorrect. A wireless attack targets vulnerabilities in wireless networks, such as exploiting weak encryption or cracking Wi-Fi passwords.

    C is incorrect. A credential replay attack involves capturing and reusing legitimate login credentials to gain unauthorized system access.

    D is incorrect. A DNS attack exploits vulnerabilities in the domain name system (DNS), such as DNS poisoning or spoofing.

64. The correct answer is **B**. Quantitative risk analysis uses numerical data, often displayed as a scoring system, to evaluate risk.

    A is incorrect. Qualitative risk analysis assesses risk based on subjective judgment and descriptive data rather than numerical values.

    C is incorrect. Probability-based risk analysis is not a standard term for risk analysis methods.

    D is incorrect. Impact-based risk analysis focuses on assessing risks' potential impact but does not primarily use numerical data for evaluation.

65. The correct answer is **C**. An acceptable use policy (AUP) defines the rules and guidelines for employees using company systems and resources, outlining acceptable behavior and prohibited actions.

    A is incorrect. A business continuity plan outlines procedures to ensure operations continue during and after a disruption.

    B is incorrect. An incident response plan details the processes for responding to identification, containment, and recovery but does not address acceptable resource use.

    D is incorrect. A disaster recovery plan focuses on restoring systems and data after a disaster but does not specify employee usage rules.

66. The correct answer is **C**. Directory traversal, also known as path traversal, is an attack in which the attacker manipulates the URL paths or inputs to access directories or files outside the intended web directory structure.

    A is incorrect. A replay attack involves intercepting and retransmitting valid data transmissions to trick the system into performing unauthorized actions.

    B is incorrect. A buffer overflow occurs when more data than required is sent by an attacker, causing memory corruption and possibly allowing arbitrary code execution.

    D is incorrect. Forgery attacks, such as cross-site request forgery (CSRF), trick users into performing actions they did not intend.

67. The correct answer is **A**. Due diligence refers to regularly assessing security to ensure compliance with any regulations, and then documenting the results.

    B is incorrect. Attestation and acknowledgment involve confirming compliance but do not specifically refer to the ongoing assessment and documentation of security practices.

    C is incorrect. Internal automation relates to using technology to automate processes, which is different from the focus of assessing and documenting security practices.

    D is incorrect. Supply chain analysis involves evaluating the security practices of vendors and suppliers.

68. The correct answer is **C**. A collision attack occurs when two different inputs produce the same hash value, compromising the integrity of the hashing algorithm. Since hashing functions are expected to produce unique hashes for different inputs, a collision undermines the algorithm's effectiveness in ensuring data integrity.

    A is incorrect. A birthday attack is a type of cryptographic attack based on the probability theory known as the birthday paradox.

    B is incorrect. A downgrade attack forces a system to abandon more robust encryption methods in favor of weaker ones, making it easier for attackers to compromise communication.

    D is incorrect. A side-channel attack exploits the physical implementation of a cryptosystem, such as power consumption or electromagnetic leaks, rather than attacking the cryptographic algorithm itself.

69. The correct answer is **B**. A brute-force attack involves systematically trying to guess a password using all possible combinations of characters. The attacker uses computational power to exhaustively search for the correct password without regard for account lockout policies or timing restrictions.

    A is incorrect. Password spraying is an attack in which the attacker tries a small set of commonly used passwords across many accounts in a system.

    C is incorrect. A dictionary attack uses a predefined list of common or likely passwords (like a dictionary) rather than trying every possible combination.

    D is incorrect. Credential stuffing uses stolen usernames and passwords, often from a data breach, to attempt logins on other systems where users may have reused the same credentials.

70. The correct answer is **C**. Impossible travel occurs when a user appears to be logged in from two locations within a time frame, making physical travel between those locations impossible. This is often a sign of compromised credentials or suspicious activity, where an attacker may use the same account from a distant location.

    A is incorrect. Out-of-cycle logging might suggest an unexpected login outside normal hours, but it does not describe simultaneous logins from different geographic locations.

    B is incorrect. Concurrent session usage occurs when a user is logged in to multiple sessions on the same system or network simultaneously.

    D is incorrect. Missing logs refers to the absence of expected log entries in an audit trail or monitoring system.

71. The correct answer is **C**. An air gap is a security measure in which critical systems are completely isolated from any external network, including the internet, to prevent unauthorized access or cyberattacks. This physical separation ensures that data cannot be accessed remotely, providing high protection against external threats.

    A is incorrect. A DMZ is a network architecture in which specific systems (such as web servers) are placed in a semi-public zone isolated from both the external internet and the internal network.

    B is incorrect. A VLAN is a logical network segmentation method for grouping devices on the same physical network into separate broadcast domains.

    D is incorrect. Subnetting is the process of dividing a network into equal-sized subnets. This improves performance and security within a network but does not involve physically isolating systems from the internet or other networks.

72. The correct answer is **D**. SMTP (Simple Mail Transfer Protocol) operates on port 25 and is used to send email. Blocking this protocol and port in the firewall will effectively stop all email traffic.

    A is incorrect. Allowing HTTP on port 80 does not impact email traffic; this protocol is used for web traffic.

    B is incorrect. DNS is used to resolve domain names and IP addresses. Blocking it would disrupt internet services but would not specifically stop email traffic.

    C is incorrect. Allowing FTP on port 21 is unrelated to email traffic. FTP is used for file transfers.

73. The correct answer is **B**. The key benefit of using an application allow list is that it only permits pre-approved and trusted applications to run on a system. This reduces the risk of malware and other unauthorized software from executing because only explicitly authorized software can operate.

    A is incorrect. Blocking all network traffic by default is a characteristic of network security configurations, such as firewall settings, not of application allow lists.

    C is incorrect. A block list allows all applications to run except those explicitly prohibited.

    D is incorrect. Although patch management is critical for maintaining system security, it is not a function of an application allow list.

74. The correct answer is **B**. Configuring a firewall with specific rules allows administrators to control which traffic is permitted or denied, enhancing the network's overall security by preventing unauthorized access and malicious activity.

    A is incorrect. The firewall's primary purpose is security, not improving speed or reducing delays in the network.

    C is incorrect. A firewall does not increase network throughput. It may reduce throughput due to the processing of rules and filtering.

    D is incorrect. A firewall does not directly improve internet speed. Its function is to secure and manage traffic.

75. The correct answer is **B**. A service-level agreement (SLA) is a formal agreement between a vendor and client that specifies the expected level of service, including performance benchmarks, uptime guarantees, and remedies or penalties for failing to meet these requirements.

    A is incorrect. A memorandum of agreement (MOA) is a formal agreement that outlines the terms and understanding between two parties regarding cooperation on a specific project or task.

    C is incorrect. A non-disclosure agreement (NDA) is a legal contract that ensures confidentiality between parties and prevents the sharing of sensitive or proprietary information.

    D is incorrect. A master service agreement (MSA) can serve as a foundational agreement, but it does not typically include specific performance metrics or service levels.

76. The correct answer is **B**. Vulnerability scans proactively identify security weaknesses in the company's network before exploiting them. They are designed to detect and report vulnerabilities in systems, applications, and network infrastructure.

    A is incorrect. Dashboards provide a summary or visualization of data from different sources but don't actively identify security weaknesses.

    C is incorrect. Packet captures analyze network traffic but are typically used for troubleshooting or investigating incidents.

    D is incorrect. Automated reports can summarize findings but don't directly identify vulnerabilities like scans do; they generally provide insights based on existing data sources.

77. The correct answer is **C**. A significant security challenge in a microservices architecture is ensuring secure communication between the many small, loosely coupled services. As microservices communicate over the network, securing these interactions becomes complex when services are distributed across multiple environments or cloud platforms.

    A is incorrect. A benefit of microservices is that they enable easier independent scaling of individual services based on demand.

    B is incorrect. Microservices require extra monitoring and logging due to the distributed nature of the services, but this is not a security challenge.

    D is incorrect. Application-level encryption is still critical in microservices, especially when sensitive data is transmitted between services.

78. The correct answer is **B**. In cloud architecture, a key consideration for scalability is using stateless applications, which do not rely on saved data between sessions, making them easier to scale horizontally.

    A is incorrect. Relying on a single server with high processing power may provide short-term performance benefits, but it does not support horizontal scaling, which is essential for cloud architectures.

    C is incorrect. Tightly integrated components can hinder scalability. In a cloud environment, loosely coupled components are preferred because they allow individual services to scale independently without affecting the entire system.

    D is incorrect. Limiting the number of users is not a viable scalability strategy.

79. The correct answer is **A**. Intellectual property (IP) refers to creations of the mind, such as inventions, designs, algorithms, and proprietary technologies that a company owns. These are protected through patents, copyrights, or trade secrets.

    B is incorrect. Regulated data refers to information governed by specific laws or regulations, such as healthcare data (HIPAA) or financial data (SOX).

    C is incorrect. Financial information refers to data regarding a company's finances, including revenues, expenses, profits, and financial transactions.

    D is incorrect. Human-readable data refers to information people can easily understand without special tools or processing.

80. The correct answer is **B**. The theoretical response to a hypothetical incident scenario is discussed during a tabletop exercise. This involves reviewing and discussing the team's steps during an actual incident.

    A is incorrect. Real-time network traffic and anomalies are not typically part of the exercise.

    C is incorrect. Detailed technical configurations of network devices are usually outside the focus of a tabletop exercise.

    D is incorrect. Discussing current performance metrics is not a key part of the tabletop exercise.

81. The correct answer is **D**. Obfuscation is scrambling or transforming data into a format that hides its original meaning, making it unreadable to unauthorized individuals. Only the correct key or decryption method can interpret the obfuscated data.

    A is incorrect. Segmentation refers to dividing a network or system into smaller, manageable sections to improve security and performance.

    B is incorrect. Masking involves replacing sensitive data with anonymized or modified data that maintains the same format but conceals the original information.

    C is incorrect. Hashing converts data into a fixed-size hash value or code, which is generally used to verify data integrity or securely store passwords.

82. The correct answer is **C**. The "Lessons Learned" phase occurs after an incident has been resolved. This phase focuses on reviewing the incident, identifying weaknesses in the response process, and implementing improvements.

    A is incorrect. The preparation phase involves creating and improving plans, tools, and processes before an incident occurs.

    B is incorrect. The eradication phase involves removing the cause of the incident and restoring systems to a secure state.

    D is incorrect. The containment phase involves stopping the spread of the incident to minimize damage.

83. The correct answer is **C**. A default deny rule will block all traffic by default unless some other rules explicitly allow it. Improving security by specifically permitting traffic that can pass through the firewall while all other traffic is automatically denied.

    A is incorrect. An allow list is a list of entities explicitly allowing access to a system or network.

    B is incorrect. A deny list lists entities explicitly blocked or denied access.

    D is incorrect. A default allow rule means that all traffic is permitted by default unless explicitly blocked by other rules.

84. The correct answer is **C**. Packet captures can allow inspection of the data being transmitted over the network in real time, providing detailed insights into each packet's contents.

    A is incorrect. Dashboards display aggregated data and metrics but do not provide detailed packet-level information.

    B is incorrect. Vulnerability scans identify potential security weaknesses in systems but do not analyze network traffic.

    D is incorrect. Automated reports summarize findings and metrics but do not offer the granular detail necessary to inspect individual packets.

85. The correct answer is **B**. XDR extends the capabilities of traditional EDR by collating other source data from networks, servers, and endpoints for comprehensive threat detection.

    A is incorrect. XDR does not primarily control user passwords; IAM solutions typically manage this.

    C is incorrect. Patch management systems, not XDR, handle automatic software updates.

    D is incorrect. Basic antivirus protection is a feature of traditional antivirus software, not XDR.

CompTIA Security+ SY0-701 Mock Exam 4

1. The correct answer is **C**. When applications actively process data, it is referred to as data in use. This is the phase where a system manipulates or uses data in real time.

    A is incorrect. Data at rest refers to data stored on physical media and not currently being accessed or processed.

    B is incorrect. Data sovereignty refers to the laws and regulations governing data, depending on the country where it is located.

    D is incorrect. Data in transit refers to data actively moving between systems or networks, such as during transmission over the internet.

2. The correct answer is **B**. The acquisition phase of digital forensics focuses on obtaining a forensically sound copy of the original data without altering the original evidence.

    A is incorrect. This describes the Analysis phase, not the Acquisition phase.

    C is incorrect. Preparing reports is part of the Reporting phase, which occurs after evidence has been collected and analysed.

    D is incorrect. Storing evidence securely is part of the Chain of Custody, which is beyond the specific scope of the Acquisition phase.

3. The correct answer is **C**. This action ensures that the appropriate personnel can investigate, warn other employees, and take necessary actions to protect the organization from potential threats.

    A is incorrect. While alerting others to suspicious emails is good, forwarding potentially malicious content can inadvertently spread the threat.

    B is incorrect. Deleting the email without reporting it may allow a threat to persist undetected.

    D is incorrect. Clicking on links in a suspicious email is a risky action that could lead to malware infection or phishing.

4. The correct answer is **C**. A business continuity plan (BCP) ensures that a company can continue operating its critical functions after a major disruption or disaster, cyberattacks, or other emergencies.

    A is incorrect. An information security policy outlines how the organization will protect its information assets, focusing on confidentiality, integrity, and availability.

    B is incorrect. A change management policy governs how changes to IT systems and processes are requested, reviewed, approved, and implemented.

    D is incorrect. An acceptable use policy defines how employees and other users can use company resources, such as computers and networks.

5. The correct answer is **B**. A honeytoken is a deceptive piece of information, such as a fake password or database entry, used to detect and alert administrators when unauthorized individuals access or use it. It helps identify and monitor unauthorized access attempts.

    A is incorrect. Encrypting data in transit involves securing data traveling across a network to prevent interception and unauthorized access. A honeytoken does not perform encryption but is used to detect unauthorized activity.

    C is incorrect. Providing real-time security updates involves sending notifications or information about security threats and changes. A honeytoken does not serve this function; it detects and alerts administrators to unauthorized activity, not to provide security updates.

    D is incorrect. User authentication involves overseeing how users log in and access different systems. A honeytoken is not involved in managing authentication but is used to detect unauthorized actions by simulating valuable data.

6. The correct answer is **B**. Security guards deter unauthorized access and can quickly respond to security incidents, making them a critical component of physical security.

    A is incorrect. Monitoring network traffic is different from the typical role of physical security guards.

    C is incorrect. Security guards do not usually configure or maintain access control systems.

    D is incorrect. Auditing security logs is more of an IT or compliance function.

7. The correct answer is **B**. These commands typically trigger the SSD's built-in mechanisms to erase data securely and efficiently across all memory cells.

    A is incorrect. Degaussing is effective for traditional magnetic hard drives but does not apply to solid-state drives (SSDs) since they do not store data magnetically.

    C is incorrect. A quick format removes the filesystem structure but does not overwrite the data. The data remains recoverable using data recovery tools.

    D is incorrect. Reinstalling the operating system does not erase or overwrite all data on the SSD. It may only affect the operating system files, leaving other data intact and recoverable.

8. The correct answer is **D**. When the ideal control cannot be implemented (in this case, upgrading the encryption standard), a compensating control is used to mitigate the risk. These controls are alternative measures that provide equivalent protection.

    A is incorrect. Physical controls involve tangible security measures not relevant to encryption issues.

    B is incorrect. Detective controls identify incidents but don't mitigate the encryption risk directly.

    C is incorrect. Preventive controls stop incidents from happening but don't address the specific limitation of upgrading the encryption standard.

9. The correct answer is **B**. Data interception and modification during transmission are significant security concerns related to the data plane, as it handles the data transmitted across the network.

    A is incorrect. Unauthorized changes to routing protocols are concerns related to the control plane.

    C is incorrect. Misconfiguration of network policies pertains to network management and the control plane.

    D is incorrect. Unauthorized access to network configuration settings relates to network management and security.

10. The correct answer is **C**. Attribute-based access control (ABAC) uses the user's attributes of resources and environment to make access decisions, providing a flexible approach to authorization.

    A is incorrect. Role-based access control (RBAC) assigns permissions based on roles, not attributes.

    B is incorrect. Discretionary access control (DAC) allows resource owners to manage access permissions.

    D is incorrect. Mandatory access control (MAC) is based on system-enforced policies and labels, not attributes.

11. The correct answer is **B**. Creating a policy is a managerial control because it involves defining and establishing the organization's security guidelines, procedures, and standards. These policies guide how security measures are implemented and managed across the organization.

    A is incorrect. Compensating controls provide alternative measures when primary controls are not feasible and not specifically related to policy creation.

    C is incorrect. Operational controls involve the day-to-day implementation of security measures but not the creation of overarching policies.

    D is incorrect. Technical controls involve using technology and software to enforce security but do not encompass policy creation and management.

12. The correct answer is **B**. Contracts, agreements, and other legal documentation are considered "legal information" and must be protected to ensure compliance and confidentiality, as they often contain sensitive or regulated content.

    A is incorrect. Trade secrets involve proprietary business information, such as formulas or strategies, but not legal documents like contracts.

    C is incorrect. Intellectual property refers to company creations, such as patents or copyrights.

    D is incorrect. Non-human-readable refers to data in formats humans do not understand easily, such as encrypted data.

13. The correct answer is **B**. Adaptive identity uses behavioral analytics to adjust access controls based on real-time behavior and risk assessments.

    A is incorrect. Static IP addresses do not adapt to changing risk conditions.

    C is incorrect. Physical security badges are unrelated to dynamic identity management.

    D is incorrect. Fixed access rights do not accommodate dynamic adjustments based on real-time risk.

14. The correct answer is **C**. Redundant systems and failover solutions involve having backup components and systems that can take over in the case of failure, ensuring that the system remains operational. This is the most effective strategy for ensuring high availability.

    A is incorrect. Strong password policies help protect against unauthorized access, enhancing security, but do not directly affect system availability.

    C is incorrect. Regular data backups are crucial for data recovery in case of data loss but do not ensure a system remains operational.

    D is incorrect. Encrypting sensitive data ensures confidentiality and protection against unauthorized access but does not address system availability.

15. The correct answer is **A**. Resource consumption is when the observed spike in CPU and memory usage indicates that the server consumes more resources than usual, leading to degraded performance and slow response times.

    B is incorrect. Resource inaccessibility refers to resources that cannot be accessed.

    C is incorrect. Out-of-cycle logging typically pertains to activities occurring outside a scheduled interval. It doesn't directly relate to spikes in CPU and memory usage.

    D is incorrect. Missing logs implies that logs are not being recorded or accessed, which is unrelated to performance issues.

16. The correct answer is **B**. Micro-segmentation involves dividing a network into smaller, isolated segments to limit attackers' movement within the network. By controlling traffic between these segments, micro-segmentation reduces unauthorized access, enhancing security within a zero-trust environment.

    A is incorrect. Encrypting data at rest involves securing stored data to protect it from unauthorized access.

    C is incorrect. Single sign-on (SSO) allows users to access multiple applications with one set of credentials.

    D is incorrect. Endpoint protection involves securing individual devices from threats. While critical for overall security, endpoint protection does not explicitly involve isolating network segments to control lateral movement within a network.

17. The correct answer is **A**. Gap analysis and vulnerability assessments serve different purposes. Gap analysis compares current practices to established standards or benchmarks to identify discrepancies and areas for improvement. In contrast, a vulnerability assessment identifies specific weaknesses or vulnerabilities within systems.

    B is incorrect. Vulnerability assessments focus on identifying and analyzing system weaknesses rather than comparing security measures to industry standards.

    C is incorrect. Gap analysis and vulnerability assessments are distinct processes. Gap analysis involves comparing current practices with standards to find gaps, while vulnerability assessments aim to identify and address technical vulnerabilities in systems.

    D is incorrect. Vulnerability assessments are designed to find and address weaknesses in systems, not to develop security policies.

18. The correct answer is **B**. This is the main advantage of using a DMZ. Placing public-facing servers in a separate, isolated network segment adds an extra layer of protection. It reduces the risk of external attackers gaining access to the internal network, even if the public-facing servers are compromised.

    A is incorrect. A DMZ's primary purpose is not to increase internal network bandwidth. Instead, it focuses on improving security by isolating public-facing services from the internal network.

    C is incorrect. A DMZ is designed to prevent unrestricted access to internal resources.

    D is incorrect. A DMZ does not remove firewalls. It requires additional firewall rules to regulate traffic between the internal network, DMZ, and the internet.

19. The correct answer is **D**. A generator is designed to provide long-term power during extended outages, making it suitable for maintaining critical infrastructure over prolonged periods.

    A is incorrect. Battery backups are typically used for short-term power needs, such as bridging the gap during brief outages.

    B is incorrect. A UPS provides immediate short-term power to protect against brief outages and allow for safe shutdown procedures.

    C is incorrect. A portable power bank is usually designed for individual devices' small, short-term power needs.

20. The correct answer is **B**. Access control is the security measure that ensures only authorized personnel can access a system or server. It involves implementing policies and mechanisms to restrict access based on user identity and permissions.

    A is incorrect. Data encryption protects data confidentiality by converting information into cipher text to prevent unauthorized access.

    C is incorrect. Asset ownership refers to the assignment of responsibility for an asset but does not directly relate to the security measures for controlling access.

    D is incorrect. Network monitoring involves observing and analyzing network traffic for security threats or performance issues but does not restrict access to specific servers or systems.

21. The correct answer is **C**. SAML is commonly used for single sign-on (SSO) to enable users to authenticate across multiple applications with a single set of credentials.

    A is incorrect. LDAP is a protocol used for directory services, not specifically for SSO.

    B is incorrect. OAuth is primarily used for authorization, not authentication for SSO.

    D is incorrect. SMTP is used for email communication, not for SSO.

22. The correct answer is **B**. OAuth is designed to grant third-party applications limited access to user resources without sharing user credentials, facilitating authorization rather than authentication.

    A is incorrect. OAuth is not primarily used for authentication but for authorization.

    C is incorrect. LDAP, not OAuth, typically handles centralized directory management.

    D is incorrect. User account synchronization is not the primary function of OAuth.

23. The correct answer is **B**. Discretionary access control (DAC) allows users to decide who can access their files or resources.

    A is incorrect. MAC involves strict control over access based on security policies, not user discretion.

    C is incorrect. RBAC assigns permissions based on roles, not user discretion.

    D is incorrect. Rule-based access control uses pre-defined rules to manage access, not user discretion.

24. The correct answer is **C**. The primary role of the asset owner is to manage its lifecycle, including acquisition, maintenance, and retirement, and to ensure its security throughout its life.

    A is incorrect. While updating software is essential, it is typically part of the responsibilities of a system administrator.

    B is incorrect. Performing security audits is usually the responsibility of security personnel or an audit team.

    D is incorrect. Monitoring network traffic is typically the responsibility of network security professionals or administrators.

25. The correct answer is **B**. A right-to-audit clause allows the company to verify that the vendor maintains security standards over time. This clause provides for audits or reviews of the vendor's security practices, helping ensure ongoing compliance and protection.

    A is incorrect. A penetration testing clause would allow the company to conduct or request penetration tests to identify security vulnerabilities, but this is unlikely.

    C is incorrect. This clause would require the vendor to provide evidence of regular vulnerability scans but does not give the company the right to audit the vendor's security processes.

    D is incorrect. A supply chain verification clause ensures that security standards are met throughout the supply chain. However, it is not the same as a right-to-audit clause.

26. The correct answer is **C**. Rule-based access control grants or denies access based on pre-defined rules.

    A is incorrect. RBAC is based on user roles, not pre-defined rules.

    B is incorrect. DAC allows users to set access permissions, not pre-defined rules.

    D is incorrect. ABAC uses attributes for access control, not pre-defined rules.

27. The correct answer is **A**. SMTP is the standard protocol for sending emails between servers. Port 25 is for SMTP communication.

    B is incorrect. The Post Office Protocol (POP3) is used by email clients to access messages from an SMTP server, not for sending outgoing emails.

    C is incorrect. Email clients use the Internet Message Access Protocol (IMAP) to retrieve and manage emails on a mail server.

    D is incorrect. The Hypertext Transfer Protocol (HTTP) is used for web traffic, not email transmission.

28. The correct answer is **B**. The primary purpose of an independent third-party audit is to provide an unbiased and objective evaluation of a company's security controls and practices. This ensures that the organization's security measures are effective and meet regulatory or industry standards.

    A is incorrect. The primary purpose is not to find cost-saving opportunities.

    C is incorrect. The role of an independent third-party audit is not just to approve internal reports but to assess the effectiveness of security practices and controls through an objective review.

    D is incorrect. Although access management might be part of the audit, this option focuses too narrowly on internal processes.

29. The correct answer is **B**. A security key is an example of "something you have" in multi-factor authentication.

    A is incorrect. A password is an example of "something you know."

    C is incorrect. A fingerprint scan is an example of "something you are."

    D is incorrect. A PIN is an example of "something you know."

30. The correct answer is **B**. Secure Shell (SSH) is a cryptographic protocol designed to provide secure access to remote servers. It encrypts the session, ensuring confidentiality, integrity, and authentication.

    A is incorrect. Telnet provides remote access but does not encrypt the session, making it insecure and susceptible to eavesdropping and attacks.

    C is incorrect. File Transfer Protocol (FTP) transfers files and does not inherently provide secure remote server access.

    D is incorrect. Hypertext Transfer Protocol (HTTP) is used for web communication and does not provide secure remote server access.

31. The correct answer is **B**. HTTPS is a secure version of HTTP, encrypting communication between a web server and a client on port 443 to ensure confidentiality and integrity.

    A is incorrect. HTTP is insecure because it transmits data in plaintext, making it susceptible to interception.

    B is incorrect. FTP is used for transferring files, not for web server connections.

    C is incorrect. Telnet is a protocol for remote command-line access, not web server communication.

32. The correct answer is **C**. In PKI, a public key is often distributed through a public directory or included in a digital certificate, making it accessible to those who need it to encrypt data or verify signatures.

    A is incorrect. Sending the public key via encrypted email is not common practice; since it is not secret, it is usually shared more openly.

    B is incorrect. Public keys do not need to be stored securely in the same way private keys do.

    D is incorrect. Public keys are not encrypted before distribution; they are meant to be openly available.

33. The correct answer is **B**. Internal automation uses automated tools and processes to monitor compliance, such as automatically collecting security logs and generating compliance reports.

    A is incorrect. This refers to an external process rather than an internal, automated approach to compliance monitoring.

    C is incorrect. The acknowledgment process typically involves individuals within the organization formally confirming that they understand and agree to certain policies or standards.

    D is incorrect. Due care refers to the steps an organization takes to ensure responsible actions regarding security and compliance.

34. The correct answer is **C**. Transport Layer Security (TLS) encrypts data during transmission over the internet, protecting it from eavesdropping and tampering.

    A is incorrect. Full-disk encryption is used for data at rest, not in transit.

    B is incorrect. File-level encryption is used to secure data at rest.

    D is incorrect. PHP is an open-source server-side scripting language used mainly in web development.

35. The correct answer is **A**. A secure enclave is a hardware-based feature that isolates sensitive computations, including cryptographic operations, from the main OS to protect against unauthorized access.

    B is incorrect. Secure enclaves are not designed for large data storage.

    C is incorrect. Secure enclaves do not manage network encryption keys but perform isolated operations securely.

    D is incorrect. Secure enclaves are not responsible for software updates.

36. The correct answer is **B**. Salting involves adding a unique value to each password before hashing it, making it difficult for attackers to crack the passwords using pre-computed tables.

    A is incorrect. Encryption is a different method of securing data and does not prevent using rainbow tables.

    C is incorrect. Digital signatures are used for verifying data integrity and authenticity, not for password storage.

    D is incorrect. Storing passwords in plain text is insecure, even with restricted access.

37. The correct answer is **A**. Digital signatures verify the sender's authenticity and ensure the email content has not been tampered with, making them the correct choice for this scenario.

    B is incorrect. Salting is related to securing passwords and not verifying email authenticity.

    C is incorrect. Key stretching is used to enhance password security, not to authenticate emails.

    D is incorrect. Blockchain could be used for secure transactions but is not directly relevant to email authenticity in this context.

38. The correct answer is **A**. The first step in obtaining a new SSL/TLS certificate is to generate a CSR, which is then submitted to a CA for issuance.

    B is incorrect. Downloading a CRL is not related to the process of obtaining a new certificate.

    C is incorrect. OCSP is for checking the status of certificates, not for requesting new ones.

    D is incorrect. Wildcard certificates can be requested, but the process begins with a CSR.

39. The correct answer is **A**. Nation-state actors are typically government-sponsored and are highly likely to engage in cyber espionage. Their targets often include national defense systems, intellectual property, and other critical infrastructure.

    B is incorrect. Hacktivists are primarily motivated by political or social causes and typically target organizations or entities they oppose.

    C is incorrect. Unskilled attackers, or "script kiddies," lack the expertise and resources to conduct sophisticated cyber espionage.

    D is incorrect. Shadow IT refers to using unauthorized technology within an organization, typically by employees looking to improve productivity.

40. The correct answer is **B**. Hacktivists are motivated by the desire to promote political or social change. They use cyberattacks to protest, raise awareness, or disrupt organizations or governments they view as unethical or unjust.

    A is incorrect. Financial gain is typically the motivation for cybercriminals or organized crime groups, not hacktivists.

    C is incorrect. Cyber espionage is typically associated with nation-state actors seeking intelligence or sensitive information.

    D is incorrect. While personal vendettas can motivate some cyberattacks, they are more characteristic of insider threats or individuals seeking revenge.

41. The correct answer is **B**. Brand impersonation involves creating a fake website or other communication that resembles a legitimate brand to get users to give up their sensitive information.

    A is incorrect. Pretexting involves creating a fabricated scenario to trick someone into giving up information.

    C is incorrect. A watering-hole attack involves compromising a legitimate website that the target group frequently visits.

    D is incorrect. Smishing is a form of phishing that involves sending fraudulent text messages (SMSs).

42. The correct answer is **B**. Disinformation involves deliberately spreading false information with the intent to deceive, often for political, financial, or competitive purposes.

    A is incorrect. Misinformation refers to the spread of false or inaccurate information, often unintentionally or without the intent to deceive.

    C is incorrect. Pretexting involves creating a fabricated scenario to obtain information.

    D is incorrect. Impersonation involves pretending to be someone else to deceive or manipulate others.

43. The correct answer is **B**. Pretexting involves creating a fabricated scenario or identity to manipulate someone into divulging information. The attacker pretends to be an employee to gain access.

    A is incorrect. Vishing involves phone calls to deceive individuals into revealing sensitive information. The pretext is the specific tactic of pretending to be someone else to gain access.

    C is incorrect. Business email compromise (BEC) typically involves using compromised or spoofed email accounts to deceive employees into transferring money or revealing sensitive information.

    D is incorrect. Smishing involves sending fraudulent text messages to fool people into revealing confidential information.

44. The correct answer is **A**. A watering-hole attack involves compromising websites visited by groups of users, such as employees of a targeted organization, to infect them with malware or gather sensitive information.

    B is incorrect. Phishing typically involves sending fraudulent emails to trick individuals into revealing sensitive information.

    C is incorrect. Typosquatting involves creating a fake website with a domain name that closely resembles a legitimate one, usually by using common misspellings.

    D is incorrect. Impersonation involves pretending to be someone else to deceive or manipulate others.

45. The correct answer is **C**. Vishing uses phone calls to deceive individuals into revealing personal or financial information. The attacker impersonates a bank representative over the phone.

    A is incorrect. Phishing typically involves sending fraudulent emails or messages to get individuals to reveal personal information.

    B is incorrect. Smishing involves sending fraudulent text messages to trick individuals into revealing personal information.

    D is incorrect. Pretexting involves creating a fabricated scenario to obtain information or access, often in person or over the phone.

46. The correct answer is **C**. Legacy systems are older technologies that are still in use, including outdated and unsupported operating systems.

    A is incorrect. Virtual machine escape refers to an attack in which a threat actor can break out of a guest operating system and gain access to the host system.

    B is incorrect. Resource reuse refers to vulnerabilities related to improper handling of system resources such as memory or CPU cache.

    D is incorrect. Firmware is the embedded software that controls a device's hardware.

47. The correct answer is **B**. End-of-life (EOL) refers to the phase when a product, such as hardware or software, is no longer supported by the vendor. This means no updates, including security patches, are provided, leaving the system vulnerable to exploitation.

    A is incorrect. Firmware refers to the software embedded in hardware devices that controls their operation.

    C is incorrect. A virtual machine escape is a vulnerability in which an attacker can break out of a virtualized environment and gain access to the host machine.

    D is incorrect. Resource reuse vulnerabilities are related to the improper clearing or reusing of system resources such as RAM.

48. The correct answer is **C**. A worm is malware that spreads across a network by exploiting vulnerabilities without requiring user interaction.

    A is incorrect. Spyware is used to gather information from a user's system but does not spread automatically like a worm does.

    B is incorrect. A Trojan disguises itself as legitimate software to trick users into running it, but it does not spread on its own across networks.

    D is incorrect. A virus requires user interaction, such as opening a file or running a program, to spread.

49. The correct answer is **A**. Environmental activity describes a physical risk related to extreme temperatures and humidity levels in the data center, which can damage the equipment.

    B is incorrect. A brute-force attack refers to a cyberattack that repeatedly tries various password combinations to gain unauthorized access, which is unrelated to physical threats such as environmental conditions.

    C is incorrect. RFID cloning involves copying data from an RFID chip, which is unrelated to the risks of temperature and humidity.

    D is incorrect. Social engineering is a psychological manipulation tactic that tricks people into revealing sensitive information. It does not relate to physical environmental risks.

50. The correct answer is **C**. An amplification attack is where DNS servers are exploited to increase the volume of traffic directed at the company's web servers, overwhelming them with data.

    A is incorrect. Also known as a man-in-the-middle (MitM) attack, this involves intercepting and possibly altering communications between two parties.

    B is incorrect. A DNS attack is a broader term for attacks targeting DNSs, such as DNS spoofing or cache poisoning.

    D is incorrect. Malicious code attack refers to attacks using malware, such as viruses or worms, unrelated to the network traffic amplification technique described.

51. The correct answer is **A**. An on-path attack involves intercepting and potentially altering communications between two parties without their knowledge.

    B is incorrect. Wireless attack refers to attacks specifically targeting wireless networks, but it doesn't describe the interception and alteration of communication between two parties as in an on-path attack.

    C is incorrect. In a credential replay attack, the attacker captures and reuses a legitimate user's credentials to gain unauthorized access.

    D is incorrect. A DDoS attack overwhelms a system with traffic to disrupt service.

52. The correct answer is **C**. Replay attacks involve intercepting and reusing valid authentication data (such as session tokens or credentials) to gain unauthorized access to a system.

    A is incorrect. Privilege escalation occurs when attackers gain higher access levels within a system than they should have. It doesn't involve intercepting and reusing valid sessions.

    B is incorrect. A buffer overflow attack exploits a system by overloading its memory buffer, potentially allowing the attacker to run malicious code.

    D is incorrect. Injection attacks involve inserting malicious code into a program to manipulate its execution, but they are unrelated to intercepting and reusing session data.

53. The correct answer is **A**. A collision attack targets the ability of a hashing algorithm to produce the same hash for different inputs. Due to the birthday paradox, this can occur more often than people realize.

    B is incorrect. A replay attack involves intercepting and reusing valid authentication data, such as session tokens, unrelated to hash functions or finding collisions.

    C is incorrect. A man-in-the-middle (MitM) attack is where an attacker secretly intercepts and potentially alters the communication between two parties without either party knowing.

    D is incorrect. A downgrade attack occurs when an attacker forces systems to use weaker, outdated cryptographic protocols, which have no direct relation to hashing collisions or birthday-based probability techniques.

54. The correct answer is **D**. Password spraying involves an attacker trying a small number of commonly used passwords across many different user accounts.

    A is incorrect. A rainbow table attack involves pre-computed tables of hash values for possible passwords used to match hashed passwords. It does not involve trying passwords directly against multiple accounts.

    B is incorrect. Credential stuffing occurs when attackers use usernames and passwords obtained from a breach to try logging into multiple accounts across different services.

    C is incorrect. A brute-force attack involves systematically trying every possible password for a single account until the correct one is found.

55. The correct answer is **A**. Blocked content of certain websites likely indicates that the system administrator or a security policy has blocked access to these sites, possibly for security or productivity reasons.

    B is incorrect. Resource consumption refers to excessive CPU, memory, or bandwidth use. It does not directly cause websites to be blocked or services to malfunction.

    C is incorrect. Account lockout typically occurs when users exceed the allowed login attempts. It would prevent users from accessing their accounts.

    D is incorrect. Published/documented information refers to data that has been made publicly available and is irrelevant to the problem of websites or services being blocked or inaccessible.

56. The correct answer is **C**. A DMZ (de-militarized zone), also known as a screened subnet, is a network segment designed to provide additional security by isolating publicly accessible servers (such as web and email servers) from the internal network and the internet.

    A is incorrect. A virtual local area network (VLAN) is used to segment internal networks at the data link layer but does not provide the same security isolation as a DMZ.

    B is incorrect. An air gap refers to a security measure in which a network is physically isolated from other networks, particularly the internet. This is not the same as a DMZ, which still allows some external access.

    D is incorrect. An intrusion detection system (IDS) monitors network traffic for suspicious activity and does not refer to a network segment.

57. The correct answer is **C**. Setting permissions involves controlling user access to files and directories based on assigned rights to read, write, or execute.

    A is incorrect. MFA is a security measure that requires different types of verification before granting access to a system.

    B is incorrect. While ACLs are used in firewalls to manage network traffic and restrict access to network resources, they do not specifically involve file access controls.

    D is incorrect. An IPS is designed to monitor malicious activity on networks or systems and can take action to block or prevent those activities.

58. The correct answer is **A**. A block list allows the company to specifically prevent known malicious applications from executing while permitting all other software to run.

    B is incorrect. While a firewall can block certain types of network traffic, it does not explicitly prevent known malicious applications from executing on the system.

    C is incorrect. A VPN creates a secure connection over a less secure network and does not provide application-level controls to prevent the execution of malicious software.

    D is incorrect. A honeypot is a security resource set that can be attacked or compromised to study attackers' behavior. It is not used to prevent the execution of malicious applications on systems.

59. The correct answer is **B**. It may allow new or unknown malicious software to run as new or previously unknown malware that isn't on the list can still execute.

    A is incorrect. Excessive false positives are not the main drawback of a block list; it primarily fails to account for new threats rather than misclassifying safe applications.

    C is incorrect. Block lists do not block all traffic by default; they only prevent specific applications or programs listed.

    D is incorrect. Managing a block list can be challenging in larger environments, but it may be easier in smaller environments.

60. The correct answer is **C**. The primary security risk associated with legacy applications is known vulnerabilities that cannot be patched. These applications may contain vulnerabilities that remain unaddressed due to the lack of updates and support.

    A is incorrect. While legacy applications might have optimizations, this does not address their security risks. The performance benefit does not outweigh the potential security vulnerabilities.

    B is incorrect. Legacy applications are often less resistant to modern threats due to outdated security practices and features.

    D is incorrect. Legacy applications often need help integrating with new systems.

61. The correct answer is **C**. The primary function of a host-based intrusion prevention system (HIPS) is to monitor the host for malicious activity and take action to block or prevent those activities.

    A is incorrect. While encryption is a security measure, it is not a function of a HIPS.

    B is incorrect. Physical security measures are outside the scope of a HIPS.

    D is incorrect. User access management is typically handled by access control systems or identity management solutions, not by a HIPS.

62. The correct answer is **A**. Default passwords are commonly available in documentation and online, making them a significant security risk if kept the same.

    B is incorrect. Default passwords are usually not encrypted.

    C is incorrect. Endpoint protection software does not manage default passwords but focuses on securing devices from malware and other threats.

    D is incorrect. Using default passwords often violates security policies aimed at strengthening security measures.

63. The correct answer is **A**. Simulations provide a realistic, hands-on experience where participants actively respond to a staged incident using tools and techniques as if they were real. Tabletop exercises, on the other hand, are discussion-based activities.

    B is incorrect. Simulations are generally more detailed and realistic, involving real-world tools.

    C is incorrect. Tabletop exercises are theoretical and discussion-based, while simulations focus on real-time actions.

    D is incorrect. Both simulations and tabletop exercises involve team participation.

64. The correct answer is **B**. The preservation phase in digital forensics focuses on protecting and maintaining the integrity of evidence. This includes securely storing evidence to prevent tampering or alteration and ensure its admissibility in legal proceedings.

   A is incorrect. Restoring normal operations falls under the Recovery phase of incident response.

   C is incorrect. Documenting findings occurs during the Reporting phase.

   D is incorrect. Interviews with involved parties would be part of the initial investigation or Preparation phase.

65. The correct answer is **B**. A significant security risk in virtualized environments is VM escape, which occurs when a virtual machine breaks out of its isolated environment and interacts with the host system or other VMs, potentially compromising its security.

   A is incorrect. Virtualization does not inherently increase physical security requirements for a data center; the primary security concerns are typically related to the software and virtual layers.

   C is incorrect. Data backup procedures are not simplified just because of virtualization.

   D is incorrect. While VMs are designed to be isolated, this isolation is not guaranteed and can be broken by vulnerabilities, such as VM escape exploits.

66. The correct answer is **B**. E-Discovery (Electronic Discovery) refers to identifying, collecting, and reviewing electronic data that may be relevant in legal proceedings. It is a critical part of the legal process, especially for litigation and compliance purposes.

   A is incorrect. The recovery of deleted files is not the primary focus of E-Discovery.

   C is incorrect. Encrypting data is a security practice related to protecting data in transit but is not directly related to E-Discovery.

   D is incorrect. Monitoring network traffic for unusual activity falls under network security and intrusion detection activities.

67. The correct answer is **D**. Information that is freely available to the public and requires no special protection should be classified as public, as it is intended to be accessible by anyone without restrictions.

   A is incorrect. Confidential information is sensitive and restricted to specific individuals or groups.

   B is incorrect. Sensitive data, such as personal information, requires protection due to its nature.

   C is incorrect. Restricted data has access limitations and is protected from public view.

68. The correct answer is **A**. This technique, also known as geolocation-based access control, restricts access based on the user's or system's geographic location. It is often used to enforce data privacy and comply with data sovereignty laws.

    B is incorrect. Hashing is a method of verifying data integrity, not restricting access based on location.

    C is incorrect. Data masking hides sensitive information by replacing it with fictional data and is commonly used in testing environments.

    D is incorrect. Permission restrictions refer to controlling access to data based on user roles or specific permissions, but they do not specifically address geographic location.

69. The correct answer is **B**. During the Analysis phase, the primary goal is to gather information about the incident, including its scope, the systems affected, the potential impact, and the nature of the threat.

    A is incorrect. Deploying patches is part of the remediation or eradication phase, not the Analysis phase.

    C is incorrect. Communication with stakeholders typically occurs during the containment or post-incident phases.

    D is incorrect. Updating security policies is part of the "Lessons Learned" phase after an incident has been resolved.

70. The correct answer is **C**. Isolation, often called network segmentation, is critical for protecting ICS/SCADA systems from external threats. These systems control essential industrial operations, and isolation minimizes the risk of unauthorized access or infection from the broader network.

    A is incorrect. While updating firmware is important, ICS/SCADA systems often have strict uptime requirements, and updates must be carefully planned.

    B is incorrect. Strong password policies are crucial for security, but isolating the network is more critical.

    D is incorrect. While antivirus software is beneficial, many ICS/SCADA systems are not designed to run traditional antivirus solutions.

71. The correct answer is **C**. Changing default credentials reduces the risk of unauthorized access, and network segmentation ensures that IoT devices are isolated from other sensitive parts of the network, improving security.

    A is incorrect. Enabling default user accounts poses a significant security risk because attackers commonly know and exploit them.

    B is incorrect. Disabling automatic updates can prevent IoT devices from receiving critical security patches, leaving them vulnerable to known threats.

    D is incorrect. Increasing device screen brightness has no impact on the security of IoT devices.

72. The correct answer is **B**. MDM allows a company to remotely configure, monitor, and secure mobile devices, ensuring compliance with security policies and managing software updates.

    A is incorrect. Connection methods refer to how devices connect to networks, such as Wi-Fi or VPN, and are not focused on managing or securing devices remotely.

    C is incorrect. Deployment models describe how devices are assigned or used within an organization but do not provide the tools to manage or secure devices remotely.

    D is incorrect. COPE is a deployment model that allows employees to use company-owned devices for work and personal purposes.

73. The correct answer is **A**. AES is a widely used encryption protocol for securing wireless networks, especially WPA2 and WPA3. It provides strong encryption and integrity checking.

    B is incorrect. RC4 is an older stream cipher that has been deprecated due to vulnerabilities, making it less secure for modern wireless encryption.

    C is incorrect. DES is an outdated encryption algorithm whose short key length renders it no longer secure.

    D is incorrect. SHA is used for hashing and integrity checking but is not an encryption algorithm.

74. The correct answer is **C**. Input validation checks and filters data entered into a web application to ensure it meets specific criteria before processing, preventing malicious data from being executed.

    A is incorrect. Code signing is a way of checking the integrity and authenticity of software by attaching a digital signature.

    B is incorrect. Secure cookies are a mechanism to ensure cookies are sent only over secure HTTPS connections.

    D is incorrect. Static code analysis involves reviewing code for potential security flaws without executing the program.

75. The correct answer is **C**. Secure cookies are designed to enhance session management security by ensuring that cookies are only transmitted over secure HTTPS connections and cannot be accessed by unauthorized scripts.

    A is incorrect. Code signing is a process used to verify the authenticity and integrity of software.

    B is incorrect. Input validation is essential for checking the data entered into a web application, but it does not prevent unauthorized scripts from accessing cookies.

    D is incorrect. Static code analysis is a technique for reviewing source code for vulnerabilities but does not directly impact the security of session management.

76. The correct answer is **D**. Sensitive data includes information that could cause harm if disclosed but may still need to be accessed regularly by authorized personnel for business purposes. Confidential indicates that the information is sensitive and should only be accessible to authorized personnel.

    A is incorrect. Public classification is meant for openly available information that does not require protection.

    B is incorrect. "Restricted" indicates that access is limited and implies higher secrecy or sensitivity than typically associated with financial records necessary for business operations.

    C is incorrect. Confidential data is often used for information that is sensitive but may not be as widely accessed in normal business operations.

77. The correct answer is **C**. Maintaining a comprehensive asset inventory helps organizations track all devices connected to the network. By knowing what devices are authorized, security administrators can more easily identify and mitigate unauthorized access and devices.

    A is incorrect. Patch management policies are essential for keeping systems secure by updating software and fixing vulnerabilities.

    B is incorrect. Regularly updating antivirus software is crucial for protecting systems from malware, but it does not prevent unauthorized devices from accessing the network.

    D is incorrect. Encrypting network communications enhances security by protecting data in transit from eavesdropping or tampering.

78. The correct answer is **A**. Data sanitization refers to processes that make data unrecoverable while allowing the hardware to remain usable. In contrast, data destruction typically involves physically destroying the hardware, rendering it unusable.

    B is incorrect. The speed of sanitization and destruction can vary depending on the methods used.

    C is incorrect. Data sanitization and destruction can apply to software (data) and hardware (storage devices).

    D is incorrect. Data destruction is meant to permanently eliminate data, often by physically damaging the storage medium, while data sanitization aims to make data unrecoverable but can leave the hardware intact and usable.

79. The correct answer is **B**. Secure data sanitization ensures that all sensitive data on the hard drives is permanently and irretrievably removed.

    A is incorrect. Rebooting the server may terminate running processes, but it does not address the issue of data security.

    C is incorrect. While reformatting may remove data, it is not reliable for ensuring that sensitive information cannot be recovered.

    D is incorrect. Changing the IP address does not affect the data stored on the server and does nothing to secure or erase sensitive information.

80. The correct answer is **B**. Different industries and jurisdictions have specific regulations governing how long data must be retained and the procedures for securely deleting it when it is no longer needed. Regulatory compliance is essential to ensure data privacy.

    A is incorrect. The color of the hardware casing does not relate to data retention policies or compliance.

    C is incorrect. While understanding who accesses data can be necessary for security and access control, it does not directly impact the compliance aspects of a data retention policy.

    D is incorrect. Although geographic location can influence the applicable laws and regulations, it is not a direct consideration for implementing a data retention policy.

81. The correct answer is **B**. The primary function of a signature in an IDS or IPS is to detect known patterns of threats and vulnerabilities. Signatures are pre-defined rules or patterns that identify specific types of attacks or malicious activity by matching them against known threat behaviors.

    A is incorrect. Encryption of sensitive data before transmission is unrelated to the function of IDS/IPS signatures.

    C is incorrect. Firewalls typically create outbound traffic rules rather than through IDS/IPS signatures.

    D is incorrect. Network bandwidth optimization is not the primary role of an IDS/IPS signature.

82. The correct answer is **C**. Block rules in a web filtering solution are designed to prevent users from accessing websites that match certain criteria, such as specific domains, content categories, or security risks. These rules help enforce content and security policies within an organization.

    A is incorrect. Block rules restrict site access based on the defined criteria, not allowing access by default.

    B is incorrect. This describes an allow list approach, where all websites are blocked by default, and only approved ones are accessible.

    D is incorrect. Block rules are not designed to manage time-based access.

83. The correct answer is **B**. Automated virtual machine deployment is an example of using automation for resource provisioning. It allows for the quick and efficient setup of virtual machines without manual intervention.

    A is incorrect. Manual hardware installation requires physical effort and human involvement, which is the opposite of automation.

    C is incorrect. Manually configuring network settings is not an automated process.

    D is incorrect. Manual software updates require human effort to check, download, and install, making them non-automated.

84. The correct answer is **A**. Resource reuse vulnerabilities occur when resources such as memory, files, or other system components are not adequately cleared or sanitized before reusing.

    B is incorrect. Firmware refers to the low-level software embedded in hardware devices, which controls their essential functions.

    C is incorrect. EOL refers to technology no longer supported by the manufacturer, meaning it does not receive updates or security patches.

    D is incorrect. Legacy systems are older technologies still in use but may not be actively supported.

85. The correct answer is **C**. A password is an example of "something you know" in multi-factor authentication.

    A is incorrect. A security key is an example of "something you have."

    B is incorrect. A fingerprint scan is an example of "something you are."

    D is incorrect. A smartcard is an example of "something you have."

CompTIA Security+ SY0-701 Mock Exam 5

1. The correct answer is **A**. Privilege escalation occurs when an attacker exploits a vulnerability to gain access to higher privileges than they are authorized for, such as accessing system files that should be restricted.

    B is incorrect. Forgery involves creating fake or tampered data, such as in a cross-site request forgery attack, in which attackers trick a user into executing unwanted actions.

    C is incorrect. A buffer overflow occurs when an attacker writes more data to a buffer than it can hold, allowing attackers to execute malicious code.

    D is incorrect. Directory traversal involves accessing files or directories outside the intended structure by manipulating file path inputs (e.g., using ../ to move up the directory tree).

2. The correct answer is **B**. A right-to-audit clause in a contract allows the company to review the third-party vendor's security practices and ensure they are conducting regular assessments of their policies and procedures. This clause also allows the company to verify compliance with security requirements and review audit findings.

    A is incorrect. Department quarterly assessments are not contractual proof that a vendor regularly reviews its policies.

    C is incorrect. Supply chain analysis reports evaluate the risks and vulnerabilities within a vendor's supply chain but do not directly confirm that the vendor regularly reviews its security policies.

    D is incorrect. Penetration testing results demonstrate that a vendor has tested its systems for vulnerabilities at a specific time but they do not provide proof of regular reviews of security policies.

3. The correct answer is **D**. Downloading malware from a suspicious email link is classified as unintentional because the employee likely did not intend to download malware. They may not have recognized the email as a threat and did not deliberately seek to engage in harmful activity.

    A is incorrect. Defensive behavior would be making deliberate choices and taking steps to avoid the risks associated with malware.

    B is incorrect. Intentional violation refers to knowingly and willingly breaching security protocols or policies. In this case, the employee did not intend to violate any rules or put the company at risk.

    C is incorrect. The behavior did not unexpectedly violate expectations or norms, as employees can often inadvertently fall victim to malware.

4. The correct answer is **D**. Bollards are sturdy, vertical posts designed to prevent vehicles from accessing restricted areas, protecting the building and pedestrians.

   A is incorrect. Bollards can be designed aesthetically, but their primary function is security.

   B is incorrect. Bollards do not monitor foot traffic.

   C is incorrect. Bollards are not used as a lighting system.

5. The correct answer is **B**. Asset management refers to the process of identifying, documenting, and tracking the ownership, status, and life cycle of physical and digital assets within an organization. This includes hardware such as computers, servers, and networking equipment.

   A is incorrect. Incident response refers to identifying, managing, and mitigating the effects of security incidents, such as breaches, attacks, or vulnerabilities.

   C is incorrect. Data encryption involves converting data into a secure format that only authorized parties can access.

   D is incorrect. Threat modeling identifies potential security threats to a system and develops strategies to mitigate those risks.

6. The correct answer is **A**. Regularly updating a software inventory lets a company track which software is installed and used. This helps ensure the company complies with licensing agreements and avoids using unauthorized or expired software.

   B is incorrect. Network performance is affected by bandwidth, hardware configuration, and network traffic, not by maintaining an up-to-date software inventory.

   C is incorrect. Power consumption is related to the hardware and software running on devices but not to maintaining an updated software inventory.

   D is incorrect. Regularly updating the software inventory helps with software management but does not directly prevent hardware failures.

7. The correct answer is **B**. Detective control is used to research how an incident happened by identifying, logging, and analyzing the event. This type of control helps in understanding the incident's details and origins.

   A is incorrect. Technical controls involve tools and systems to protect or detect but not specifically for researching post-incident.

   C is incorrect. Corrective controls focus on fixing issues and restoring systems after an incident, not investigating the cause.

   D is incorrect. Administrative controls involve policies and procedures, not the actual process of investigating an incident.

8. The correct answer is **B**. Loss of license refers to a situation where a company can no longer operate in specific sectors due to regulatory non-compliance. Regulatory bodies issue licenses or permits, and non-compliance with industry regulations can revoke those licenses.

    A is incorrect. Contractual impacts refer to the consequences of breaching the terms of a contract, such as losing clients or partners.

    C is incorrect. Reputational damage refers to the harm caused to a company's public image or brand due to negative publicity or failure to meet legal or ethical standards.

    D is incorrect. Fines are financial penalties imposed for non-compliance with regulations. They are not as severe as the loss of a license.

9. The correct answer is **B**. Cyber insurance is designed to provide financial protection against losses that result from cyber incidents, such as data breaches, network interruptions, and other security-related events. This helps companies manage the financial impact of incidents that could arise despite their best security efforts.

    A is incorrect. Purchasing cyber insurance does not directly affect the need for vulnerability scans.

    C is incorrect. Cyber insurance does not exempt a company from applying patches.

    D is incorrect. Cyber insurance does not directly improve the effectiveness of compensating controls.

10. The correct answer is **A**. Network logs provide detailed information on device communications, including IP addresses, protocols, ports, and traffic patterns. These logs are essential for monitoring internal and external network traffic, allowing security analysts to track communications and identify unusual activity.

    B is incorrect. Application logs capture details about specific software operations, including errors, performance issues, and user activities within the application.

    C is incorrect. Operating system security logs focus on security events related to the operating system, such as login attempts, system errors, and permissions changes.

    D is incorrect. Intrusion detection system (IDS) and intrusion prevention system (IPS) logs capture data about potential or actual security incidents by monitoring network traffic and flagging suspicious patterns. However, they don't offer the full traffic detail that network logs provide.

11. The correct answer is **A**. Employee security training programs are examples of directive controls because they aim to influence and guide user behavior to ensure adherence to security policies and best practices.

    B is incorrect. Intrusion detection systems are examples of detection controls.

    C is incorrect. Firewalls are considered preventive controls as they block unauthorized access.

    D is incorrect. Data encryption is a protective control that secures data.

12. The correct answer is **C**. Multi-factor authentication (MFA) requires two or more forms of verification, such as something you know (password) and something you have (one-time code sent to a mobile device).

    A is incorrect. A username and password alone are single-factor authentication (SFA).

    B is incorrect. A password and PIN are considered SFA as both are knowledge-based factors.

    D is incorrect. A password alone is an SFA method.

13. The correct answer is **D**. Code signing is a process that involves attaching a digital signature to software applications or executables. A digital signature is created using a private and public key pair.

    A is incorrect. Secure cookies protect data in transit, particularly for session management in web applications.

    B is incorrect. Input validation is a security practice that ensures that only properly formatted data is used by other application processes.

    C is incorrect. Static code analysis involves examining source code for vulnerabilities without executing it.

14. The correct answer is **A**. Implementing encryption algorithms enhances confidentiality by protecting data from unauthorized access. However, these algorithms can slow down system performance, potentially reducing the system's availability and responsiveness. This scenario illustrates a conflict between maintaining confidentiality and ensuring availability.

    B is incorrect. Digital signatures verify the authenticity and integrity of data, ensuring it has not been altered.

    C is incorrect. Backing up data to multiple locations enhances availability and data recovery in case of failure, but it does not directly impact confidentiality.

    D is incorrect. Enforcing strict access controls enhances confidentiality by restricting unauthorized access to data. Speeding up access does not have a direct conflict with system availability, as it improves access.

15. The correct answer is **C**. Anomaly-based detection identifies suspicious behaviour by comparing network activity against a baseline of normal activity. When this baseline is deviated from, it triggers an alert for potential threats or attacks.

    A is incorrect. Signature-based systems identify threats based on predefined attack patterns.

    B is incorrect. Normal behaviour suggests an absence of deviations, which is not the focus of anomaly-based detection.

    D is incorrect. This is IP-based filtering, which isn't directly related to anomaly-based detection.

16. The correct answer is **C**. A SIEM tool is designed to collect and aggregate security events and logs from various systems, devices, and applications across a network. It provides real-time monitoring, alerts, and reporting, helping companies detect potential security incidents or threats.

     A is incorrect. Providing secure remote access is typically the role of a VPN or other tunneling protocols, not a SIEM tool.

     B is incorrect. Spam filtering is a function of email security solutions or dedicated anti-spam systems.

     D is incorrect. Managing user identities and access rights is an identity and access role, not a SIEM tool.

17. The correct answer is **B**. Comparing current security measures with industry standards or regulations is a typical step in performing a gap analysis. This process helps identify discrepancies between the organization's existing security practices and the best practices or compliance requirements, thus highlighting areas that need improvement.

     A is incorrect. Developing an incident response plan involves creating procedures and alerts for responding to security incidents. This is not a typical step in gap analysis.

     C is incorrect. Implementing encryption across data systems is a specific security measure to protect data confidentiality. While encryption may be a solution to address gaps identified in the analysis, it is not a step in the gap analysis process itself.

     D is incorrect. Conducting a vulnerability assessment involves identifying and analyzing weaknesses in a network to mitigate potential security risks. While it can provide valuable information for gap analysis, there are other steps in the gap analysis process.

18. The correct answer is **A**. Capacity planning involves assessing and ensuring the infrastructure can handle the necessary load and requirements during peak disaster recovery scenarios. The security administrator is likely focusing on whether the current infrastructure can support the demands of recovery operations when they are most critical.

     B is incorrect. Incident response refers to the processes and procedures for managing and addressing security incidents as they occur.

     C is incorrect. Data encryption protects data by converting it into an unreadable secure format without the appropriate key.

     D is incorrect. Access control involves managing who can access specific resources or information within an organization.

19. The correct answer is **C**. Static code analysis involves examining an application's source code without executing it. This practice helps identify security vulnerabilities and coding errors and ensures adherence to security best practices early in development.

    A is incorrect. Code signing is a security measure using digital certificates to verify the software code.

    B is incorrect. Input validation is a security measure that ensures the application accepts only correctly formatted data.

    D is incorrect. Secure cookies enhance cookie security by preventing their access by unauthorized scripts or over non-secure channels.

20. The correct answer is **B**. The control plane manages and routes traffic based on network policies and routing protocols. It handles the decision-making process regarding how data should be routed.

    A is incorrect. Handling user data traffic is the primary function of the data plane.

    C is incorrect. Encryption and decryption are tasks typically handled by security mechanisms rather than the control plane.

    D is incorrect. Physical security measures are unrelated to the control plane's functions.

21. The correct answer is **B**. Adaptive identity management adjusts access controls dynamically based on real-time risk assessments and user behavior, providing a more flexible approach to security.

    A is incorrect. Enforcing rigid policies does not adapt to changing risk conditions, contrary to the concept of adaptive identity.

    C is incorrect. Monitoring network traffic is related to threat detection, not adaptive identity management.

    D is incorrect. Providing a static set of permissions does not account for the adaptive nature of this approach.

22. The correct answer is **B**. It is risky behavior because using weak passwords increases the possibility of unauthorized access to accounts. It reflects a conscious choice to use passwords that do not meet security standards, thereby putting the organization's data and systems at risk.

    A is incorrect. Unexpected behavior refers to actions that deviate from normal or anticipated behavior. It is not unexpected among users who may need to be made aware of the importance of strong passwords.

    C is incorrect. Unintentional behavior implies that the individuals were unaware of their actions and did not mean to compromise security.

    D is incorrect. Users with weak passwords typically do not have malicious intent; they may be uninformed about password security.

23. The correct answer is **B**. To protect the private key, it is commonly encrypted with a strong passphrase or stored in a hardware security module (HSM), ensuring it remains secure and inaccessible to unauthorized users.

    A is incorrect. Private keys should never be stored on publicly accessible servers.

    C is incorrect. Sharing private keys, even with trusted parties, is not recommended due to the risk of compromise.

    D is incorrect. The private key should never be distributed.

24. The correct answer is **B**. Symmetric encryption uses one key for encryption and decryption and is more efficient for large amounts of data than asymmetric encryption, which uses a key pair.

    A is incorrect. Symmetric encryption uses a single key, but asymmetric uses a key pair.

    C is incorrect. Asymmetric encryption is typically used for digital signatures, while symmetric is used for bulk data encryption.

    D is incorrect. Full-disk encryption typically uses symmetric encryption for performance reasons.

25. The correct answer is **B**. TPMs are often integrated into individual devices, such as laptops and desktops, while HSMs are external hardware devices used in enterprises for secure key management and cryptographic operations.

    A is incorrect. Both TPMs and HSMs are hardware-based security solutions.

    C is incorrect. TPMs and HSMs can handle various types of keys, but TPMs are not specifically for cloud-based keys.

    D is incorrect. TPMs and HSMs can handle encryption tasks, not just storage.

26. The correct answer is **B**. Key stretching increases the computational effort needed to crack a password, making brute-force attacks more difficult.

    A is incorrect. Key stretching increases processing time to enhance security, not shorten it.

    C is incorrect. Key stretching doesn't increase password length but the time required to hash the password.

    D is incorrect. Key stretching is not about generating key pairs; it's about enhancing password hash security.

27. The correct answer is **B**. A public ledger in blockchain technology ensures that transactions are transparent and immutable, meaning they cannot be altered once recorded. This feature is key to ensuring the integrity and transparency of financial transactions.

    A is incorrect. While encryption secures data, it does not inherently provide transparency or immutability.

    C is incorrect. Digital signatures ensure authenticity and integrity, but they do not alone provide the transparency and immutability needed.

    D is incorrect. Salting is a technique used in password security, not securing or making blockchain transactions transparent.

28. The correct answer is **B**. A wildcard certificate is designed to secure multiple subdomains under a single domain, making it the ideal choice for this scenario.

    A is incorrect. Self-signed certificates are not ideal for public-facing subdomains due to trust issues.

    C is incorrect. EV certificates provide higher trust levels but do not cover multiple subdomains.

    D is incorrect. Code-signing certificates authenticate software code, not domains.

29. The correct answer is **C**. Shadow IT refers to employees using unauthorized hardware, software, or cloud services within an organization. These activities are typically done without malicious intent but unintentionally expose the organization to security risks.

    A is incorrect. Hacktivists are individuals or groups that intentionally conduct cyberattacks to promote political or social causes.

    B is incorrect. Nation-state actors are typically government-sponsored groups that conduct cyber operations for strategic purposes.

    D is incorrect. Organized crime groups are involved in coordinated, intentional activities for financial gain through illegal means, including cybercrime.

30. The correct answer is **C**. Organized crime groups are most likely to target financial institutions as they seek substantial financial gain. These groups are often involved in fraud, theft, and extortion, which can be highly profitable.

    A is incorrect. Targeting government secrets is characteristic of nation-state actors engaged in espionage or strategic intelligence gathering.

    B is incorrect. While organized crime groups may use social media for various purposes, they are more likely to target larger, more profitable entities.

    D is incorrect. Often targeted by hacktivists, protest organizations are less likely to be the focus of organized crime groups.

31. The correct answer is **C**. Configuring strong access controls ensures that only authorized personnel can access the router's settings while turning off unnecessary web interfaces. This reduces the attack surface by preventing potential vulnerabilities from being exploited through the router's management interfaces.

    A is incorrect. VLANs primarily focus on managing traffic within the network rather than hardening the router's security settings.

    B is incorrect. Routers typically do not run traditional operating systems that support anti-malware software.

    D is incorrect. Defragmentation is irrelevant to routers, as they generally have different file storage and fragmentation issues than traditional computers.

32. The correct answer is **B**. Phishing involves sending fraudulent emails that appear to be from a legitimate source to fool people into revealing personal information, such as login credentials.

    A is incorrect. Business email compromise (BEC) typically involves compromising or spoofing legitimate business email accounts to trick employees into transferring sensitive information.

    C is incorrect. To deceive users, brand impersonation involves creating fake websites, emails, or other communications that closely mimic a legitimate brand.

    D is incorrect. Pretexting involves creating a fabricated scenario to manipulate victims into divulging information.

33. The correct answer is **A**. Phishing is the act of sending deceptive emails that appear to come from a legitimate source, with the goal of tricking individuals into providing personal information or credentials. In this scenario, the attacker impersonates a well-known company to trick recipients into updating their account information on a fraudulent website.

    B is incorrect. Smishing involves sending fraudulent text messages to trick individuals into revealing personal information.

    C is incorrect. Typosquatting involves creating a fake website with a domain name that seems like a legitimate one.

    D is incorrect. Brand impersonation describes the act of mimicking a brand; however, the specific act of sending deceptive emails to gather personal information is more accurately described as phishing.

34. The correct answer is **A**. The Containment phase in incident response aims to limit the spread and impact of a security incident. By isolating affected systems or networks, it prevents further damage and minimizes the risk of the incident spreading to other parts of the infrastructure.

    B is incorrect. Removing the incident's root cause occurs in the Eradication phase, not the Containment phase.

    C is incorrect. Restoring systems to regular operation occurs during the incident response Recovery phase.

    D is incorrect. Reviewing and improving the incident response plan happens during the Lessons Learned phase.

35. The correct answer is **A**. Vishing involves using phone calls to deceive individuals into revealing sensitive information. The attacker uses a fake caller ID to impersonate a customer support rep to obtain sensitive information.

    B is incorrect. While impersonation is a technique used in vishing, it is a broader concept that involves pretending to be someone else in various contexts.

    C is incorrect. Smishing involves sending fraudulent text messages to trick individuals into revealing personal information.

    D is incorrect. A watering hole attack compromises a website frequented by a specific group to infect users or gather information.

36. The correct answer is **B**. A regulatory examination is an audit by a government agency or regulatory body to verify that a company complies with specific industry regulations.

    A is incorrect. The government agency, not an independent third party, assigns auditors directly.

    C is incorrect. The company would perform a self-assessment internally to evaluate its compliance or security measures.

    D is incorrect. A departmental audit does not refer to an audit conducted by a regulatory body.

37. The correct answer is **A**. Firmware is the low-level software embedded in hardware devices. It is responsible for controlling and managing the hardware's functions.

    B is incorrect. Hardware refers to physical components within the computer system, such as processors, memory, and storage devices.

    C is incorrect. MTTR stands for mean time to repair, a metric used to describe the average time required to repair a system or component after a failure.

    D is incorrect. Ransomware is malicious software designed to encrypt data on a victim's system and demand a ransom for its release.

38. The correct answer is **D**. In virtual environments, improper handling of memory reuse can allow sensitive data to be inadvertently shared between virtual machines, leading to significant security risks.

    A is incorrect. Firmware refers to the low-level software that controls hardware devices. It is not related to the management of virtual machine memory.

    B is incorrect. Virtual machine sprawl refers to the uncontrolled proliferation of virtual machines in an environment, which can lead to management and security challenges.

    C is incorrect. MTBF stands for mean time between failures, a metric used to predict the reliability of hardware or systems.

39. The correct answer is **B**. End-of-life refers to a stage where a product, such as firmware or software, is no longer supported by the vendor, meaning it will not receive updates, including security patches.

    A is incorrect. ALE stands for annualized loss expectancy, a metric used to quantify the expected monetary loss from a specific risk over a year.

    C is incorrect. CSRF stands for cross-site request forgery, a type of web security vulnerability in which an attacker causes a user to perform actions they did not intend to perform. This is unrelated to firmware updates or the risks associated with end-of-life software.

    D is incorrect. SQLi stands for SQL injection, a type of attack that involves inserting or injecting malicious SQL queries into input fields to manipulate a database.

40. The correct answer is **A**. A rootkit is a type of malware designed to provide attackers with administrative-level access to a system while hiding its existence. Rootkits are difficult to detect because they conceal themselves deep within the system, making it harder for traditional antivirus tools to find and remove them.

    B is incorrect. Bloatware refers to software that comes pre-installed on a device and takes up storage or system resources without providing much value.

    C is incorrect. A logic bomb is a piece of malicious code that triggers a harmful action based on specific conditions or at a particular time.

    D is incorrect. Spyware is malware that secretly collects user information, often maliciously.

41. The correct answer is **C**. Environmental interference refers to disruptions caused by physical or environmental factors, such as radio frequency interference (RFI) or electromagnetic interference (EMI), which can affect wireless communication.

    A is incorrect. Brute-force attacks involve repeatedly trying different combinations of words until the correct one is found.

    B is incorrect. RFID cloning involves duplicating the data from a radio frequency identification (RFID) tag to create a counterfeit tag. This type of attack does not disrupt wireless communication signals.

    D is incorrect. SQL injection is an attack that involves injecting malicious SQL code into a database query to manipulate or access data.

42. The correct answer is **D**. Mitigation involves implementing measures to reduce the impact or likelihood of a risk. In this case, adding security controls such as encryption and access control helps minimize the chances of a data breach or lessen its potential damage.

    A is incorrect. Risk acceptance means that the company is aware of the risk but does not take any action to reduce it.

    B is incorrect. Risk avoidance involves eliminating the risk by not engaging in the activity that presents the risk.

    C is incorrect. Risk transference involves shifting risk to a third party by purchasing insurance or outsourcing certain operations.

43. The correct answer is **C**. A credential replay attack occurs when attackers capture valid authentication credentials (such as a username and password) and reuse them to gain unauthorized access to systems.

    A is incorrect. A DNS attack manipulates the Domain Name System, usually redirecting users to malicious sites or disrupting network services.

    B is incorrect. A malicious code attack involves using malware (viruses, trojans, or ransomware) to compromise systems.

    D is incorrect. An amplified attack generally refers to increasing the traffic sent to a target (as in DDoS attacks) by leveraging other systems (such as DNS servers) to amplify the traffic.

44. The correct answer is **B**. Virtual local area networks (VLANs) allow the segmentation of a network into smaller, isolated sections. This enables traffic isolation based on departments, organizational units, or functions, limiting the spread of internal threats.

    A is incorrect. VLANs primarily segment network traffic and do not provide system redundancy. Redundancy usually involves failover systems or backups.

    C is incorrect. VLANs are designed to isolate and control traffic, not to provide unrestricted access.

    D is incorrect. VLANs operate on the switch network and do not directly impact physical access to devices.

45. The correct answer is **A**. Access control lists (ACLs) allow administrators to define specific rules governing who can access certain resources, such as financial records. Configuring an ACL to only permit access from the finance team's group role ensures that only authorized users can access the financial data.

    B is incorrect. Disabling all network shares would prevent everyone, including the finance team, from accessing shared resources.

    C is incorrect. Network segmentation must be combined with other controls (such as ACLs) to achieve the desired outcome.

    D is incorrect. Granting full control permissions to all employees would allow unrestricted access to the financial records, directly contradicting the goal of limiting access to the finance team.

46. The correct answer is **C**. An application allow list specifies a list of approved and trusted applications permitted to run on a company's systems.

    A is incorrect. A block list works oppositely to an allow list by specifying a list of applications that are denied from running.

    B is incorrect. Content filtering refers to controlling the data types accessed or transmitted over the network, such as blocking specific websites or filtering out inappropriate content.

    D is incorrect. Data loss prevention (DLP) is a security strategy for preventing the unauthorized transmission of sensitive data outside the organization.

47. The correct answer is **B**. During the decommissioning process, it is crucial to ensure that all data is securely migrated to new systems or completely erased to prevent unauthorized access or data breaches.

    A is incorrect. Backing up legacy applications is not the key consideration when decommissioning, as the goal is to retire these systems to reduce risks.

    C is incorrect. Keeping them running defeats the purpose of decommissioning, which is to remove outdated, vulnerable software from the environment.

    D is incorrect. The goal of decommissioning is to remove legacy applications, not update them.

48. The correct answer is **B**. A host-based firewall is a protective barrier for the workstation, filtering incoming and outgoing traffic based on predefined security rules to prevent malicious activities.

    A is incorrect. Encryption of data during transmission is not the function of a firewall.

    C is incorrect. A host-based firewall is designed to manage and filter network traffic, not to manage software installed on a workstation.

    D is incorrect. Firewalls focus on controlling network traffic, not managing user permissions.

49. The correct answer is **B**. Many IoT devices are designed for convenience and connectivity rather than security, which can lead to vulnerabilities that attackers exploit to gain access to the network.

    A is incorrect. Automatic updates for IoT devices are not always guaranteed, and many devices may not receive timely or frequent security patches.

    C is incorrect. While some IoT devices may include encryption capabilities, not all do, and those that do might not always use robust encryption standards.

    D is incorrect. IoT devices generally do not provide enhanced control over network traffic. Instead, they often require additional security measures to protect the overall network.

50. The correct answer is **B**. Endpoint logs are critical in an insider threat investigation because they record the actions taken on individual devices, such as file access, login attempts, software execution, and system changes.

    A is incorrect. Firewall logs track network traffic entering and leaving the organization's network. They don't provide granular details about actions performed on specific devices.

    C is incorrect. Metadata refers to data that provides information about other data, such as file creation dates, modification history, or email headers.

    D is incorrect. Network logs capture data about the flow of traffic across a network, such as IP addresses, protocols, and packet transfers.

51. The correct answer is **B**. ICSs/SCADA systems frequently rely on proprietary protocols and legacy systems designed without modern security considerations. This can lead to vulnerabilities, as these systems may not support contemporary security features or best practices, making them attractive targets for attackers.

    A is incorrect. Consumer-grade antivirus software is generally unsuitable for ICS/SCADA environments, requiring specialized security measures.

    C is incorrect. ICS/SCADA systems often do not have automatic updates due to system stability and downtime concerns.

    D is incorrect. While some ICS systems may be air-gapped, this is not universally true. Many ICS/SCADA systems are connected to corporate networks or the internet, which creates potential security risks.

52. The correct answer is **B**. Risk transference involves shifting the responsibility for certain risks to another party. By selecting a cloud service provider (CSP) with comprehensive security certifications and adequate insurance coverage, a company can transfer some risks associated with data breaches, compliance, and infrastructure failures to the CSP.

     A is incorrect. While backups and disaster recovery plans are important for ensuring data availability and integrity, they do not directly support risk transference.

     C is incorrect. Having an in-house IT team does not support risk transference. It takes responsibility for security incidents within the organization.

     D is incorrect. Avoiding cloud services may reduce certain risks associated with third-party providers, but it does not effectively support risk transference.

53. The correct answer is **A**. Regularly scheduled backups ensure the most current data is saved and can be restored during a data loss incident. Testing recovery procedures is critical because it confirms that backup data can be reliably restored.

     B is incorrect. While a faster internet connection can improve the speed of data transfers during recovery, it is not a primary factor in the overall ease of recovery.

     C is incorrect. Physical security measures are essential for protecting data from theft or damage, but they do not directly contribute to the ease of data recovery.

     D is incorrect. A complex network architecture can hinder recovery efforts, complicating restoring services and data.

54. The correct answer is **B**. Active monitoring engages with the network and systems, often performing actions such as testing or probing for vulnerabilities and responding to detected threats. In contrast, passive monitoring involves collecting and analyzing data without interacting with or altering the network traffic, making it a less intrusive method of gathering information about network activity.

     A is incorrect. This incorrectly defines both active and passive monitoring.

     C is incorrect. This reverses the roles of active and passive monitoring.

     D is incorrect. This option inaccurately assigns functions to active and passive monitoring.

55. The correct answer is **B**. The firewall actively enforces security policies by blocking real-time unauthorized access based on predefined rules. It interacts with network traffic to protect the system.

     A is incorrect. An IDS only logs activities without taking any action.

     C is incorrect. A network traffic analyzer that observes and records traffic does not intervene or take action to protect the network.

     D is incorrect. Generating reports on network activity without real-time interaction indicates that the system is not actively monitoring or intervening to mitigate potential threats.

56. The correct answer is **B**. IPSec is a suite of protocols designed to secure Internet Protocol (IP) communications by providing the confidentiality, integrity, and authentication of data packets. It is widely used in VPNs to ensure secure data transmission over IP networks.

    A is incorrect. HTTP is a protocol for transmitting hypertext over the web but does not provide security features such as encryption, confidentiality, or integrity.

    C is incorrect. FTP transfers files over a network but does not provide built-in security features for confidentiality or integrity.

    D is incorrect. SNMP is primarily used to manage and monitor network devices.

57. The correct answer is **A**. One of SD-WAN's main advantages is its ability to provide centralized management of network traffic, enabling organizations to optimize their wide area network (WAN) performance more effectively. It can also enhance security through features such as encryption, firewalls, and cloud-based security solutions.

    B is incorrect. SD-WAN does not directly enhance physical security for data centers.

    C is incorrect. SD-WAN is primarily concerned with optimizing and securing data in transit across WANs, not encrypting data at rest.

    D is incorrect. SD-WAN is specifically designed to manage and optimize WAN traffic.

58. The correct answer is **C**. A warm site is a backup site with some hardware and infrastructure already set up, allowing it to be operational more quickly than a cold site. It must be fully equipped and operational at all times but have enough resources to be brought online relatively quickly in case of a disaster.

    A is incorrect. A hot site is always fully equipped and operational, with all necessary hardware, software, and data readily available for immediate use.

    B is incorrect. A cold site is a backup location without active equipment that requires significant time and effort to set up before it can be operational.

    D is incorrect. Geographic dispersion refers to spreading resources across many locations to reduce the risks associated with localized disasters.

59. The correct answer is **D**. Geographic dispersion refers to distributing resources across different locations, such as data centers. This reduces the risk of data loss and downtime caused by localized disasters.

    A is incorrect. A warm site does not inherently involve spreading data centers across multiple geographic locations.

    B is incorrect. A cold site is a backup location without active equipment that requires significant setup time to become operational.

    C is incorrect. A hot site offers rapid recovery but needs to address the specific issue of spreading resources across various locations.

60. The correct answer is **C**. A simulation testing method creates a realistic scenario to mimic a real-world cyberattack. It involves engaging employees and systems in an environment replicating an actual incident's conditions.

    A is incorrect. A tabletop exercise involves discussing a hypothetical scenario in a group setting, usually around a table, to assess the response strategies and communication plans.

    B is incorrect. Failover refers to switching to a backup system or resource in the event of a failure of the primary system. It is not a testing method for assessing responses to cyberattacks.

    D is incorrect. Parallel processing involves performing multiple processes simultaneously. It is often used in computing and data-processing contexts.

61. The correct answer is **C**. Parallel processing tests validate that both systems can operate effectively under load and help identify any discrepancies or performance issues that may arise when both systems are active.

    A is incorrect. Simulation testing creates a controlled environment to mimic real-world scenarios and evaluate the response to a disaster or incident. However, it does not involve running applications on both systems simultaneously.

    B is incorrect. A tabletop exercise is a discussion-based session where team members gather to discuss their roles and responses to hypothetical scenarios.

    D is incorrect. Failover refers to switching to a backup system when the primary system fails. It does not involve the simultaneous operation of both systems.

62. The correct answer is **C**. Encryption during the backup process ensures that everything remains secure, even if it is accessed by unauthorized individuals. This is crucial for protecting the confidentiality and integrity of the data being backed up.

    A is incorrect. Replication involves creating copies of data across different locations to ensure availability and redundancy. It does not inherently secure sensitive data.

    B is incorrect. Frequency adjustment refers to changing how often backups are performed.

    D is incorrect. Onsite storage involves keeping backup data in the same physical location as the primary data. This can be convenient but poses significant risks if that location is compromised.

63. The correct answer is **C**. Replication involves continuously copying data from the primary storage system to a secondary system in real time or near-real time. This strategy ensures that any changes to the data are immediately reflected in the backup, minimizing the risk of data loss during a failure.

    A is incorrect. A full backup involves making a complete copy of all data at a specific point in time. It does not occur in real time and can take a significant amount of time to complete.

    B is incorrect. Incremental backups involve saving only the data that has changed since the last backup. While efficient in terms of storage space and backup time, they do not provide real-time data protection.

    D is incorrect. A snapshot is a point-in-time copy of data that captures a system's state at a specific moment. Snapshots can provide quick recovery options, but they do not offer continuous real-time backups.

64. The correct answer is **C**. A UPS offers short-term power, typically allowing systems to run for several minutes depending on the load and UPS capacity. This gives users enough time to save work and safely shut down equipment.

    A is incorrect. Generators typically take some time to start up and are used for longer-term backup rather than short-term, immediate power needs.

    B is incorrect. Solar panels convert sunlight into electricity but require sunlight to generate power and do not provide immediate backup during a power outage.

    D is incorrect. A power strip distributes electricity from a wall outlet to multiple devices and does not provide backup power during an outage.

65. The correct answer is **C**. Wi-Fi is the most commonly used connection method for mobile devices to connect to corporate networks. Organizations typically implement secure Wi-Fi protocols (such as WPA3) to ensure encryption and security for the data transmitted over the wireless network.

    A is incorrect. While cellular connections provide secure access to the internet, there are other methods for connecting to a corporate network.

    B is incorrect. Bluetooth is generally used for short-range device-to-device connections and is not commonly utilized for connecting mobile devices to corporate networks.

    D is incorrect. Mobile device management (MDM) is not a connection method but a solution for managing mobile devices in an organization.

66. The correct answer is **B**. "Restricted" is a classification level used for highly sensitive data that could cause significant harm or damage if disclosed, whether accidentally or maliciously. This classification typically applies to information that requires the highest levels of protection and is only accessible to a limited group of authorized personnel.

    A is incorrect. Public data is information that can be freely shared with anyone and does not need any protection.

    C is incorrect. "Unrestricted" refers to data that requires no protection; it can be made freely available.

    D is incorrect. Internal data is typically accessible to employees within the organization but is not intended for public release.

67. The correct answer is **C**. Ownership assignment refers to designating a specific individual or team responsible for managing, maintaining, and securing an asset, such as an application.

    A is incorrect. Role-based access control (RBAC) is a security model in which access permissions are granted based on a user's role within an organization.

    B is incorrect. Application patching is applying updates or patches to software to fix vulnerabilities, improve performance, or add features.

    D is incorrect. Data classification refers to organizing and categorizing data based on its sensitivity and the protection level required.

68. The correct answer is **B**. When selecting a destruction method, the sensitivity of the data being destroyed is paramount. Data classified as highly sensitive requires more rigorous destruction methods to ensure that it cannot be recovered.

    A is incorrect. While the size of the hard drive may impact the time it takes to perform a data destruction process, it is not a critical consideration in determining the method used for destruction.

    C is incorrect. The age of the hardware may affect its reliability or compatibility with certain destruction methods, but it is not a critical consideration for data destruction.

    D is incorrect. The operating system may influence the tools available for data destruction, but it is not a critical consideration when selecting a data destruction method.

69. The correct answer is **C**. Overwriting hard drives with random data ensures that any data stored on the hard drives is irretrievable. By overwriting the existing data with random data multiple times, the security administrator effectively prevents unauthorized access to sensitive information.

    A is incorrect. This is highly insecure. Selling the laptops without any changes means that the new owners will have access to all the data on the devices.

    B is incorrect. Standard file deletion does not securely remove data. It typically only removes pointers to the data, making it possible to recover the deleted files using data recovery tools.

    D is incorrect. Reinstalling the operating system may remove some user data but it does not guarantee that all data has been permanently erased.

70. The correct answer is **C**. Shredding involves physically destroying the storage media by breaking it into small pieces. This process ensures that the data stored on the media is irretrievable and makes data recovery impossible.

    A is incorrect. Disk encryption protects by converting data into a secure format accessed only with a specific key or password. However, it does not destroy the data or the storage media.

    B is incorrect. Data wiping or sanitization involves using software to overwrite existing data using new data patterns. While it effectively removes data, it does not physically alter the storage media.

    D is incorrect. Data backup creates copies of data to prevent loss in case of failure or destruction. This method does not involve any destruction of data.

71. The correct answer is **B**. A certificate of destruction is formal documentation that the data stored on the decommissioned hardware has been securely destroyed in compliance with relevant security and privacy standards.

    A is incorrect. A certificate of destruction does not pertain to warranty status.

    C is incorrect. The certificate of destruction does not provide information about the cost or value of the hardware.

    D is incorrect. The main goal of obtaining a certificate of destruction is to document the secure destruction of data, not simply to count how many devices have been decommissioned.

72. The correct answer is **A**. The primary purpose of package monitoring in vulnerability management is to track and identify vulnerabilities within software packages, including whether they are up to date and contain known vulnerabilities that attackers could exploit.

    B is incorrect. Monitoring network traffic is related to network security and intrusion detection, not specifically to package monitoring in vulnerability management.

    C is incorrect. Assessing the physical security of server rooms pertains to physical security measures and controls, not vulnerability management related to software packages.

    D is incorrect. Updating operating systems is an important part of maintaining security, but it is separate from package monitoring.

73. The correct answer is **B**. It refers to a collective group or community that collaborates to share insights, experiences, and data regarding vulnerabilities and threats. Such organizations enhance security by allowing members to learn from each other's findings, improving threat awareness and response strategies.

    A is incorrect. Static analysis involves examining code without executing it, typically during the software development phase, to identify potential vulnerabilities.

    C is incorrect. Penetration testing is not a method for sharing information about vulnerabilities and threats among organizations.

    D is incorrect. Dynamic analysis focuses on assessing software but does not involve sharing information about threats and vulnerabilities within a community.

74. The correct answer is **C**. Open source intelligence (OSINT) involves collecting and analyzing publicly available information. OSINT can include data from websites, forums, social media, and vulnerability databases to identify potential vulnerabilities that could affect an organization.

    A is incorrect. Scanning the internal network does not involve using publicly available information.

    B is incorrect. Engaging a third-party firm typically involves an external assessment that may utilize proprietary tools and methodologies.

    D is incorrect. A bug bounty program invites individuals to find and report vulnerabilities in exchange for rewards.

75. The correct answer is **B**. A false negative occurs when a security measure fails to detect an actual threat or attack, indicating that there is no problem when, in fact, there is one. This can lead to serious security breaches since the real threat goes unnoticed.

    A is incorrect. A false positive occurs when a security measure incorrectly identifies a benign situation as a threat.

    C is incorrect. A true positive is when a security measure correctly identifies an actual threat.

    D is incorrect. A true negative is when a security measure correctly identifies a benign situation as non-threatening.

76. The correct answer is **B**. Classifying vulnerabilities allows organizations to prioritize their responses based on each vulnerability's severity and potential impact. This ensures that critical vulnerabilities are addressed first, effectively managing risk and resource allocation.

    A is incorrect. Classifying vulnerabilities does not ensure all systems are running the latest operating systems.

    C is incorrect. Limiting access to sensitive data pertains more to access control policies than vulnerability classification.

    D is incorrect. Cost considerations come into play after vulnerabilities have been classified and prioritized.

77. The correct answer is **B**. CVSS provides a standardized way to assess and communicate the severity of vulnerabilities. It assigns scores to vulnerabilities based on various metrics, helping administrators prioritize which patches to apply first.

    A is incorrect. A risk assessment matrix is not explicitly designed to prioritize patching based on the severity of vulnerabilities.

    C is incorrect. Firewall logs are useful for monitoring traffic and identifying suspicious activity but they do not provide information about the severity of vulnerabilities.

    D is incorrect. Encryption software does not assist in assessing or prioritizing vulnerabilities for patching.

78. The correct answer is **B**. After applying patches and updating controls, the next step would be to conduct an audit to ensure that these actions have been effective and that compliance with security policies is maintained.

    A is incorrect. Reporting remediation does not directly contribute to ongoing security.

    C is incorrect. Segregating patched systems can be a good practice for additional security; however, it is not a direct next step in the vulnerability management process.

    D is incorrect. Acquiring cyber insurance does not directly address the immediate need to verify the effectiveness of vulnerability management.

79. The correct answer is **A**. Misinformation refers to the spread of false or incorrect information, often without malicious intent.

    B is incorrect. Disinformation involves the deliberate spreading of false information with the intent to deceive.

    C is incorrect. Phishing involves sending fraudulent emails or messages to trick individuals into revealing sensitive information.

    D is incorrect. Impersonation involves pretending to be someone else to deceive individuals.

80. The correct answer is **D**. After applying patches, perform a vulnerability scan to ensure that the patches have successfully addressed the vulnerabilities they were intended to fix. This step helps confirm that the system is secure.

    A is incorrect. The primary goal of scanning after patching is to confirm that the vulnerabilities have been resolved, not to identify new ones.

    B is incorrect. System segmentation is typically a separate security consideration unrelated to the immediate results of a vulnerability scan after patching.

    C is incorrect. Reporting on vulnerabilities is not the main purpose of performing a scan after patching.

81. The correct answer is **B**. When a vulnerability cannot be patched immediately, implementing compensating controls is the best course of action. These controls can help mitigate the risk associated with the vulnerability, such as increasing monitoring, applying access controls, or implementing other security measures until a patch is available.

    A is incorrect. Ignoring the vulnerability poses a significant risk to the organization.

    C is incorrect. Additional insurance coverage does not directly mitigate the vulnerability risk.

    D is incorrect. Performing an audit is not the best immediate action when a vulnerability cannot be patched.

82. The correct answer is **B**. Auditing is critical because it verifies whether the remediation actions taken after identifying vulnerabilities, such as patching or applying compensating controls, have been effective. Compliance with internal policies and regulatory standards is ensured, confirming that security measures are operating as intended.

    A is incorrect. Audits focus more on the effectiveness of the remediation process and compliance than on discovering new vulnerabilities.

    C is incorrect. Auditing does not replace the need for rescanning systems. Vulnerability scans are necessary to identify new vulnerabilities and ensure that patches or mitigations have been applied correctly.

    D is incorrect. The main purpose is to ensure the effectiveness and compliance of security controls, not just report generation.

83. The correct answer is **B**. An evil twin attack involves setting rogue access points that mimic a company's wireless network to trick users into connecting. The attacker then intercepts network traffic or steals sensitive data.

    A is incorrect. A DNS attack targets the Domain Name System. Attackers manipulate DNS queries or responses to redirect users to malicious sites or disrupt services.

    C is incorrect. A credential replay attack occurs when an attacker intercepts valid authentication credentials and reuses them to gain unauthorized access.

    D is incorrect. A malicious code attack refers to deploying harmful software designed to damage systems or steal data, such as viruses or trojans.

84. The correct answer is **C**. A system resource monitoring tool is specifically designed to track system performance metrics such as CPU usage, memory consumption, disk I/O, and network bandwidth. It helps administrators identify bottlenecks or underused resources.

    A is incorrect. A hypervisor runs virtual machines on a single physical host.

    B is incorrect. A load balancer distributes incoming network traffic across multiple identical servers.

    D is incorrect. A domain controller responds to authentication requests within a network and validates user credentials.

85. The correct answer is **B**. SAML is a type of XML that securely exchanges authentication and authorization data between a user and a service provider.

    A is incorrect. LDAP is used for directory services, not for exchanging authentication data.

    C is incorrect. HTTP is a protocol for transferring data over the web, not specifically for authentication.

    D is incorrect. POP3 is used for email retrieval, not for authentication and authorization.

CompTIA Security+ SY0-701 Mock Exam 6

1. The correct answer is **D**. SAML allows users to log in once and gain access to multiple applications and services without needing to re-authenticate, facilitating single sign-on (SSO).

    A is incorrect. LDAP is used for directory services and does not provide SSO.

    B is incorrect. OAuth is used for authorization and not primarily for SSO.

    C is incorrect. TLS is used for securing communication, not for SSO.

2. The correct answer is **B**. Port 25 is used for Simple Mail Transfer Protocol (SMTP). It is responsible for sending emails.

    A is incorrect. Port 443 is used for HTTPS (secure web traffic).

    C is incorrect. Port 21 is used for FTP (File Transfer Protocol) and is related to file transfers, not email.

    D is incorrect. Port 22 is used for SSH (Secure Shell), typically for secure remote administration.

3. The correct answer is **A**. An intrusion detection system is used to monitor network traffic, detecting signs of suspicious or malicious activity in real time. It uses predefined rules to analyze network packets, generating alerts if threats are detected.

    B is incorrect. A data loss prevention (DLP) system prevents sensitive data from leaving a company through unauthorized channels.

    C is incorrect. An application firewall is not designed for real-time network-wide monitoring and alerting.

    D is incorrect. Secure Sockets Layer (SSL) is a protocol for encrypting data in transit between a server and a client.

4. The correct answer is **D**. When encountering a suspicious email, the most appropriate action is to report it to the security team and avoid interacting with the email, its links, or attachments.

    A is incorrect. Responding to a phishing email increases the risk of further engagement with attackers.

    B is incorrect. Opening attachments in a phishing email is dangerous as they often contain malware or malicious software.

    C is incorrect. Marking as spam and deleting does not allow the organization's security team to investigate the email.

5. The correct answer is **C**. Access badges control and monitor physical access to different areas in a company, meaning only authorized personnel can enter secure zones.

    A is incorrect. While access badges can be used for time tracking, their primary function in physical security is access control.

    B is incorrect. Access badges are typically used for physical access.

    D is incorrect. Access badges are used to identify individuals.

6. The correct answer is **B**. A memorandum of understanding (MOU) is between two companies outlining the terms and details of the understanding, including each party's roles and responsibilities, but it is not a legal obligation.

    A is incorrect. A business partnership agreement (BPA) is a legally binding agreement that outlines business partners' roles, responsibilities, and obligations in an ongoing partnership.

    C is incorrect. A statement of work (SOW) is a document that details the specific tasks, deliverables, and timelines involved in a project.

    D is incorrect. A non-disclosure agreement (NDA) is a legally binding contract designed to protect confidential information shared between parties.

7. The correct answer is **C**. Key stakeholders from various departments, including IT, security, and management, should be involved in a gap analysis. This diverse involvement ensures that all relevant perspectives are considered and the analysis is comprehensive.

    A is incorrect. There must be more than the IT department for a comprehensive gap analysis.

    B is incorrect. While external auditors can provide valuable insights and an objective perspective, there are better options than relying solely on them for a gap analysis.

    D is incorrect. While the compliance team is crucial in following standards and regulations, they should not be the only ones involved in a gap analysis.

8. The correct answer is **A**. Single sign-on (SSO) allows users to authenticate once and gain access to multiple systems or applications, simplifying the login process for large organizations.

    B is incorrect. Manual verification is impractical for many users and must be more scalable.

    C is incorrect. Shared credentials pose security risks and do not provide individual user accountability.

    D is incorrect. Role-based access lists are used for authorization, not authentication.

9. The correct answer is **C**. Port 445 is used for Microsoft Server Message Block (SMB) file-sharing services. Blocking traffic on this port will prevent file-sharing services from being used on the network.

    A is incorrect. Port 22 is used for SSH (Secure Shell), typically for secure communication.

    B is incorrect. Port 80 is used for HTTP web traffic and blocks web browsing.

    D is incorrect. Port 53 is used for DNS (Domain Name System) queries.

10. The correct answer is **A**. HTTPS (Hyper Text Transfer Protocol Secure) encrypts data transmitted between the user's browser and the web server, ensuring the data remains confidential and cannot be intercepted by unauthorized parties. Therefore, the primary goal of using HTTPS is to provide data confidentiality.

    B is incorrect. Data availability refers to ensuring that data and services are accessible when needed. While HTTPS enhances security, it does not specifically address keeping the web application available.

    C is incorrect. Data integrity ensures that data has not been altered or tampered with. While HTTPS provides some integrity checks through encryption and digital certificates, its primary focus is securing the communication to ensure confidentiality.

    D is incorrect. System redundancy involves having backup systems to maintain service in case of failure. HTTPS does not address redundancy; it focuses on securing data in transit.

11. The correct answer is **A**. Report any remaining vulnerabilities and outline mitigation strategies to stakeholders. This ensures transparency and helps with decision-making about the next steps in the vulnerability management process.

    B is incorrect. Applying older patches that have already been replaced or are outdated can reintroduce vulnerabilities.

    C is incorrect. Compensating controls should only be removed if it's certain that all vulnerabilities have been effectively mitigated.

    D is incorrect. Increasing insurance coverage is only one of the immediate next steps after patching and rescanning.

12. The correct answer is **B**. Confirm that the vulnerabilities detected during the initial scan have been successfully patched or mitigated. This ensures that remediation efforts are effective and that no security gaps remain.

    A is incorrect. Auditing security controls is a separate process.

    C is incorrect. User compliance with security policies is generally not the focus of a vulnerability scan.

    D is incorrect. Rescanning is not intended to apply older patches. Its goal is to verify that existing patches and mitigation efforts were effective.

13. The correct answer is **B**. In SAML, the identity provider (IdP) authenticates the user and provides an assertion to the service provider, allowing access to resources.

    A is incorrect. Managing a database of user credentials is typically done by the directory service, not the IdP.

    C is incorrect. Managing user sessions is a function of the service provider, not the IdP.

    D is incorrect. The service provider or access control mechanisms handle granting access permissions based on roles.

14. The correct answer is **A**. Policy-driven access control uses predefined rules to dynamically manage access based on various factors, unlike traditional methods that often rely on static permissions.

    B is incorrect. Manual configuration is not characteristic of policy-driven access control, which aims to automate and manage access based on rules.

    C is incorrect. Policy-driven access control still requires user authentication; it uses policies to manage access.

    D is incorrect. Physical security measures are separate from policy-driven access control, focusing on logical and dynamic access management.

15. The correct answer is **B**. An incident response plan provides a structured approach for identifying, containing, eradicating, and recovering from such incidents. It ensures that the organization minimizes damage and resumes normal operations as quickly as possible.

    A is incorrect. A business continuity plan (BCP) outlines how an organization will continue its essential functions during and after a disaster. It does not focus specifically on responding to security incidents.

    C is incorrect. A disaster recovery plan (DRP) focuses on restoring IT systems and data after a significant disruption, such as a natural disaster.

    D is incorrect. A change management policy manages and documents changes in an organization's IT environment. It is not related to responding to security incidents.

16. The correct answer is **A**. By addressing the causes of false positives, organizations can refine their detection methods, leading to more accurate vulnerability assessments and reducing unnecessary alerts.

    B is incorrect. Updates are based on new vulnerabilities or patches rather than the accuracy of detection tools.

    C is incorrect. Risk tolerance is a broader strategic decision influenced by various factors, including business objectives and compliance requirements.

    D is incorrect. The primary purpose is not to classify vulnerabilities but to enhance the overall accuracy of the detection mechanisms.

17. The correct answer is **B**. Encryption and decryption of data packets can impact the performance of the data plane because these processes add computational overhead, potentially affecting the speed and efficiency of data transmission.

    A is incorrect. Configuration of network routing protocols affects the control plane.

    C is incorrect. Updates to network security policies are related to network management and control.

    D is incorrect. The physical security of network devices is a concern for physical security and does not directly impact the performance of the data plane.

18. The correct answer is **C**. In a zero-trust model, continuously monitoring and logging network activity is crucial. This allows for analyzing and detecting suspicious behavior, ensuring that potential security incidents can be quickly identified and addressed. Continuous monitoring and logging align with zero-trust's ongoing verification and assessment emphasis.

    A is incorrect. Traditional security models focus on establishing a strong network perimeter to protect against external threats.

    B is incorrect. zero-trust does not assume that devices are trustworthy, even after authentication. It continuously verifies and validates devices, users, and their access requests.

    D is incorrect. While simplifying access controls can improve user experience, Zero Trust focuses on rigorous, dynamic, and often more complex access controls to ensure thorough security.

19. The correct answer is **B**. Passive security monitoring observes and analyzes network traffic without interacting with or altering it. This makes it less intrusive, as it does not impact the flow of traffic or system performance.

    A is incorrect. Real-time alerts and automated responses are typical features of active monitoring.

    C is incorrect. Active monitoring generally requires more complex hardware and software for real-time detection and response, which can be more expensive.

    D is incorrect. Passive monitoring is primarily for observation and analysis, not for actively defending against attacks.

20. The correct answer is **A**. Key escrow is beneficial when encrypted data needs to be recovered in situations where the private key is lost or an employee leaves the company, ensuring continuity and access.

    B is incorrect. Key escrow does not involve distributing public keys; it is about securely storing private keys.

    C is incorrect. Key escrow is about securing private keys, not making them accessible to all staff.

    D is incorrect. Key escrow is unrelated to issuing digital certificates. It is about key recovery.

21. The correct answer is **D**. Public key infrastructure (PKI) is commonly used over insecure channels to securely exchange encryption keys, using asymmetric encryption methods.

    A is incorrect. Symmetric key exchange over an insecure channel with an additional secure method is safe.

    B is incorrect. Plaintext transmission is insecure and not used for key exchange.

    C is incorrect. TLS is an encryption protocol, and it would be incorrect to refer to it as "TLS without any encryption."

22. The correct answer is **B**. Role-based access control (RBAC) is suitable for organizations where access is based on departmental roles and policies.

    A is incorrect. Attribute-based access control (ABAC) is more flexible with attributes rather than roles.

    C is incorrect. Location-based access control (LAC) is not a standard security access control.

    D is incorrect. Mandatory access control (MAC) uses strict policies rather than departmental roles.

23. The correct answer is **B**. Secure enclaves enhance security by generating and storing encryption keys within a secure, isolated environment inaccessible to the main OS, reducing the risk of key compromise.

    A is incorrect. Secure enclaves do not make keys accessible to all applications. They are isolated.

    C is incorrect. Secure enclaves are typically local to the device, not cloud-based.

    D is incorrect. Secure enclaves are designed to limit access, not allow remote access to keys.

24. The correct answer is **D**. Internal classification is typically used for documents and emails meant for internal use within the organization that do not contain sensitive or classified information. While these materials are not for public consumption, they do not require the highest level of protection.

    A is incorrect. Restricted information is highly sensitive and could cause significant harm if disclosed.

    B is incorrect. Public information is intended for distribution outside the organization and poses no risk if disclosed.

    C is incorrect. Confidential data refers to sensitive information that requires protection and limited access, such as employee records or financial reports.

25. The correct answer is **C**. A public ledger in blockchain technology records all transactions transparently and immutably, ensuring that all participants can verify the data.

    A is incorrect. A public ledger is decentralized and does not maintain a centralized database.

    B is incorrect. While blockchain transactions can be encrypted, the public ledger focuses on transparency and integrity.

    D is incorrect. Private keys are not stored in the public ledger; individual participants securely hold them.

26. The correct answer is **B**. A public ledger in blockchain technology ensures that all transactions are recorded transparently and are tamper-proof, making it a key feature for maintaining integrity.

    A is incorrect. Salting is not used in blockchain for transaction integrity.

    C is incorrect. Key stretching enhances password security, not transaction transparency.

    D is incorrect. While encryption may be used, the public ledger is the primary feature ensuring transparency and integrity in the blockchain.

27. The correct answer is **A**. The appropriate action is to generate new certificate signing requests (CSRs) to renew the expiring certificates, ensuring continued secure communications.

    B is incorrect. Adding certificates to a certificate revocation list (CRL) is for revocation, not renewal.

    C is incorrect. Disabling online certificate status protocol (OCSP) would reduce security by not checking the certificate status in real time.

    D is incorrect. While wildcard certificates can be useful, they still need to solve the issue of certificate expiration and renewal.

28. The correct answer is **D**. An employee with knowledge of internal systems and processes is the most likely type of insider threat. This individual has authorized access to the organization's resources and information, which can be exploited.

    A is incorrect. External threat actors (nation-state) are typically government-sponsored and conduct cyber operations for strategic or intelligence purposes.

    B is incorrect. Unskilled attackers are generally external and need deep knowledge of internal systems.

    C is incorrect. Political or social motivations drive hacktivists and are usually external to their target organization.

29. The correct answer is **C**. Shadow IT refers to employees' use of unauthorized software, devices, and services that bypass official IT policies and controls.

    A is incorrect. Nation-state actors are usually involved in sophisticated cyber operations targeting strategic or intelligence goals.

    B is incorrect. Organized crime groups focus on financial gain through criminal activities such as fraud, theft, and extortion.

    D is incorrect. While insider threats involve individuals within an organization who may misuse their access, the specific issue of using unauthorized software and devices is more accurately described as shadow IT.

30. The correct answer is **B**. A self-assessment is an internal review where a company's security team evaluates its own practices, controls, and policies without involving external parties.

    A is incorrect. A compliance audit is an external review performed by an independent entity or regulatory body to ensure the company is following legal, industry, or internal regulations.

    C is incorrect. An external audit involves an independent third party assessing the company's practices.

    D is incorrect. A third-party assessment is conducted by an external organization that evaluates the security of another entity.

31. The correct answer is **B**. Managed service providers (MSPs) often have extensive access to a company's network and systems, making them a significant risk if compromised. Attackers can exploit this trusted relationship to gain access to the company's network.

    A is incorrect. Open service ports can be a security risk but they are not directly related to the exploitation of third-party relationships.

    C is incorrect. Default credentials pose a security risk within the company but are not specifically related to third-party relationships.

    D is incorrect. Although insider threats involving company employees are a concern, the risk here involves exploiting third-party relationships.

32. The correct answer is **C**. Open service ports that are not required for a server's operation can be exploited by attackers to gain unauthorized access or conduct attacks on the server.

    A is incorrect. Default credentials are a security concern but they relate to weak authentication practices rather than the specific issue of unnecessary open ports on a server.

    B is incorrect. Vulnerable software can be exploited but the concern is specifically about the open port providing a potential entry point for attackers.

    D is incorrect. Insider threats involve malicious activities by employees or trusted individuals.

33. The correct answer is **B**. A vendor-related threat occurs when a company's third-party vendor has poor security practices, which can lead to attackers exploiting vulnerabilities, potentially affecting the company.

   A is incorrect. Default credentials refer to factory-set usernames and passwords that are often easily exploitable if not changed.

   C is incorrect. Phishing attacks involve tricking individuals into providing sensitive information through deceptive emails or messages.

   D is incorrect. A watering hole attack compromises a specific website or online resource frequently visited by the target organization.

34. The correct answer is **D**. Default credentials are a well-known security risk because they are often easily guessed or found in public documentation, making them a likely attack vector if not changed.

   A is incorrect. Managed service providers (MSPs) can introduce security risks if compromised but they are not directly related to the issue of using default credentials.

   B is incorrect. While suppliers can pose a security risk, this question specifically relates to the internal management of network devices.

   C is incorrect. Open service ports can be a security risk but they are not the primary concern regarding default usernames and passwords on network devices.

35. The correct answer is **A**. Legacy systems refer to outdated platforms, hardware, or software that are still in use but are no longer supported or updated by the vendor.

   B is incorrect. Cloud platforms are environments where applications and services are hosted remotely on internet servers.

   C is incorrect. On-premises refers to software and hardware located and managed within an organization's physical premises. It does not explicitly indicate that a system needs to be updated or supported.

   D is incorrect. Resource overuse refers to the excessive consumption of computing resources, leading to potential performance issues.

36. The correct answer is **C**. The exposure factor is a metric that indicates the potential impact of a vulnerability on a system. It is expressed as a percentage that represents the expected loss in the event of a successful vulnerability exploit.

   A is incorrect. Risk tolerance is the level of risk that any company is willing to accept. It does not measure the potential impact of a vulnerability.

   B is incorrect. Vulnerability classification involves categorizing vulnerabilities based on characteristics such as severity or type.

   D is incorrect. A false negative rate does not measure the impact of a vulnerability but, instead, indicates the effectiveness of detection mechanisms.

37. The correct answer is **B**. Port 23 is used by Telnet, a protocol for remote access to devices. Telnet is often considered insecure because it transmits data, including passwords, in plaintext.

    A is incorrect. Port 80 is used for HTTP (Hypertext Transfer Protocol), which handles web traffic.

    C is incorrect. Port 443 is used for HTTPS, which secures web traffic. Blocking this port would stop secure web traffic.

    D is incorrect. Port 110 is used by POP3 (Post Office Protocol version 3), responsible for retrieving emails.

38. The correct answer is **A**. Misconfiguration is a common vulnerability in cloud environments where improper access controls can lead to unauthorized access to sensitive data. Ensuring that security settings are correctly configured is essential to prevent such risks.

    B is incorrect. A zero-day vulnerability refers to a security flaw that is unknown to the software vendor and has no available fix.

    C is incorrect. Cryptographic vulnerabilities involve weaknesses in encryption methods or implementations. They are not typically related to misconfigurations of access controls in cloud environments.

    D is incorrect. Jailbreaking refers to removing restrictions on mobile devices, typically installing unauthorized software.

39. The correct answer is **B**. A zero-day vulnerability is a flaw in the system's hardware or software that is unknown to the vendor and has no available patch or fix. It represents a significant risk because attackers can exploit it before it is discovered and mitigated.

    A is incorrect. Sideloading refers to installing apps from sources other than the official repository.

    C is incorrect. Cloud-specific vulnerabilities, such as improper configurations or access controls, are unique to cloud environments and services.

    D is incorrect. Supply chain vulnerabilities arise from weaknesses in the security of suppliers and third-party vendors, potentially impacting the end product.

40. The correct answer is **B**. Sideloading installs applications on a mobile device from sources other than the official repository. This practice can expose devices to malware and other security risks, as the apps may not have undergone the same security checks as those from authorized sources.

    A is incorrect. AIS typically stands for Automated Indicator Sharing, a tool for sharing cyber threat indicators between organizations.

    C is incorrect. RTO stands for recovery time objective, a business continuity metric representing the maximum time a system or service can be down after a failure or disaster.

    D is incorrect. Vendor diversity uses multiple vendors for similar services or products to reduce risk.

41. The correct answer is **C**. Supply chain vulnerabilities arise when third-party vendors, service providers, or software providers introduce security risks into an organization's environment. This can happen through compromised software, hardware, or services, leading to potential breaches or attacks.

    A is incorrect. Cloud-specific vulnerabilities relate to security issues unique to cloud environments, such as misconfigured cloud storage or improper access controls.

    B is incorrect. Cryptographic vulnerabilities involve weaknesses in encryption algorithms, key management, or cryptographic implementations that attackers could exploit.

    D is incorrect. FDE stands for full disk encryption, a method of encrypting all data on a disk drive.

42. The correct answer is **B**. File integrity monitoring (FIM) is a tool for checking changes to critical system files and configurations. It works by comparing the current state of files against a known, trusted baseline and alerting administrators if any unauthorized modifications, deletions, or additions are detected.

    A is incorrect. A configuration management database (CMDB) stores information about an organization's assets and configuration items.

    C is incorrect. A virtual local area network (VLAN) segments network traffic for better security and management. It does not monitor or detect changes to system files or configurations.

    D is incorrect. A content delivery network (CDN) is a distributed network that delivers web content quickly to users by caching it closer to their location.

43. The correct answer is **D**. Jailbreaking is the practice of modifying a smartphone's operating system to remove restrictions imposed by the manufacturer or carrier. This allows the installation of unauthorized apps and access to the filesystem, which can pose significant security risks as it can bypass built-in security measures.

    A is incorrect. A zero-day vulnerability is a security flaw that is unknown to the software vendor and has no patch available, making it vulnerable to exploitation.

    B is incorrect. XSS (cross-site scripting) is a security vulnerability commonly found in web applications. In this vulnerability, attackers inject malicious scripts into web pages viewed by other users.

    C is incorrect. An application allow list is a security feature that restricts application execution to only those explicitly allowed by an administrator.

44. The correct answer is **A**. Weak encryption protocols refer to vulnerabilities in cryptographic systems where data protection is inadequate due to outdated or insecure encryption methods. This makes the data susceptible to unauthorized access or breaches.

    B is incorrect. Public cloud refers to cloud services provided by third-party vendors over the internet.

    C is incorrect. Mobile device vulnerabilities could involve issues such as insecure apps or unauthorized access, but weak encryption protocols are more specifically related to cryptographic vulnerabilities.

    D is incorrect. Sideloading is installing apps from sources other than the official app store, which can introduce malware.

45. The correct answer is **B**. The primary purpose of using access control lists (ACLs) is to control and restrict access to network resources by specifying which IP addresses or ranges of addresses can send or receive traffic.

    A is incorrect. ACLs are primarily used for access control, not as a logging tool.

    C is incorrect. ACLs do not perform encryption; they allow or deny traffic based on predefined rules.

    D is incorrect. ACLs are not designed to inspect traffic contents to detect malware; they are used to manage which traffic is permitted or denied based on predefined rules.

46. The correct answer is **B**. The allow list ensures that only authorized and necessary applications can run, while the block list specifically prevents known malicious or risky applications from executing.

    A is incorrect. Relying solely on a block list can leave the system vulnerable to threats yet to be identified.

    C is incorrect. Encryption is a separate process to secure data in transit, ensuring privacy and protection from interception.

    D is incorrect. Allow and block lists are helpful for application control but do not directly relate to network segmentation.

47. The correct answer is **B**. A factory reset may remove configurations but wiping the disks ensures that all data is permanently erased and cannot be recovered through forensic methods.

    A is incorrect. Disconnecting servers from the network does not address the risk of sensitive data remaining on the disks.

    C is incorrect. When decommissioning servers, it's essential to wipe the data completely.

    D is incorrect. Disconnecting servers from the internet does not eliminate the risk of data recovery from the physical drives after decommissioning.

48. The correct answer is **C**. The risk management strategy of avoidance is used when a company decides not to engage in an activity or stops an existing activity to completely eliminate the associated risks.

    A is incorrect. Risk transfer involves shifting the risk to another party, often by purchasing insurance or outsourcing.

    B is incorrect. Risk acceptance means acknowledging the risk and dealing with its consequences without additional mitigation efforts.

    D is incorrect. Risk mitigation involves taking steps to reduce the impact or likelihood of a risk. For example, implementing security controls to protect sensitive customer data could be a good option.

49. The correct answer is **B**. Real-time operating systems (RTOSs) are designed for high-performance, time-sensitive tasks, often at the expense of security. Many RTOS environments lack built-in advanced security features such as strong encryption, access control, or intrusion detection, and may therefore require additional hardening.

    A is incorrect. RTOS environments are typically designed for efficiency and speed rather than for providing user-friendly interfaces.

    C is incorrect. RTOS environments do not automatically encrypt data by default. Many RTOS implementations lack native encryption capabilities due to their lightweight design.

    D is incorrect. RTOS environments are not designed to support multiple operating systems simultaneously.

50. The correct answer is **A**. Reputational damage occurs when a company's public image is harmed due to negative publicity, such as being reported in the media for a data breach or non-compliance with security protocols. This often leads to a loss of customers and business partners.

    B is incorrect. Contractual impacts refer to the legal consequences of failing to meet contractual obligations, such as service-level agreements.

    C is incorrect. Fines are typically imposed for violating laws or regulations, for example, data protection regulations such as GDPR.

    D is incorrect. A loss of license occurs when a company is no longer permitted to operate in a certain field due to non-compliance with regulatory requirements.

51. The correct answer is **C**. A key security challenge with embedded systems is their limited resources, such as memory, processing power, and storage, which makes it difficult to implement complex security protocols such as encryption and access control.

    A is incorrect. Embedded systems are optimized for specific tasks and often lack the computational power to handle complex security measures such as encryption or MFA.

    B is incorrect. Embedded systems generally have minimal or no user-friendly management interfaces.

    D is incorrect. Embedded systems typically require additional security configurations to ensure safe integration with other systems.

52. The correct answer is **B**. Cloud providers typically follow their own update schedules and patching policies, which can impact when security updates are available. It's important for users to stay informed about the provider's patching policies to maintain a strong security posture.

    A is incorrect. While some cloud providers may automatically apply patches in specific environments (such as SaaS), in IaaS and PaaS models, users are often responsible for applying patches to applications running on virtual machines.

    C is incorrect. Patch availability is critical to the security posture of any system, including cloud environments.

    D is incorrect. Patches in cloud environments are typically released as frequently, if not more frequently, than in traditional on-premises environments.

53. The correct answer is **B**. Legacy systems often run on outdated software and hardware without vendor support or security updates. As newly discovered vulnerabilities cannot be patched, these systems are vulnerable to attacks, making them a significant concern for security teams.

    A is incorrect. Modern applications and operating systems still supported by vendors typically receive regular security updates and patches.

    C is incorrect. Cloud service providers usually follow a rigorous patching schedule and provide frequent updates to maintain the security of their infrastructure.

    D is incorrect. Applications with built-in patch management can automatically or quickly receive updates, ensuring they stay protected against vulnerabilities.

54. The correct answer is **D**. Ensuring that the data center has sufficient power capacity and redundant power and cooling systems is critical for reliability, performance, and uptime. Without proper power and cooling, the servers and networking equipment can overheat or fail, leading to service disruptions and data loss.

    A is incorrect. Office space does not directly impact the computing and power needs of the data center.

    B is incorrect. The aesthetic design of a data center does not affect its power or computing capabilities.

    C is incorrect. The geographic location of the data center is separate from the power and computing needs.

55. The correct answer is **B**. The primary purpose of a jump server (or jump box) is to act as an intermediary for accessing and managing systems in a restricted or isolated network. By requiring administrators to use a jump server, organizations can enforce strong authentication and logging before allowing access to critical or sensitive systems.

A is incorrect. Protocols such as SSL/TLS or VPNs are responsible for providing encrypted communication, not a jump server.

C is incorrect. Load balancing is the function of a load balancer, spreading the load across multiple servers to improve performance.

D is incorrect. Monitoring and blocking malicious traffic is typically the role of a firewall or intrusion prevention system (IPS), not a jump server.

56. The correct answer is **C**. A web proxy server acts as an intermediary between users and the internet, allowing it to filter requests, cache responses for improved performance, and log traffic for auditing and monitoring purposes.

A is incorrect. The main role of a web proxy is to manage traffic rather than encrypt it.

B is incorrect. While a proxy server can filter content, it does not typically block malicious traffic directly.

D is incorrect. Proxy servers are not primarily designed for real-time threat detection.

57. The correct answer is **A**. Secure access service edge (SASE) combines networking and security functions into a single cloud service. It enables organizations to securely connect users to applications and data, regardless of location.

B is incorrect. SASE primarily focuses on network and cloud security rather than physical security.

C is incorrect. SASE does not concentrate solely on endpoint protection or antivirus solutions.

D is incorrect. SASE does not specialize only in user authentication.

58. The correct answer is **A**. A VPN creates an encrypted connection over a less secure network, such as the public internet. It allows users to work with data as if their devices were directly connected to a private network, ensuring the data's confidentiality and integrity.

B is incorrect. Cloud access security brokers (CASBs) focus on managing security in cloud environments rather than establishing secure communication channels.

C is incorrect. Network access control does not create secure communication channels over public networks.

D is incorrect. An intrusion detection system (IDS) is a security tool that monitors network activities for malicious actions or policy violations.

59. The correct answer is **A**. Data related to a company's earnings, transactions, and budgets falls under financial information. This data type typically includes revenue reports, expenditures, and other monetary records that are essential for business operations and regulatory compliance.

    B is incorrect. Intellectual property (IP) refers to patents, trademarks, and copyrighted works.

    C is incorrect. A trade secret refers to confidential business information (such as formulas, processes, or designs) that gives a company a competitive edge.

    D is incorrect. Human-readable refers to data that humans can easily interpret, such as text or certain data formats. This is not a specific type of data classification, such as financial information.

60. The correct answer is **B**. Directive controls are designed to direct or influence behavior to ensure the follow-through of security policies and procedures. They help guide users and systems in complying with established security requirements.

    A is incorrect. Monitoring and recording security events fall under monitoring controls.

    C is incorrect. Providing physical barriers is the function of physical controls.

    D is incorrect. Detecting and responding to threats is the role of detection and response controls.

61. The correct answer is **B**. Human-readable data refers to information people can easily understand without needing decoding or transformation, such as plain text, CSV files, or HTML documents.

    A is incorrect. Regulated data refers to information governed by laws or regulations and requires specific handling or protection.

    C is incorrect. Non-human-readable data refers to data that requires decoding or transformation to be understood by humans.

    D is incorrect. Legal information refers to laws, contracts, or regulations data. It is also not easily interpreted by others.

62. The correct answer is **C**. Private data refers to personal information about individuals, such as employees. Privacy laws protect that data. This type of information, including Social Security numbers, medical records, and personal contact details, should not be disclosed without the individual's consent.

    A is incorrect. Public data refers to information intended for open access and does not require special protection.

    B is incorrect. Restricted data typically refers to sensitive information that may be classified due to its importance to national security or proprietary business interests.

    D is incorrect. Unrestricted data refers to information that can be freely accessed without restrictions. This is the opposite of what applies to personal information protected by privacy laws.

63. The correct answer is **D**. Restricted data classifications apply to highly sensitive information such as intellectual property and trade secrets. This data type is critical to a company's competitive advantage and must be tightly controlled to prevent unauthorized access.

    A is incorrect. Public data is information for open access, such as press releases or marketing material.

    B is incorrect. Secure is not a formal data classification category.

    C is incorrect. Open data is accessible to anyone without restrictions.

64. The correct answer is **B**. Data sovereignty refers to data that is subject to the regulations of the country in which it is stored. Cloud services must comply with regional laws regarding where data is stored and how it is accessed.

    A is incorrect. Data in use refers to data actively being processed or utilized by a system, not to the legal concerns of where data is stored or the jurisdiction that governs it.

    C is incorrect. Data at rest refers to data that is stored but not currently in use.

    D is incorrect. Geolocation refers to identifying the physical location of a device or user. However, it is not the primary consideration when ensuring compliance with regional laws about data storage.

65. The correct answer is **C**. Geolocation involves using GPS technology to determine the physical location of devices and facilities. By tracking the location, the organization can enhance its security measures and ensure that devices and data storage facilities are secure and monitored.

    A is incorrect. Data sovereignty refers to the legal implications of data storage and management based on geographical boundaries.

    B is incorrect. Data in transit refers to data actively being transferred over a network.

    D is incorrect. Data in use refers to data actively being processed by a system.

66. The correct answer is **B**. Masking involves replacing sensitive data with placeholder values. This technique is commonly used in test environments to protect sensitive information while allowing the application to function properly.

    A is incorrect. Tokenization involves replacing all sensitive data with unique identifiers (tokens), not just part of it, and usually through a token service provider.

    C is incorrect. Encryption does not replace data with random values but secures it through a transformation process.

    D is incorrect. Segmentation refers to dividing a network into smaller, manageable parts to enhance security.

67. The correct answer is **A**. Segmentation involves dividing a network into smaller, isolated segments. This method enhances security by controlling data access and limiting the impact of security breaches within the network.

    B is incorrect. Hashing is a method used to convert data into a fixed-size string of characters, typically a digest that cannot be easily reversed.

    C is incorrect. Tokenization involves replacing sensitive data with unique identifiers that can be securely mapped back to the original data.

    D is incorrect. Obfuscation makes data or code difficult to understand or interpret.

68. The correct answer is **B**. Cellular networks provide a more secure connection than public Wi-Fi or Bluetooth when mobile devices are outside the corporate network. Cellular data is generally encrypted by default, making it safer for secure communication.

    A is incorrect. Bluetooth is primarily used for short-range device connections and is less secure for data transmission over long distances.

    C is incorrect. Wi-Fi can be secure if configured properly but public or untrusted Wi-Fi networks pose significant risks.

    D is incorrect. Mobile device management (MDM) is a tool for managing and securing mobile devices but does not provide the actual connection method.

69. The correct answer is **C**. Classifying data according to sensitivity and confidentiality helps an organization determine the appropriate security controls to protect the data. Different levels of classification guide decisions on access controls, encryption, and monitoring.

    A is incorrect. Software license management focuses on ensuring that the organization has proper software licenses, not data security.

    B is incorrect. Network traffic management involves controlling data flow across a network. It is unrelated to data classification for security purposes.

    D is incorrect. Asset management involves keeping an inventory of hardware and software assets.

70. The correct answer is **B**. Asset tracking involves maintaining an up-to-date inventory of all hardware and software used within an organization. Documenting software versions is a key part of asset management, helping the organization ensure that all systems are compliant and secure by tracking software and its versions across the company.

    A is incorrect. Network segmentation refers to dividing a network into smaller, isolated segments to improve security.

    C is incorrect. Access control manages who can access specific systems or data.

    D is incorrect. Incident response deals with handling security incidents, such as malware infections.

71. The correct answer is **C**. The primary purpose of using automated tools to find all the workstations in a large organization is to track and manage hardware assets effectively.

    A is incorrect. Reducing purchasing costs is not the primary purpose of using automated tools.

    B is incorrect. Ensuring hardware compatibility is typically a part of software deployment planning.

    D is incorrect. Automated asset management tools do not directly aim to improve employee productivity.

72. The correct answer is **B**. Creating and enforcing a data retention policy ensures that the company retains its data for the necessary period as required by compliance laws. This policy will specify how long different types of data must be stored.

    A is incorrect. Data encryption is related to protecting data confidentiality, not determining how long data should be retained.

    C is incorrect. Upgrading hardware is unrelated to data retention policies or compliance laws.

    D is incorrect. Network firewalls are used to control network traffic based on security rules.

73. The correct answer is **B**. A secure erase tool ensures that data is permanently overwritten and cannot be recovered, even with specialized recovery tools.

    A is incorrect. Formatting does not completely remove all data from the hard drive. Some data may still be recoverable with forensic tools.

    C is incorrect. Deleting user accounts only removes server access, not the data stored on hard drives.

    D is incorrect. Removing the server from the network only prevents it from being accessed remotely.

74. The correct answer is **B**. Third-party assessments are typically conducted to identify vulnerabilities in externally developed software or services. They ensure that external providers or partners maintain security standards and that their software does not introduce risks.

    A is incorrect. Gathering real-time threat data from external sources does not require a third-party assessment.

    C is incorrect. Internal teams perform daily vulnerability scans using automated scanning tools.

    D is incorrect. Monitoring software packages for updates is usually an internal task that can be automated with patch management tools.

75. The correct answer is **B**. Static analysis tools analyze source code or compiled code for vulnerabilities before it is deployed. These tools help detect coding errors, security flaws, and potential vulnerabilities without executing the code.

    A is incorrect. Simulating potential attacks on a live system is typically done using penetration testing.

    C is incorrect. Subscribing to external threat feeds involves obtaining real-time data on emerging threats from external sources.

    D is incorrect. Tools such as intrusion detection systems (IDSs) or security information and event management (SIEM) systems typically monitor network traffic for anomalies.

76. The correct answer is **D**. The chain of Custody process involves maintaining an unbroken record of the evidence from collection to presentation in court. It is essential to update the chain of custody documentation each time evidence is transferred.

    A is incorrect. Encryption is not a specific requirement of the Chain of Custody process.

    B is incorrect. Notifying all users is unnecessary in the context of the Chain of Custody process.

    C is incorrect. Performing a system backup before transferring evidence is not standard for the Chain of Custody process.

77. The correct answer is **B**. A Legal Hold is a directive issued to preserve relevant evidence in the event of an investigation or litigation. It ensures that evidence is not deleted or altered while the investigation is ongoing.

    A is incorrect. Limiting access to sensitive areas of the network is not the purpose of a Legal Hold.

    C is incorrect. Legal hold does not involve taking legal action against individuals. It is a procedural step in preparing for legal action if necessary.

    D is incorrect. Legal Hold does not recover lost or deleted data.

78. The correct answer is **B**. Third-party assessments are typically conducted to identify vulnerabilities in externally developed software or services. They ensure that external providers or partners maintain security standards and that their software does not introduce risks.

    A is incorrect. Gathering real-time threat data from external sources does not require a third-party assessment.

    C is incorrect. Internal teams perform daily vulnerability scans using automated scanning tools.

    D is incorrect. Monitoring software packages for updates is usually an internal task that can be automated with patch management tools.

79. The correct answer is **B**. After identifying the root cause of a security incident, the next critical step is implementing corrective actions to address the issue and prevent it from happening again.

    A is incorrect. A financial impact analysis is not the next critical step after identifying the root cause.

    C is incorrect. Notification to external bodies may be required depending on legal or regulatory obligations, but this step does not directly address the incident's root cause.

    D is incorrect. Reassessing security policies is not the immediate next step after identifying the root cause.

80. The correct answer is **B**. This includes evaluating whether the vulnerabilities were successfully mitigated and identifying any remaining risks needing further attention. This ensures that management clearly understands the current security posture and any residual concerns.

    A is incorrect. Cost data might be included in a broader report but differs from the core information needed for a security assessment.

    C is incorrect. Management will not need a detailed description of each vulnerability. The focus should be on the outcome of the remediation actions and the overall risk reduction.

    D is incorrect. Naming specific employees responsible for systems is optional for the report.

81. The correct answer is **A**. Rescan the network to confirm that the segmentation was correctly implemented and the vulnerability has been effectively isolated.

    B is incorrect. Compensating controls should only be turned off if it's confirmed that the network segmentation has fully mitigated the vulnerability.

    C is incorrect. Reinstallation is usually reserved for more severe cases such as malware infections rather than standard vulnerability mitigation through segmentation.

    D is incorrect. Purchasing cyber insurance is not a direct follow-up step to network segmentation.

82. The correct answer is **A**. Audit logs are the best method for ensuring that patches are applied correctly and effectively. They provide a detailed record of actions and help validate whether the remediation steps were followed as planned.

    B is incorrect. The focus should be on verifying that patches and vulnerabilities were addressed rather than just checking for malware.

    C is incorrect. Once the remediation is completed, the focus should be on validating the solution's effectiveness, not applying additional controls.

    D is incorrect. Decreasing insurance coverage is unrelated to validating the remediation process.

83. The correct answer is **B**. Rule-based access controls restrict access based on the time of day or other temporal constraints.

    A is incorrect. Mandatory access control (MAC) is based on classifications, not time constraints.

    C is incorrect. Attribute-based access control (ABAC) uses attributes for access control, not time constraints.

    D is incorrect. Discretionary access control (DAC) is based on user discretion, not time restrictions.

84. The correct answer is **A**. The primary purpose of conducting a gap analysis is to identify and document the differences between an organization's current security practices and its desired security goals. This process helps understand the changes or improvements needed to align current practices with the desired standards or requirements.

    B is incorrect. While creating new security policies might address gaps identified in a gap analysis, the primary purpose of the gap analysis itself is not to create policies but to identify differences between current practices and required goals.

    C is incorrect. Increasing physical security is a specific security measure that protects the organization's physical assets and facilities.

    D is incorrect. Managing and allocating the security budget involves financial planning and resource allocation to support security initiatives.

85. The correct answer is **B**. Changing rules on a host firewall is a technical control because it involves configuring and managing hardware or software to protect against security threats.

    A is incorrect. Administrative controls involves policies and procedures, not technical configuration.

    C is incorrect. Detective controls identifies and reports security incidents but doesn't involve active configuration changes.

    D is incorrect. Alternative controls refers to different or compensating controls not directly related to firewall rule changes.

‹packt›

www.packtpub.com

Subscribe to our online digital library for full access to over 7,000 books and videos, as well as industry-leading tools to help you plan your personal development and advance your career. For more information, please visit our website.

Why Subscribe?

- Spend less time learning and more time coding with practical eBooks and videos from over 4,000 industry professionals
- Improve your learning with Skill Plans built especially for you
- Get a free eBook or video every month
- Fully searchable for easy access to vital information
- Copy and paste, print, and bookmark content

At www.packtpub.com, you can also read a collection of free technical articles, sign up for a range of free newsletters, and receive exclusive discounts and offers on Packt books and eBooks.

Other Books You May Enjoy

If you enjoyed this book, you may be interested in these other books by Packt:

CompTIA® Security+® SYO-701 Certification Guide, Third Edition

Ian Neil

ISBN: 978-1-83546-153-2

- Differentiate between various security control types
- Apply mitigation techniques for enterprise security
- Evaluate security implications of architecture models
- Protect data by leveraging strategies and concepts
- Implement resilience and recovery in security
- Automate and orchestrate for running secure operations
- Execute processes for third-party risk assessment and management
- Conduct various audits and assessments with specific purposes

CompTIA A+ Practice Tests Core 1 (220-1101) and Core 2 (220-1102)

Ian Neil and Mark Birch

ISBN: 978-1-83763-318-0

- Expertly diagnose and resolve hardware, software, and networking issues
- Navigate Microsoft Windows, macOS, Linux, and more with confidence
- Secure wireless networks and protect against threats
- Troubleshoot problems related to motherboards, RAM, CPU, and power
- Skillfully use Microsoft command-line tools
- Implement workstation backup and recovery methods
- Utilize remote access technologies with ease
- Assess your proficiency in communication techniques and professional conduct

Share Your Thoughts

Now you've finished *CompTIA Security+ SY0-701 Practice Tests*, we'd love to hear your thoughts! Scan the QR code below to go straight to the Amazon review page for this book and share your feedback or leave a review on the site that you purchased it from.

https://packt.link/r/1836646852

Your review is important to us and the tech community and will help us make sure we're delivering excellent-quality content.